Libya

Libya

From Colony to Independence

RONALD BRUCE ST JOHN

ONEWORLD

OXFORD

A Oneworld Paperback Original

Published by Oneworld Publications 2008

Copyright © Ronald Bruce St John 2008

All rights reserved
Copyright under Berne Convention
A CIP record for this title is available
from the British Library

ISBN 978–1–85168–598–1

Maps and Illustrations by Nathan Bailey St John
Typeset by Jayvee, Trivandrum, India
Cover design by Design Deluxe
Printed and bound in the United States
by Thomson-Shore Inc, Dexter, MI

Oneworld Publications
185 Banbury Road
Oxford OX2 7AR
England
www.oneworld-publications.com

To Carol

CONTENTS

PREFACE

This book is aimed at the general reader, casual traveler, business executive, and university undergraduate student of the Great Socialist People's Libyan Arab Jamahiriya, generally known as Libya. It attempts to make the history of Libya understandable, interesting, and perhaps occasionally even exciting. In so doing, I have tried to provide a widely comprehensive presentation in the space available, including economic, social, and cultural as well as diplomatic and political history.

The Libyan experience, especially in modern times, has been rich and diverse, but it was not always unique. Where appropriate, I have underlined the special qualities of the Libyan experience, but I have also pointed out where the process of change in Libya shared much with that of other economies, societies, and states. Common patterns are to be expected, and within them we find Libyan particularities formed by specific contingencies.

The target audience, combined with the inherent space limitations of a general history covering more than three millennia, necessitates a book focused on the analysis of events, providing only enough detail to make them understandable. In the process, I make liberal use of my own research on Libya which spans a period of four decades. I also rely heavily on the research of others, bringing to the general reader the results of wonderfully detailed research previously accessible only to the specialist. Because of this approach, students of Libya may find some of what I say familiar, in part because I've drawn from their work and in part because I've repeated or expanded upon things I've said in my own.

For those interested in further reading, the bibliographical essay at the end of the book provides a road map to the most important literature available on Libya. Given the anticipated audience, only English-language books, with a few exceptions, are cited. In addition to the individual bibliographies listed at the beginning of the essay, all of the books cited therein contain a substantial bibliography, often involving works in languages other than English, and provide those interested with a springboard for further reading. For additional detail, the reader is referred to the latest edition of my *Historical Dictionary of Libya* (2006) which includes the most extensive bibliography of Libya available today, listed by subject to facilitate the location of desired materials.

A very large number of people, in and out of Libya, have encouraged and assisted my research and writing over the many years. I will not try to name them as that would take far too much space; however, I do want to acknowledge their generosity and support. I also want to thank our son, Nathan Bailey St John, for illustrating this book. The illustrations and maps he has created add much to our understanding of the history of Libya. I would also like to thank my wife, Carol, to whom this volume is dedicated, for her encouragement and support over a lifetime together.

MAPS AND ILLUSTRATIONS

NOTE ON TRANSLITERATION

The transliteration of personal and place names from Arabic into English is widely recognized as a frustrating and imprecise exercise. It is made more difficult when it involves source materials stretching over three millennia and drawing on both European and non-European languages. This is particularly true in the case of Libya where the Latin spelling of personal and place names has not been standardized. On the contrary, early explorers, travelers, diplomats, and other officials, most of whom were not linguists, too often fixed the spelling of Arabic names and places in the Latin alphabet. As a result, many of the Latin spellings in use are a mixture of English, Italian, and French adaptations.

The issue of place names is an especially difficult one. To call places what they were called in the past is to invite confusion for modern readers. The past names have often disappeared completely from the memory of all but a few specialists in the area or subject. The use of past names would be historically accurate but overly confusing for the general reader. Therefore, in this text, I have preferred to refer to places according to general international usage, employing conventional, contemporary spellings whenever possible. When it is not possible, I try to make clear the connection between ancient and contemporary place names.

The convention for place names adopted in this book has the advantage of clarity, but it is not intended to endorse necessarily the policies of the people who changed the names. That said, it should enable students of Libya to consult standard international atlases and maps and easily find the places mentioned in the book.

SELECT CHRONOLOGY OF LIBYAN HISTORY

Twelfth century BCE	Phoenicians active throughout Mediterranean Basin.
ca. 2700–2200 BCE	Earliest written documentation of Libyan history.
632 BCE	Foundation of Cyrene, first Greek city in North Africa.
500 BCE–CE 500	Garamantes a power in southern Libya.
264–241 BCE	First Punic War.
218–202 BCE	Second Punic War.
149–146 BCE	Third Punic War.
115–117	Jewish revolt in Cyrenaica.
300	Provinces of Upper Libya and Lower Libya formed.
429	Vandals enter North Africa.
644–646	Arabs occupy Cyrenaica and Tripolitania.
661–750	Umayyad dynasty.
750–1258	Abbasid dynasty.
910–1171	Fatimid dynasty.
Eleventh century	Hilalian invasion.
1073–1147	Almoravid dynasty.
1147–1267	Almohad dynasty.
1228–1574	Hafsid dynasty.
1517	Ottomans occupy Cyrenaica.
1551	Ottomans occupy Tripoli.
1711–1835	Karamanli dynasty.
1835	Second Ottoman occupation.

1842	Sanusi Order establishes first *zawiya* in Cyrenaica.
1908	Young Turk revolt.
1911–1943	Italian occupation.
1912	Congress of Aziziyyah.
November 1918	Tripoli Republic created.
October 1919	*Legge Fondamentale* promulgated.
1929	Cyrenaica, Tripolitania, and Fezzan united as Libya.
September 1931	Libyan resistance ends with execution of Umar al-Mukhtar.
1938	Italy embarks upon large-scale agricultural settlements.
1943	British Military administration in Cyrenaica and Tripolitania and French Military Administration in Fezzan.
November 1949	United Nations General Assembly passes a resolution creating an independent and sovereign state of Libya.
December 1951	United Kingdom of Libya, headed by King Idris al-Sanusi, proclaims its independence.
February 1953	Libya joins Arab League.
July 1953	Libya concludes military agreement with Great Britain.
September 1954	Libya concludes military agreement with United States.
1955	Libyan petroleum law comes into effect.
October 1961	Oil exports begin.
1962	Libya joins Organization of Petroleum Exporting Countries(OPEC).
April 1963	Federal government abandoned in favor of a unitary state.
September 1969	One September Revolution overthrows monarchy.
December 1969	Constitutional Proclamation.

June 1970	American forces evacuate Wheelus Airbase.
June 1971	Arab Socialist Union (ASU).
April 1973	Issuance of Third Universal Theory marks beginning of Popular Revolution.
August 1973	Libya nationalizes Occidental Petroleum followed shortly by nationalization of all foreign oil companies.
April 1974	Qaddafi resigns to devote himself to revolutionary activities.
September 1975	Imposition of first U.S. economic sanctions against Libya.
September 1976	Publication of part one of *The Green Book.*
March 1977	Declaration of the Establishment of the People's Authority.
November 1977	Publication of part two of *The Green Book.*
June 1979	Publication of part three of *The Green Book.*
December 1979	Mob attacks U.S. embassy in Tripoli.
January 1980	Mob burns French embassy in Tripoli.
February 1980	United States closes its embassy in Libya.
May 1981	United States orders Libya to close its diplomatic mission in Washington, DC.
April 1984	London police besiege Libyan embassy and a police officer is killed by shots fired from inside the embassy.
August 1984	Libya and Morocco sign Treaty of Oujda, declaring a union between the two states.
April 1986	United States carries out air strikes against targets around Benghazi and Tripoli.
August 1986	Morocco withdraws from union with Libya.
October 1988	United States first accuses Libya of building chemical weapons plant.
December 1988	Pan Am flight 103 explodes over Lockerbie, Scotland.

February 1989 Algeria, Libya, Mauritania, Morocco, and Tunisia create Arab Maghrib Union.

March 1989 Libya complains Islamist groups, like the Muslim Brotherhood, are using religion to obtain political power.

September 1989 UTA flight 772 explodes over Niger.

August 1991 Libya marks opening of Great Manmade River.

April 1992 United Nations imposes sanctions on Libya.

November 1992 Libya demands compensation from Italy for its thirty-two-year occupation.

November 1994 Libya sets multiple exchange rate for Libyan dinar one week after the currency is devalued.

September 1995 Islamists clash with government forces in Benghazi.

April 1996 Qaddafi announces Libya will cease doing business with Western companies.

March 1997 Vatican establishes full diplomatic relations with Libya.

October 1998 South Africa bestows Order of Good Hope on Qaddafi in recognition of his support in the fight against apartheid.

April 1999 United Nations Security Council suspends Libya sanctions.

March 2000 Libya abolishes most central government executive functions, devolving responsibility to twenty-six municipal councils constituting General People's Congress.

September 2000 Widespread racial violence reported in Libya.

January 2001 Lockerbie court finds one of two Libyan defendants guilty.

October 2001 Libya selected for seat on United Nations Social and Economic Council.

March 2003	Secret talks open in London aimed at dismantling Libya's unconventional weapons programs.
September 2003	United Nations Security Council lifts Libya sanctions.
December 2003	Libya abandons unconventional weapons programs.
March 2004	General People's Congress discusses measures to liberalize Libyan economy.
June 2004	United States and Libya restore diplomatic relations.
September 2004	United States revokes trade embargo on Libya.
October 2004	European Union lifts arms embargo on Libya.
January 2005	Libya abolishes People's Courts.
March 2005	Qaddafi argues United Nations reforms should abolish Security Council.
May 2005	United States plans to restore military cooperation with Libya.
June 2005	Libyan opposition gathers in London to discuss plans to remove Qaddafi from power.
March 2006	General People's Committee creates a human rights office.
May 2006	United States removes Libya from its list of state sponsors of terrorism.
June 2006	Colony Capital purchases controlling interest in Tamoil, the largest sale of a Libyan-owned asset to that time.
July 2006	World Bank describes Libya as one of the least-diversified oil-producing economies in the world.
October 2006	Libya announces the country's 1.2 million students will receive inexpensive computers as part of the One Laptop per Child project.

December 2006	Libyan court sentences five Bulgarian nurses and a Palestinian doctor to death for the alleged deliberate HIV infection of 426 children at a Benghazi hospital.
March 2007	Libya refuses to attend an Arab summit in Saudi Arabia.
May 2007	Prime Minister Tony Blair visits Libya as part of a farewell tour of Africa.
June 2007	Qaddafi criticizes U.S. plans to deploy AFRICOM, a newly created American military command for Africa.
July 2007	Libya releases six foreign medics charged with the deliberate HIV infection of children in a Benghazi hospital.

Map 1 Libya

1

EARLY HISTORY

Much of the history of north-west Africa is the history of foreigners. Its civilizations have been imposed on its indigenous people largely from outside, and it was usually conquered from outside. Yet they have endured with considerable vigour.

Susan Raven, *Rome in Africa*, 1993

In Libya, you are made aware the whole time of the abandonment of things, the material leftovers of receding cultures.

Anthony Thwaite, *The Deserts of Hesperides*, 1969

Because Libya rests on the periphery of three worlds – Arab, African, and Mediterranean, geography has been an important influence on the historical development of its principal regions. The Gulf of Sirte, also known as the Gulf of Sidra, is centered on the country's Mediterranean coastline, forming a deep but irregular salient on its headlands. The desolate Sirte Basin, a remote desert tract known as Sirtica, extends three hundred miles along the Libyan coast below the Gulf of Sirte, dividing the country into two parts.

Formidable sea and land barriers, combined with vast deserts in the southeast and southwest of the country, resulted in the early delineation of Libya into three regions, Cyrenaica in the east, Tripolitania in the west, and Fezzan in the southwest. Historically,

Cyrenaica tended to look eastward toward the Mashriq or eastern Islamic world while Tripolitania looked westward toward the Maghrib or western Islamic world. With southern Libya extending well into the Sahara Desert and sharing selected socioeconomic features with neighboring African states, Fezzan naturally looked south to central and western Africa.

The very word "Libya," which derives from the name of a single Berber tribe known to the early Egyptians, embodies a misconception. The Greeks applied the term to most of North Africa and the name Libyan to its Berber inhabitants. It was later applied to former Ottoman provinces by Italy in 1911 as an integral part of an imperialist policy aimed at justifying colonialism by linking it to the Roman Empire and then adopted by the United Nations in 1951 to refer to the newly created United Kingdom of Libya. No European, Ottoman, or indigenous authority used the term "Libya" before the beginning of the last century. And it was not formally adopted as the name of Italy's colony in North Africa until 1929 when the separately administered provinces of Cyrenaica, Tripolitania, and Fezzan were joined under a single Italian governor. We will speak of Libyan history for reasons of convenience, but it is important to remember that Libya as an integrated administrative, economic, and political reality, is less than sixty years old.

HISTORICAL SETTING

The prehistory of Libya is shrouded in mystery with the available archeological evidence both complex and controversial. In addition, it should be recognized at the outset that the early history of Libya is known to us only through Greco-Latin literature. The early peoples of the region, from Berbers to Vandals, had no written language. Therefore, while they were described by Greek and Roman officials, geographers, and other travelers, the knowledge we have of them is indirect, through the eyes of others, and has nothing to do with the ancient peoples themselves.

The coastal plain of Libya from at least 7000 BCE shared in a Neolithic culture, skilled in the cultivation of crops and the domestication of cattle, which was common to the Mediterranean littoral. In the south of the country in what is now the Sahara Desert, nomadic herdsmen and hunters roamed large, well-watered grasslands, abounding in game. The savanna people flourished until worsening climatic conditions around 2000 BCE caused the region to desiccate. Fleeing the encroaching desert, they either migrated to the Sudan or were absorbed by local Berbers.

We also know very little about the origins of the Berber people. Egyptian inscriptions dating from the Old Kingdom (ca. 2700–2200 BCE) are the first recorded testimony of Berber migrations and the earliest written documentation of Libyan history. At least as early as this time, Berber tribes, one of which was known to the Egyptians as the Lebu or Libyans, were raiding eastward as far as the Nile Delta. During the Middle Kingdom (ca. 2200–1700 BCE), the Egyptians succeeded in establishing some dominance over these eastern Berbers and extracting tribute from them. Around 950 BCE, a Berber is thought to have seized control of Egypt and ruled as pharaoh under the name Shishonk I. His successors, the so-called Libyan dynasties, are also believed to have been Berbers.

It remains unclear when the Berber peoples reached modern-day Libya, but they were known to the writers of classical Greece and Rome who applied the name Libyan to all of them. The Greek historian, Herodotus, who visited North Africa in 450 BCE, described their social and political organization in some detail. Gaius Sallustius Crispus, the Roman historian known as Sallust, described their life in the first century BCE in a detailed account, many of whose particulars remain accurate today. Berber speakers are now a minority in the Maghrib in general and Libya in particular; nevertheless, the area in which they are found remains immense, testifying to the size of the original population. Small clusters are found at Siwa, in the western desert of Egypt, and in Fezzan in southern Libya. From the Jebel Nefousa in northwestern Libya, a large Berber-speaking area stretches southwest into southern Algeria, eastern Mali, and western Niger. Numerous Berber speakers also exist in northern Algeria and throughout Morocco.

The Garamantes were a tribal confederation of Saharan people living in what is now Fezzan. Little is known about them, including what they called themselves. Garamantes was a Greek name which the Romans later adopted. A local power between 500 BCE and CE 500, the Garamantes first appeared in written record in *The Histories* by Herodotus. The political power of the Garamantes was limited to a chain of oases some 250 miles long in the Wadi Ajal. However, because the Garamantes occupied the oases on the most direct route from the Mediterranean Sea to central Africa, the so-called Garamantean Road, they controlled trans-Saharan trade from Ghadames south to the Niger River, east to Egypt, and west to Mauritania. The valleys of Fezzan are rich in archeological sites; part of Germa (Garama), the capital of the Garamantes, was excavated in the 1960s.

PHOENICIAN SETTLEMENTS IN TRIPOLITANIA

The Phoenicians, or Punics, were an eastern Mediterranean people whose homeland included the coastal regions of contemporary Syria, Lebanon, and northern Israel. Skillful navigators and accomplished merchants, the Phoenicians were active throughout the Mediterranean Basin before the twelfth century BCE, founding commercial outposts based on an enterprising maritime trading culture. Carthage, founded in the ninth century BCE along the Mediterranean coast of what is now Tunisia, was among the most successful of the Punic colonies.

The region of Tripolitania was settled by the Phoenicians as part of an effort to extend the influence of Carthage throughout the west coast of North Africa. The Punics established permanent set-tlements, building three large coastal cities, Oea (Tripoli), Labdah (later Leptis Magna), and Sabratha, known collectively as Tripolis (three cities). By the fifth century BCE, Carthage, the greatest of the

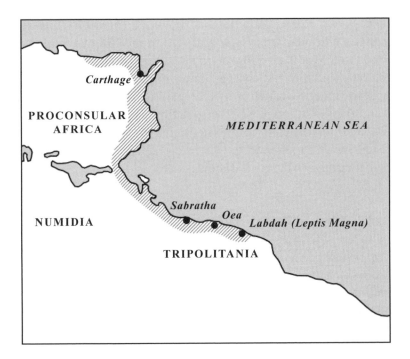

Map 2 Punic Settlement in Libya

overseas Punic colonies, had extended its hegemony across much of North Africa.

From its coastal location a few miles northeast of modern-day Tunis, Carthage exerted an especially strong influence on surrounding Berber populations. Essentially a maritime power, the Punics in Tripolitania, unlike the Greeks in Cyrenaica, also established and cultivated excellent relations with the Berbers, trading with them as well as teaching and learning from them. As a result, the Berbers eventually became somewhat Punicized in language and custom although the full extent of Punic influence on the Berbers remains a subject of historical debate. What is clear is that Carthage, together with Tripolis, later drew support from Berber tribes during both the first Punic War (264–241 BCE) and second Punic War (218–202 BCE).

The early Punic Wars doomed Carthage, ending its former glory. The Romans later sacked the city at the conclusion of the third Punic War (149–146 BCE) to forestall a Carthaginian revival. Nevertheless, the influence of Punic civilization on the North African region remained strong. Displaying a remarkable gift for cultural assimilation, the Berbers readily synthesized Punic cults into their folk religion. In the late Roman period, the Punic language was still spoken in the towns of Tripolitania as well as by Berber farmers in the coastal countryside.

GREEK INFLUENCE IN CYRENAICA

The region of Cyrenaica, occupying the eastern half of Libya, derives its name from Cyrene, the first Greek city in North Africa, founded in 632 BCE. Within two centuries, four more cities had been founded on the North African shore, thereby bringing the entire littoral of Cyrenaica under Greek influence. The four new cities were Barce (Al Marj), Euesperides (later Berenice, present-day Benghazi), Teuchira (later Arsinoe, present-day Tukrah), and Apollonia (later Susa, the port of Cyrene). Collectively, these five cities, all of which eventually became republics and experimented with a variety of democratic institutions, came to be known as the Pentapolis, a federation of five cities that traded together and shared a common coinage. Often in competition, they found it difficult to cooperate even when faced with a common enemy.

The early history of Cyrene, built approximately nine miles from the sea with a population at its peak of some three hundred thousand, is shrouded in legend. The first settlers are believed to have come from the island of Thera (present-day Santorini), possibly because the population had become too large for the limited economic resources of a small island. Whatever its origins, the city flourished; by the fifth century BCE, it was one of the largest cities in Africa. Today, Cyrene generally is considered, after Leptis Magna, the second most important archeological site in Libya. It is the most splendidly preserved of the five Greek cities of the

Pentapolis with buildings originally modeled after those at Delphi. Archeological highlights from the Greek era include the Agora, Sanctuary of Apollo, and the Temple of Zeus. Apart from the ruins themselves, the location of the ancient city of Cyrene is noteworthy as it sits on a bluff overlooking the sea. Cyrene covers a large area and is still not completely excavated.

The old city of Apollonia, founded at the same time as Cyrene, was named after the principal god of the city. Built to provide a port for Cyrene, it was initially a dependency of the former. As the mother city declined, it increased in stature in the second and third centuries, becoming the capital of Upper Libya. After Cyrene, the ruins at Apollonia are probably the most rewarding archeological site in Cyrenaica. Situated on the coast with the sea in front and hills behind, the site features several important monuments, including a

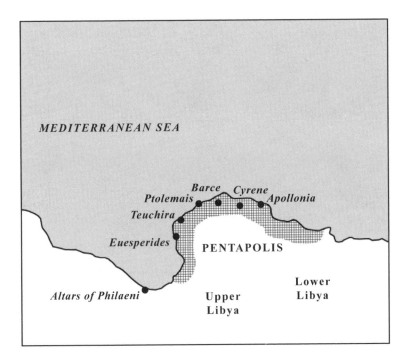

Map 3 Greek Settlement in Libya

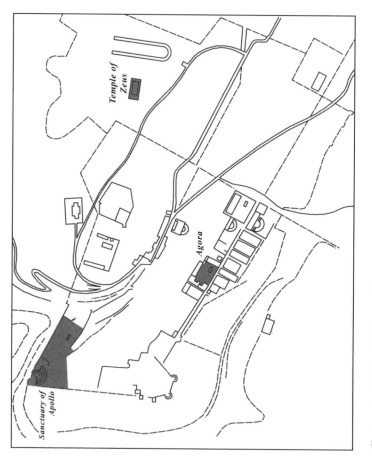

Illustration 1 Greek Ruins at Cyrene

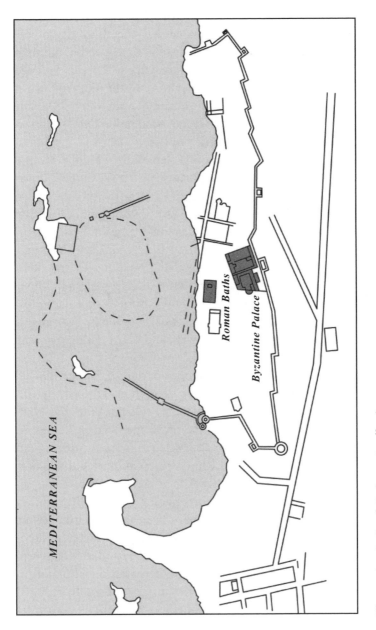

Illustration 2 Greek Ruins at Apollonia

complex of Roman baths and a sumptuous Byzantine palace. The ancient city also hosts the remnants of five Byzantine churches.

Founded around 560 BCE, Barce was the third city of the Pentapolis. An early focal point of dissent, by the end of the sixth century BCE Barce had lost its independence to Cyrene. Situated inland, its original location is now occupied by the modern town of Al Marj; nothing of Barce remains. Al Marj, site of considerable European settlement during the Italian occupation (1911–43), was severely damaged by an earthquake in 1963.

Teuchira was the fourth city of the Pentapolis. Founded around 510 BCE, it was one of the first ports settled from Cyrene. It was renamed Arsinoe, after the first wife of Ptolemy II, and later known as Cleopatris, after the daughter of Mark Anthony and Cleopatra. At various stages in its history, it enjoyed a gymnasium, baths, temples, and private houses. Consisting mostly of soft sandstone, Teuchira was not built to withstand the earthquakes and other natural and man-made calamities that visited Cyrenaica in subsequent centuries. Nothing remains of the city today except for a few Greek and Roman columns in various stages of repair, the remains of Roman tombs cut into a rock wall, and a fort dating from the Ottoman and Italian eras.

Located on the edge of contemporary Benghazi, Euesperides did not figure large in history. It was first mentioned in 515 BCE in connection with the revolt of Barca from the Persians. A punitive expedition sent from Egypt to quell the revolt marched as far west as Euesperides. The settlement was subjected to sporadic attacks from Libyan tribes over the next three centuries; and around 405 BCE, new settlers arrived from the Greek town of Naupactus to supplement a population devastated by ongoing conflict. The earliest occupation of the city seems to have been in the north, on the slightly higher ground, but these early levels probably do not predate the mid-sixth century BCE. The lower city and the walls were laid out between 375 and 350 BCE, and there was more building in the area in 350–325 BCE. Occupation of the city apparently dropped beginning around 275 BCE. In the latter fourth century, Euesperides backed the losing side in the revolt led by Thibron, a Spartan adventurer defeated by Cyrene in alliance with Berber tribes. Extensive archeological excavations have been conducted at Euesperides, especially by the Ashmolean Museum at Oxford University.

The city of Benghazi, capital of Cyrenaica and today the second largest city in Libya, was founded by Greek settlers moving westward. Built in part over the ancient city of Euesperides, Benghazi later became a part of the Roman Empire; unfortunately, very little is known of its early history. Like many North African cities, Benghazi suffered extensive damage at the hands of the Vandals; and after a brief period of repair under the Byzantines, it fell into obscurity. Rediscovered in the fifteenth century, Tripolitanian merchants helped return Benghazi to a new and prosperous phase.

Tradition has it that the citizens of Carthage and Cyrene agreed to set the border between their competing spheres of influence at the point where runners starting from either city should meet. When the brothers Philaeni, representing Carthage, met the runners from Cyrene on the southern shore of the Gulf of Sirte, the Greeks refused to believe the Carthage runners had run a fair race. To demonstrate to Cyrene the good faith of Carthage, the two Philaeni brothers agreed to be buried alive on the spot. In ancient as in contemporary times, the Altars of Philaeni, which the Greeks built over the graves of the two brothers, are regarded as the traditional boundary between Cyrenaica and Tripolitania. The Emperor Diocletian (ruled 284–305) later marked the spot with four marble columns bearing statues, two tall ones for Augusti and a shorter pair for the Caesars. During the Italian occupation, Italy erected a grandiose monument on the spot which British soldiers during World War II jokingly referred to as the Marble Arch; it was later dismantled.

For a time, the inhabitants of the five cities constituting the Pentapolis successfully resisted aggressive invaders from both east and west; however, due to intense intercity rivalries, they were seldom able to mount a common front against their foes. This weakness led to their eventual conquest by the army of the Persian king,

Cambyses III, fresh from his conquest of Egypt, in 525 BCE. Pentapolis existed as the westernmost province of the Persian Empire for the next two centuries, but it returned in 331 BCE to Greek rule under Alexander of Macedonia. Eight years later, upon the death of Alexander, the region was incorporated with Egypt and given to Ptolemy I, trusted chief of Alexander's general staff and first king of the Ptolemaic dynasty (323–285 BCE).

Cyrenaica remained under Greek rule, its kings drawn from the Ptolemaic royal house, until its last king, Ptolemy Apion, bequeathed it to Rome in 96 BCE. Cyrene's early Roman period (96 BCE–CE 115) was marked by the creation of the province of Cyrenaica in 74 BCE. Cyrenaica was combined with Crete as a Roman province in 67 BCE. While a part of the Roman Empire, Cyrene suffered serious damage during the Jewish revolt in Cyrenaica in CE 115–17. The revolt was brutally suppressed by Emperor Trajan (ruled 98–117), but it fell to his successor, Emperor Hadrian (ruled 117–38), to set about rebuilding what was destroyed. Major earthquakes in 262 and 365 again caused widespread destruction to the city. As part of a reorganization of the empire in 300, Emperor Diocletian separated the administration of Crete from Cyrenaica, forming the provinces of Upper Libya and Lower Libya and marking the first time the name Libya was used as an administrative designation. In 303, Diocletian transferred the capital of Cyrenaica to Ptolemais. With the definitive partition of the empire in 324, Tripolitania was attached to the western empire while control of eastern Libya passed to Constantinople and the Byzantines.

The socioeconomic life of the Greeks of Pentapolis appears to have been less affected by the political turmoil plaguing Cyrenaica than might have been expected. The region grew rich from the production of grain, wine, wool, and from stockbreeding as well as from silphium, an herb that grew only in Cyrenaica and which was widely regarded as an aphrodisiac. The city of Cyrene became one of the great intellectual and cultural centers of the Greek world, rightly famous for its medical school, learned academies, and architecture. It was also home to a school of thinkers, the Cyrenaics, who expounded a doctrine of moral cheerfulness, defining happiness as the sum of human pleasures. In its intellectual prime, three of Cyrene's native sons made names for themselves elsewhere, Callimachus the poet (305–240 BCE) and Eratosthenes the scientist (275–194 BCE) in Alexandria, and Carneades the philosopher (214–129 BCE) in Athens.

ROMAN INFLUENCE IN LIBYA

In the third century BCE, Rome and Carthage entered into a competition for control of the central Mediterranean, a struggle ending with Rome's destruction of its rival at the close of the third Punic War in 146 BCE. At the time, the Roman provinces of Africa corresponded roughly to the territory previously controlled by Carthage. In 46 BCE, Julius Caesar (100–44 BCE) awarded land grants in North Africa to the soldiers who had defeated Juba, the Numidian king who had allied with Pompey in the civil wars that left Caesar the undisputed master of the Roman world. By 27 BCE, Roman rule had expanded to encompass virtually all of the coastal areas of contemporary Tunisia.

Early Roman efforts at North African colonization were haphazard, consisting mostly of large agricultural estates. The systematic colonization of the region did not begin until approximately one century later. In Tripolitania, settlement in the Roman period divided fairly neatly into three zones: the coastal plain, the high plateau to the south where limited rainfall permitted some cultivation, and the pre-desert to the southeast where agriculture necessitated irrigation to be viable. On the coastal plain, olive oil developed into a very important cash crop. Tripolitania produced a significant quantity of olive oil from the time of Julius Caesar until at least 363. Further south, enormous labor was devoted to large estates to catch as much rainfall as possible through terracing and dams. Because early Roman settlers fully exploited the agricultural possibilities of the land, North Africa became an important granary for Rome. The numerous references to the plight of Rome anytime there was an interruption in the food supply from Africa

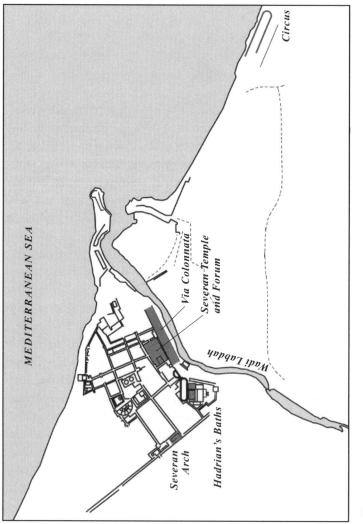

Illustration 3 Roman Ruins at Leptis Magna

attests to the importance of the region as a food source. The Romans also employed their legions to complete public works such as building roads, ports, aqueducts, and baths.

Leptis Magna, one of the three large coastal cities founded by the Phoenicians and known as the Tripolis, developed into the finest remaining example of an African city during the Roman period. The importance of Leptis Magna lay in its geographical position in relationship both to the Mediterranean and the relatively well-watered hinterland of Tripolitania. Sheltered by a promontory at the mouth of the Wadi Labdah, Leptis Magna exemplified the growth progression familiar to other Roman towns – a nuclear core with divergent though mostly rectilinear enlargements. Leptis soon overshadowed in importance its sister ports of Oea and Sabratha.

Wealthy private citizens in the first century contributed to the early development of Leptis Magna. In the second century, Emperor Septimius Severus (ruled 193–211), a native son, together with his son, Emperor Caracalla (ruled 211–17), made significant contributions to the architectural and cultural development of the city in a period widely considered to be the apogee of Leptis Magna. With the decline in seaborne trade that followed serious economic crises at the end of the third century, attacks by Berber tribes, in particular the Austuriani, became bolder and more ruthless. The raids by the Austuriani, which began in 363–65, continued off and on for the next four decades. Following an invasion of the city by the Vandals, commerce came to a halt, the harbor silted up, and Leptis Magna was abandoned.

Widely regarded as the best Roman site on the Mediterranean, Leptis Magna is clearly the most impressive archeological site in Libya. The Severan Arch, thought to have been erected in honor of a visit from Emperor Septimius Severus in 203, is a grand affair. Decorative carvings adorn the upper levels although most of the carved marble friezes that formerly decorated the top of the arch are now in a museum. The Hadrianic Baths complex, the largest outside Rome, is thought to have been dedicated around 126 and later extended. In the center of the building, a *frigidarium* or cold room paneled with marble has a roof supported by eight massive columns. Other important buildings on the site include the colonnaded street, Severan Forum, and the circus and amphitheater.

Little remains today of Oea, the second city of the Tripolis, which is buried under the modern city of Tripoli. The capital of Libya, contemporary Tripoli is much built over, destroying whatever grandeur once distinguished ancient Oea. The only monument surviving from antiquity is the magnificent four-way arch of Emperor Marcus Aurelius (ruled 161–80) and Emperor Lucius Verus (ruled 161–69). Situated near the port, the northeast side of the arch faces Tripoli harbor. Oea had a single triumphal arch while Leptis Magna had five and Sabratha had none, a probable reflection of Oea's relative importance in the Tripolis.

Like Leptis Magna and Oea, Sabratha began life as a Phoenician trading post, perhaps as early as the eighth century BCE. It later fell under Carthaginian influence in the fourth century BCE. The core of the Roman city was established around the forum and dates from the first and second centuries. Well-preserved, the ruins are less attractive than those found at Leptis Magna; however, the site enjoys a spectacular view of the sea. The Austuriani sacked the city in the late fourth century, and the Vandals later destroyed it in the fifth century. Rebuilt during the Arab occupation, it was neglected during the Ottoman period and then excavated and partially restored during the Italian era.

The earliest parts of the city are in the western area, which corresponds roughly to the original Punic city. The theater is Sabratha's glory and is considered by many to be the most striking Roman monument in North Africa. Built in the late second century, it has been beautifully restored with an unusual backdrop consisting of 108 Corinthian columns. The design is reputed to be a replica of the palace in Rome built by Emperor Septimius Severus, native son of Leptis Magna. It also bears a passing resemblance to the magnificent ruins at Petra in Jordan. Other monuments include the great forum, which dates from a fourth-century restoration. The Basilica of Apuleius, which originally served as a law court, dates from around 440 in its final form as a church.

The heavy tax burden imposed by imperial Rome sparked a revolt in the major cities of North Africa in the year 238. Order was eventually restored, but the bloody suppression of the revolt devastated many of the important towns of the Maghrib. Consequently, the region's economic center of gravity shifted for a time to the smaller towns of the interior, spared the worst effects of the revolt. This projection of imperial rule into the interior antagonized relations between Romans and native Berbers. Between 294 and 305, the region was granted autonomy under Emperor Diocletian; and sometime in the early fourth century, Tripolitania became a Roman province.

The rapid spread of Christianity into the African interior in the first and second centuries further complicated an already explosive situation. Christianity came to be viewed as a means of dissent, and many Berbers converted to the faith, not out of conviction, but because they regarded Christian beliefs as a challenge to Roman rule. Early in the fourth century, the Donatist schism with the hierarchy of the mainstream Catholic Church split Christians in North Africa. The Donatists were not heretics; they largely believed what Catholics believed and shared common forms of organization and worship. The schism originated in a difference in emphasis with the Donatists, so-called after Donatus, the sect's most important figure, holding extremely rigorous views concerning purity and sanctity. For more than a century, revolts flared in Berber areas under the banner of Donatism.

With North Africa an important granary, imperial policy toward the Donatists was influenced heavily by agricultural policy. Rome permitted a surprising amount of religious freedom throughout the province for much of the period as long as the supply of African foodstuffs was not interrupted. The first law proscribing the Donatists was not passed until the year 377. Subsequent laws, extending over forty years, ended in the victory of Catholicism, if not the complete dissolution of Donatism. At the same time, the ongoing religious conflict weakened Rome's authority in North Africa, expediting the Vandal takeover in the early fifth century.

The Vandals were a group of Germanic tribesmen who entered North Africa from Spain, crossing the Strait of Gibraltar in 429. Within a year, Carthage, Hippo, and Cirta were the only Roman cities that had not fallen to the Teutonic onslaught. At the beginning of 435, the Vandal leader Gaiseric concluded a treaty with Emperor Valentinian III (ruled 425–55) in which Rome retained Carthage and its province but surrendered the surrounding provinces to the Vandals. Four years later, Gaiseric attacked Carthage, capturing the city in 439. In 442, Valentinian III made a new treaty with the Vandals, ceding to them North Africa from Tripolitania to eastern Numidia. More than fourteen centuries would pass before the Italians again ruled a part of North Africa, defeating the Turks in 1911–12 to begin their occupation of Libya. In 455, the Vandals sailed to Italy and sacked Rome itself.

The Vandals occupied North Africa for almost a century, settling along the coast and immediate hinterland. In 533, Emperor Justinian I (ruled 527–65), who attempted to rebuild the Roman Empire after succeeding to the throne of the eastern Roman Empire in 527, sent an army under Count Belisarius to reimpose Roman rule in North Africa. Belisarius defeated the Vandals in 534, ending the Vandal Kingdom; however, Byzantine rule never reached the extent of the old Roman Empire. The fortifications around their cities, abundant traces of which still exist, bear witness to the disintegrating authority of the Byzantines. They were forced to fortify any land they occupied to protect themselves from the indigenous population.

ARAB INVASIONS

Following the death of the Prophet Muhammad in 632, a generation of Arab armies carried Islam from the Arabian Peninsula north and east into modern-day Iran as well as west into North Africa. The Byzantine provinces of Egypt, Syria, and Persia were the richer prizes with the remote regions of North Africa almost a footnote. Alexandria was occupied in 643 and Cyrenaica in 644. Two years later, the Arabs moved into Tripolitania where isolated Byzantine garrisons on the coast were overrun and Arab control of the region consolidated. Uqba bin Nafi later invaded the Fezzan in 663, forcing the capitulation of Germa, capital of the Garamantes.

Berber resistance in the Tripolitanian hinterlands delayed the Arab advance westward; however, when the Arabs recognized the Maghrib offered a promising theater of operations against the Byzantine Empire, Arab armies in 670 surged into present-day Tunisia. Stiff Berber resistance twice compelled the Arabs to retreat to Tripolitania; but with the assistance of converted Berber tribesmen, they returned each time in greater force. When Uqba finally reached the Atlantic coast in 682, he allegedly rode his horse into the sea, crying "Oh God! if the sea had not prevented me, I would have coursed on for ever like Alexander the Great, upholding your faith and fighting all who disbelieved!"[1] Apocryphal or not, the story exemplifies the Arab claim to be the chosen people to expand the dominion of Islam; only natural, not human forces, could stand in their way. The Arab empire by 715 stretched to the Pyrenees; and in North Africa it conformed to the limits of the old Roman Empire.

Of all the historical phases through which Libya passed, the seventh century arrival of the Arabs, bringing with them the Arabic language, Islam, and a new way of life, had the most lasting effect on contemporary Libyan society. Cyrenaica and Tripolitania, together with the rest of the Maghrib and Muslim Spain, were systematically organized under the religious and political leadership of the Umayyad caliphate in Damascus. From 661 to 750, members of the Umayyad family, among the most prominent merchants in pre-Islamic Mecca, held the office of caliph (*khalifa*), the successor or deputy to the Prophet Muhammad and the supreme secular and religious head based on this succession. The Umayyads succeeded in extending their power and influence into North Africa, Spain, and southern France; however, while they imposed Arab sovereignty, that did not mean Arabization or Islamization. As the

Moroccan historian Abdallah Laroui has noted, "Arabization required many centuries and Islamization was the work of the Berbers themselves. Even the recognition of Arab sovereignty was ambiguous since the authority of the local chiefs was also recognized."[2]

In North Africa, Arab rule sought the establishment of religious and political unity governed by a legal system administered by religious judges to which all other considerations, including tribal loyalties, were subordinated. Founded on the *shari'a* or traditional code of Islamic law, this legal system was based on the Qur'an, the sacred book of Muslims containing the word of God as revealed to and recited by the Prophet Muhammad, and the *hadith*, the traditions or collected sayings of the Prophet. It addition, it was a system derived in part from traditional Arab tribal and market law.

Islam at the outset was largely an urban religion because Arab rule was most easily imposed on the towns and farming areas along the North African coast. Townsmen valued the increased security that enabled them to practice trade and commerce in peace while Punicized farmers looked to the Arabs to protect their lands. Berber tribal institutions, on the other hand, clashed frequently with the authoritarian government adopted under Byzantine influence by the Arabs. In a cultural clash of considerable proportions, the Arabs came to view the Berbers as barbarians while the Berbers saw the Arabs as arrogant, brutal soldiery consumed with collecting taxes. Many Berbers fled into the desert to escape the Arab occupiers; consequently, Islam initially was confined almost exclusively to the littoral of North Africa.

Following a period of turmoil in the Arab world, the Abbasid dynasty (750–1258) overthrew the Umayyads and relocated the caliphate to Baghdad. The Abbasid caliphs based their claim to the caliphate on their descent from Abbas ibn Abd al-Muttalib (566–652), one of the youngest uncles of the Prophet Muhammad. Even though the Abbasids claimed legitimacy based on membership in the Prophet's family, the Shi'is asserted they were from the wrong lineage, highlighting a perpetual conflict in Islamic history. Genealogical descent from the Prophet has long proved a powerful claim to legitimacy, but it has never been the only one with different groups at different times demanding a caliphate based upon justice. Recognizing the difficulty of governing their vast domains from Baghdad, the Abbasids made little effort to deter regional governors and military officers from asserting their autonomy as long as they recognized the spiritual leadership of the caliph and paid an annual tribute. The fragmentation of the Abbasid empire eventually weakened the power of the caliphs, diluting their political authority and leaving them with only attenuated spiritual powers.

In line with the practice of appointing largely autonomous governors, the Abbasid caliph Harun al Rashid (ruled 786–809) in 800 appointed Ibrahim ibn Aghlab the amir or ruler of what is today a part of the Maghrib. The Aghlabids established a hereditary dynasty at Kairouan, a holy city in northeastern Tunisia, from which they ruled Tripolitania and present-day Tunisia, proclaiming formal allegiance to Baghdad and promoting mainstream Sunni Islam, but otherwise acting as an autonomous state. They successfully restored the economic prosperity of the region, repairing its irrigation system and restoring the vitality of its towns and cities. The Aghlabids later challenged Byzantine control of the central Mediterranean, conquering Sicily and playing an active role in the politics of the Italian peninsula.

FATIMIDS (910–1171)

In the seventh century, a serious conflict developed between the supporters of rival claimants to the caliphate, eventually splitting Islam into two branches, the Shi'is and the Sunnis. The Shi'is supported the claims of the direct descendants of Ali, the fourth caliph and son-in-law of the Prophet Muhammad, arguing the office of caliph should be confined to Ali's descendants. The Sunnis favored the claims of Ali's rival, leader of a collateral branch of the Prophet's tribe, together with the principle of election of the fittest from the ranks of the *shurfa*, the Prophet's descendants through his daughter, Fatima. The Shi'is had their greatest appeal among non-Arab Muslims, found in large numbers in Iran and southern Iraq today, who were scorned by aristocratic desert Arabs.

At the end of the ninth century, missionaries of the Ismali sect of Shi'i Islam converted the Kutama Berbers of the Kabylie region of Algeria to a militant brand of Islam and led them on a crusade against the Sunni Aghlabids. With the fall of Kairouan in 909, the Fatimids ruled over much of North Africa, including Tripolitania. The Fatimids were the only important Shi'i caliphate in Islamic history, and the Abbasids were their principal enemy although the Umayyads also realized the danger they posed. Coastal merchants were the foundation of a Fatimid state founded by religious enthusiasts and imposed by Berber tribesmen. A slow but steady economic revival in Europe fuelled a demand for goods from the East, which North African ports like Tripoli were ideally situated to supply.

With three caliphates splitting the Islamic world, the Maghrib was a battleground in a struggle generally contested by surrogates and local allies. For a time, the Fatimids looked west, threatening Morocco with invasion; however, they eventually turned east, completing their conquest of Egypt by 969. Moving their capital to Cairo, they established a Shi'i caliphate to rival the Sunni caliph in Baghdad. Largely abandoning the Maghrib, the Fatimids left the region to their vassals, the Zirids, a Berber dynasty that ruled the northern parts of present-day Algeria, Libya, and Tunisia from the late tenth to the mid-twelfth century. Effectively confined to the North African coast, Zirid rule proved disastrous. They neglected the agriculture-based coastal economy at the same time as shifting trade patterns gradually depressed the once thriving commerce of coastal towns. In an effort to retain the allegiance of urban Arabs, the Zirid amir in 1049 rejected Shi'i Islam, broke with the Fatimids, and initiated a Berber return to Sunni orthodoxy.

HILALIAN INVASION

Responding to the rebellious Zirids, the Fatimid caliph in Cairo invited the Bani Hilal and Bani Salim, Bedouin tribes from Saudi Arabia known collectively as the Hilalians, to migrate to the Maghrib. In addition to the politics of the time, ideological and religious considerations were long thought to be the primary impetus for the Hilalian invasion; however, contemporary research suggests that economic considerations in the form of severe droughts and famine in Upper Egypt also encouraged their migration. Invading Cyrenaica and then Tripolitania, the Hilalians imposed their Islamic faith and nomadic way of life.

The impact of the Hilalian invasion was devastating in demographic, economic, and social terms. Tripoli was sacked, and life in once-great Greek and Roman cities was snuffed out. The Arabs assimilated or displaced coastal Berbers, devastated settled agricultural life, converted farmland to pasturage, and perpetuated nomadism as the dominant form of social organization until the beginning of the twentieth century. The Hilalian migration was prompted by a complex mix of economic, political, and religious considerations. Other factors, such as a weak central state, nomadic migration, and a prolonged process of climate change, also contributed to the decline in settled agriculture and the spread of pastoralism.[3]

Authorities disagree as to the total number of Arabs to arrive in North Africa during the first two migrations, but the number likely did not exceed 700,000 and may have been much less. Assuming such numbers are directionally correct, the Arab population was no more than ten percent of the whole as late as the twelfth century. While Arab blood was later reinforced from Spain, the Berbers continued to outnumber the Arabs throughout North Africa for a prolonged period. On the other hand, waves of Arabs reached Libya earlier than elsewhere in the region because Libya was situated closest to the Middle East; consequently, the Arabization of the Berbers undoubtedly advanced more quickly in Libya than elsewhere in the Maghrib.

Arab tribes thus have occupied Libya for at least nine centuries, to say nothing of the Arabs that arrived before the Hilalian migration in the eleventh century. Tripolitania has three tribes that trace their origins to the Bani Hilal and five tribes that go back to the Bani Salim. Cyrenaica and Fezzan were occupied mainly by the Bani Salim family of tribes. In addition to the *Saadi* or dominant tribes, Tripolitania had two tribes and Cyrenaica six tribes of mixed origin, known as *Marabtin*. Client vassals, the Marabtin comprised a mix of Berbers and Arabs from the conquest period. The economic dependence of the subordinate Marabtin on the dominant Saadi was the essence of a patron–client relationship. The Marabtin were required to request permission from the Saadi to use pastoral lands and water resources, and they paid tribute for the privilege in animals and land. In turn, the Saadi looked to the Marabtin to protect their herds and wells as well as to join them in fighting other tribes in times of war.

In the wake of the Hilalian migration, tribal life became the predominant pattern of existence in Libya for an extended period of time. Each tribe had its own homeland, soil, pasture, and wells. These areas had no frontiers or definite boundaries, and the main concern of all tribes was the source of water. Most of the tribes in Libya were semi-nomadic, combining herding, cereal cultivation, and date collection in a traditional cycle of annual migration. Private property existed in urban towns and oases, but collective ownership of land and water was the norm in the hinterland. Individual ownership was generally limited to movable property, such as animals and equipment.

As tribes divided into two or more primary divisions and then into subdivisions, the essential characteristics of each division or subdivision remained its lineage and geographical area. Divisions and subdivisions of tribes defended their homeland from encroachment by another division or subdivision just like a tribe would defend itself against encroachment from another tribe. Intertribal wars were common with ownership of land and water resources the normal source of conflict.

In the aftermath of the Hilalian invasion, Zirid rule was confined to a small strip of territory along the Tunisian coast. When the Norman rulers of southern Italy arrived, the Zirids put up little resistance, accepting the dominance of Roger II (1095–1154), the Norman king of Sicily, by around 1150. After occupying Malta, Roger II invaded Tripolitania in the twelfth century with the intent to build an African empire. Initially successful, he was later forced out by the Almohads.

ALMORAVIDS, ALMOHADS, AND HAFSIDS IN TRIPOLITANIA

The eleventh and twelfth centuries witnessed the rise of two Berber tribal dynasties in Morocco, the Almoravids (1073–1147) and the Almohads (1147–1267). Both were founded by religious reformers, and together they dominated the Maghrib and Muslim Spain for over two hundred years. The state apparatus of the Almoravids, who made Marrakesh their capital, had a two-fold foundation. It rested on a militant version of the Maliki school of Sunni Islam, which interpreted the Qur'an literally, together with a military and administrative elite recruited among the Sanhaja Berbers of the middle Atlas and western Sahara. The Maliki school of Islam allowed the Almoravids to portray their defense of Islam as one combining a strict implementation of Islamic law with a zealous propagation of the faith. At its height, the Almoravid state stretched from southern Morocco east to Algiers and north into Spain.

The spiritual and political leader of what became the Almohad dynasty, Abu Abdullah Muhammad Ibn Tumart (ca. 1080–1130), gave the Almohads a theocratic, centralized government, respecting but transcending ancient tribal structures. His military commander and the founder of the new dynasty, Abd al-Mu'min bin Ali al-Kumi (ruled 1130–63), captured Fez and Marrakesh in 1147, signaling the end of the Almoravid dynasty. By 1160, he had forced the withdrawal of the Normans from their strongholds in Ifriquiya and Tripolitania. The Almohads also reasserted Islamic rule in a number of Spanish cities that had turned against the Almoravids, rescuing Córdova in 1146 and retaking Almería in 1157. At its height, the Almohad empire embraced all of North Africa from Tripoli in Libya to Tinmallal in Morocco and from Islamic Spain to the western Sahel.

Despite the military prowess of the Almohads, the Andalusian states of Spain and the city-states of Italy launched uncoordinated, albeit eventually successful, counterattacks over the next two centuries. Through a combination of economic and military means, their combined efforts led to the eventual expulsion of Islam from Spain in 1492 and the subsequent creation of small Christian political and trading enclaves in North Africa. In the interim, the Almohad empire imploded as the periphery filled a growing vacuum at the center and then split off into three competing dynasties: the Marinids (1244–1420) who ruled principally in Morocco, the Zayinids (1236–1318) in Algeria, and the Hafsids (1228–1574) in Tunisia and Tripolitania.

With the demise of the Almohad dynasty, the office of autonomous viceroy in the east became hereditary in the line of Muhammad ben Abu Hafs (ruled 1207–21), descendant of a companion of Ibn Tumart. The Hafsids adopted the titles of caliph and sultan and considered themselves the legitimate successors to the Almohads, keeping alive the memory of Ibn Tumart and promoting the ideal of Maghribi unity from their capital in Tunis. With their economic strength and political support rooted in coastal towns like Tripoli, the Hafsids ceded the hinterland to indigenous tribes which made only nominal submission to the sultan. Although the Hafsid era spanned more than thee hundred years, a combination of tribal states, theocratic republics, and coastal enclaves progressively defied the sultan's authority. As one example, the merchant oligarchy of Tripoli, as early as 1460, declared Tripoli an independent city-state.

In 1510, Spanish forces captured Tripoli; and in 1524, Emperor Charles V (1500–58) entrusted its defense to the Knights of St. John of Malta. Turkish forces drove the knights out of Tripoli in 1551. In the following year, Draughut Pasha, a Turkish pirate captain named governor by the Ottoman sultan, restored order in the coastal towns of Tripolitania and undertook the pacification of the Arab nomads in the interior. By the end of the sixteenth century, North Africa had been converted into a series of Ottoman provinces roughly corresponding to the modern states of Algeria, Libya, and Tunisia. Tripoli was the capital of a new dominion, comprising initially Tripolitania and Cyrenaica and later Fezzan.

MEDIEVAL CYRENAICA AND FEZZAN

From the twelfth to the sixteenth centuries, Cyrenaica was outside the orbit of the Maghribi dynasties controlling Tripolitania. Oriented to the east, a succession of Mamluk dynasties in Egypt claimed suzerainty over Cyrenaica even though they exercised at most nominal political control. The Bedouin tribes of Cyrenaica readily accepted no authority beyond that of their own chieftains. Merchants from Tripoli revived some of the region's markets in the fifteenth century; however, the main source of income for Cyrenaica's Bedouins remained protection money paid by caravans and pilgrims traveling between Egypt and the Maghrib.

In Fezzan, the tribal chieftains of the Beni Khattab, operating from their capital at Zawilah, dominated the region. Like the Garamantes, they derived their power from control of the oases on the trading routes from Sudan to the markets of the Mediterranean. The Moroccan Muhammad al-Fasi displaced the last of the Beni Khattab around 1550, founding a line at Murzuq that continued as the undisputed rulers of the region under Ottoman suzerainty. The rulers of Fezzan pledged their allegiance to the Ottoman sultan in the 1580s, but the Ottoman administration in Tripoli wisely refrained from otherwise trying to exercise any authority in the region. It was only later that the richness of Fezzani markets prompted Ottoman officials to send troops to Fezzan for the purpose of collecting tributes. Ottoman authority was similarly absent from Cyrenaica even though a bey or commander was stationed at Benghazi in the late seventeenth century to act as an agent of the government in Tripoli.

LASTING IMPRESSIONS

Contemporary Libya occupies a region of the African continent subject since the beginning of recorded history to successive waves of empire-builders. Repeatedly, it was a colony, state, or province of empires ruled from Africa, Asia, or Europe. At the same time, foreign rule was mostly confined to the Mediterranean coastlands with the interior of the country populated by long-established and largely independent Berber communities, recognizing the authority of their own leaders. Under some form of foreign rule until independence in 1951, Libya has endured a long history of subjugation to external domination and influence. One of the few positive results of this extended period of foreign rule is a country rich in the haunting ruins of its Phoenician, Greek, Roman, Byzantine, Ottoman, and Italian occupiers.

While the early history of Libya left the countryside pock-marked with the remnants of past empires, successive Arab incursions left the most lasting impression on the Libyan people. Beginning with the Arab invasions in the seventh century and reinforced by the Hilalian migration in the eleventh century, Islam penetrated North Africa in general and Libya in particular, marking Libyan society with a distinct and lasting Arab-Islamic character.

2

OTTOMAN OCCUPATION, 1551–1911

Ottoman Libya was a regency removed from the central government, as well as a poor and marginal one when compared with those of other provinces such as Syria and Egypt. The regency was composed of many communities competing with the central state in Tripoli. Tribal confederations, as independent socioeconomic and political organizations, were able to compete with the weak states in Tripoli from the sixteenth century onwards.

Ali Abdullatif Ahmida, *Forgotten Voices*, 2005

Turkey, having obtained the acknowledgment of the European Powers regarding her suzerainty over Tripolitania and Cyrenaica, endeavoured not only to establish and gradually improve the system of local government but also the economic conditions of the two colonies generally.

Anthony J. Cachia, *Libya under the Second Ottoman Occupation*, 1945

The Ottoman Empire emerged around 1300 in western Asia Minor not too far from the site of modern Istanbul. For over a millennium, this region had belonged first to the Roman Empire and later to the Byzantine Empire, its successor in the eastern Mediterranean world. In a remarkable process of state building, the Ottoman Empire expanded west and east, conquering Byzantine, Serb, and Bulgarian kingdoms as well as Turkish nomadic principalities in Anatolia (Asia Minor) and the Mamluk sultanate based in Egypt. By the mid-seventeenth century, the Ottomans ruled vast lands in western Asia, northern Africa, and southeast Europe.

Ottoman armies attempted to conquer Hapsburg Vienna in 1529 and again in 1683. In their second attempt, the Ottoman forces suffered a catastrophic defeat, an event that permanently reversed power relations between the Ottoman and Hapsburg empires. Soundly defeated in 1683, the Ottomans never again threatened central Europe even though they managed to occupy southeast Europe for another two hundred years. The Ottoman Empire endured even longer in its Asian and African provinces. The bulk of contemporary Turkey, Syria, Lebanon, Iraq, Israel, Palestine, Jordan, and Saudi Arabia were part of the Ottoman Empire until World War I.

FIRST OTTOMAN OCCUPATION (1551–1711)

In the sixteenth century, the regions east of Morocco were provinces under the direct control of the Ottoman Empire. The Sublime Porte formally divided the region into the three regencies of Algiers, Tunis, and Tripoli. In the seventeenth century, local military commanders seized control of what is now Algeria, Tunisia, and Libya, and these areas became vassal states of varying sorts. Ottoman diplomacy aimed to regulate the behavior of their nominal vassals or to mediate in struggles among the vassals or between them and the neighboring sultanate of Fez in modern Morocco. Contemporary Libya was thus Ottoman territory, in one form or another, for most of the period from 1551 to 1911.

The territory controlled by the regency of Tripoli approximated northern Libya today, stretching some sixteen hundred kilometers (one thousand miles) along the coast from the border with Tunisia in the west to Tobruk in the east. After 1565, the Ottomans governed Libya through a pasha appointed by the sultan in Istanbul.

The pasha was dependent upon the *janissaries*, an elite military caste stationed in Libya in support of Ottoman rule. Once an effective military force generally stationed at the center of Ottoman armies, the janissaries by the eighteenth century had evolved into a self-governing military guild, subject to its own laws, and protected by the *divan*, a local council of senior officers.

With mutinies commonplace in the far-flung provinces of the vast Ottoman Empire, the janissaries generally remained loyal to whomever paid them the most. In 1611, local chiefs staged a successful *coup d'état* in which they forced the pasha to appoint their leader, Suleiman Safar, head of government. Thereafter, Safar and his successors retained the title *dey* or local chief; and occasionally, the dey was also designated pasha. The regency was autonomous in internal affairs, even though succession to power often involved intrigue and violence, but remained dependent on the sultan for fresh recruits to the janissary corps. In addition to advising the pasha, the sultan also allowed the divan considerable autonomy in matters of taxation and foreign policy.

While the janissaries were responsible for maintaining order and collecting taxes, it was the Barbary corsairs who supplied the regency's treasury with steady income from corsairing or privateering, a practice wrongly described as piracy or terrorism. Operating openly under the instructions of recognized governments, the Barbary corsairs followed a formal set of rules that the European powers, and eventually the United States, accepted and honored. Taking a businesslike approach, the corsairs were interested in booty and ransom for profit, not murder or assassination for political means. As Richard B. Parker noted in his study of *Uncle Sam in Barbary*, "the Barbary corsairs appear to have been no worse than their European colleagues, and in some cases may have been more humane."[1]

The Barbary corsairs represented an important extension of Ottoman naval strategy in the Mediterranean as they regularly contributed men and vessels to the Ottoman fleet. British, Dutch, or French fleets occasionally bombarded Tripoli in reprisal for depredations against their shipping, but the European powers also found the Barbary corsairs to be a useful check on their commercial competitors among the Italian maritime states. The British in the late eighteenth and early nineteenth centuries also found them a useful restraint on the nascent commercial activities of the United States.

There are no reliable census figures, but a French estimate at the end of the seventeenth century put the population of Tripoli, the only city of any size in the regency of the same name, at approximately forty thousand. The bulk of its inhabitants, estimated at thirty-five thousand, were Arabs. There were also around thrity-five hundred Ottoman officials, mainly consisting of Turks and a large component of *khouloughlis*, the offspring of Ottoman soldiers and Arab women, who traditionally held high administrative offices. The khouloughlis also staffed the officer corps of the *spahis*, provincial cavalry units that augmented the janissaries. Viewed as a distinct caste, the khouloughlis lived outside the city, identified with local interests, and were generally respected by the Arabs. A sizeable Jewish community was active as craftsmen and merchants. A smaller number of European traders clustered around the compounds of the foreign consuls posted to Tripoli to sue for the release of captives brought there by the Barbary corsairs. Large numbers of enslaved blacks en route from Africa to markets in the east were a ubiquitous feature of seventeenth-century life in Tripoli.

The history of the Ottoman state in Libya has been relatively well documented, but socioeconomic life in the sixteenth to the nineteenth centuries has been largely ignored. This is true in the case of the coastal cities and more so in regards to the tribes of the interior which depended largely on the oral transmission of knowledge. Very little is known about the social life of the common man, and knowledge of the economic life of cities, villages, and oases is also incomplete. Moreover, much of the information available on this early period of Libyan socioeconomic history is drawn from the journal accounts of European diplomats, businessmen, and travelers. The journals of Thomas Baker, English consul in Tripoli in 1677–85, exemplify this format.[2] Concerned primarily with matters of commerce and trade, these few sources are often enlightening; but they provide an incomplete picture, limited in focus, difficult to confirm, and often biased.

In urban areas, commercial and economic life was regulated to a degree by *qadas*, districts supervised by *qaimmaqam* and responsible to the military governor, and *sanjaks*, administrative units governed by a *sanjak dey*. The qada-sanjak unit was the basic Ottoman administrative unit and was found throughout the empire. The regulation of economic life included the price-fixing of retail commodities and imports, inspection of weights and measures, and supervision of the public weighing station. To ensure compliance, Ottoman officials conducted regular inspections of city markets.

In reality, the regency of Tripoli consisted of two parallel societies evolving side by side but largely separate. Focused on the cities, urban areas, and coastal regions, the ruling elite was small in number and largely foreign. With the economy of the Ottoman state oriented toward trade and corsairing, its survival in the seventeenth and eighteenth centuries was based largely on the expropriation of revenue by means other than the actual taxation of the indigenous population. Consequently, the orbit of the concerns and relations of Ottoman officials was the Mediterranean world and Europe. In sharp contrast, the indigenous peoples of Libya looked inward and focused on internal commerce, trade, and pastoralism, together with domestic issues and concerns.

After 1661, Ottoman power declined and the janissaries, together with local corsairs, often manipulated the divan. The role of the pasha was reduced to that of ceremonial head of state and figurehead representative of Ottoman suzerainty, with real power in the hands of the military. In the end, the janissaries began designating a dey among themselves. Between 1672 and 1711, some twenty-four deys attempted to control the increasingly chaotic political situation in Libya. Absent firm direction from the Ottoman government in Istanbul, Tripoli lapsed into a period of military anarchy in which *coup* followed *coup* and few deys survived more than one year in office.

KARAMANLI DYNASTY (1711–1835)

Ahmad Karamanli, a khouloughli cavalry officer, overthrew the Ottoman pasha in 1711, founding the Karamanli dynasty which governed Libya for the next 124 years. Once he had seized control, Karamanli immediately swore allegiance to the Ottoman sultan and purchased from the Sublime Porte his confirmation as pasha with goods stolen from Ottoman officials murdered during the *coup d'état*. Even as he continued to recognize nominal Ottoman suzerainty, Ahmad Pasha Karamanli created a quasi-independent, dynastic military garrison with a government largely Arab in composition. Ahmad proclaimed his son Muhammad head of military forces, as well as heir to the throne.

Reigning from 1711 to 1745, Ahmad Pasha pursued active, occasionally enlightened foreign and domestic policies. Expanding commercial and diplomatic relations with Europe, improvements to the armed forces increased the power and prestige of Tripoli. Extending his political authority into Cyrenaica and Fezzan, Ahmad unified the country through a series of campaigns to suppress rebellious Arab and Berber tribes in the interior. By 1745, Fezzan was a tributary to Tripoli and the remainder of the country was pacified, facilitating trans-Saharan trade for which Tripoli was the main outlet. Of the four major caravan routes in the eighteenth and nineteenth centuries, three of them passed through Libya with the fourth in Morocco. Two routes, Tripoli–Fezzan–Kawar–Bornu and Tripoli–Ghadames–Ghat–Air–Kano, passed through western Libya; and the third, Benghazi–Kufrah–Wadai, crossed eastern Libya. The caravan trade long constituted a major source of revenue for Tripoli. Ahmad also encouraged Turks to emigrate to Tripoli which increased agricultural productivity, both for domestic consumption and export, and stimulated the overall economy.

Ahmad Pasha did much to bring political stability and economic prosperity to Libya; unfortunately, his achievements did not long survive him. Although Libya enjoyed until 1835 a largely independent status recognized by the Ottoman Empire, the Karamanli dynasty began its decline immediately after

Ahmad's death in 1745. His successors, beginning with his son, Muhammad, who ruled until 1754, were men of inferior caliber and industry. Moreover, the issue of dynastic succession repeatedly disturbed the political life of Tripoli with the ruling family constantly engaged in internal disputes and power struggles. Recognizing the weakness at the center of the regime, the Arab and Berber tribes of the interior severed their political ties to Tripoli, asserting local independence through revolts in the second half of the eighteenth century. The Libyan economy also deteriorated after 1745, especially during the periods of acute political crisis in the later 1770s and mid-1780s. For example, Tripoli in 1778–80 suffered famine, currency depreciation, and economic stagnation. The years 1784–86 saw another famine followed by a plague epidemic that reduced the population by an estimated twenty-five percent. A reduction of that magnitude clearly meant a real decline in agricultural and commercial output.

The reign of Ali I (1754–93) was corrupt and inefficient, ending in heightened political paralysis and a confused civil war. In 1793, a renegade Turkish officer, Ali Benghul (Ali al-Jazairly) took advantage of the political turmoil to overthrow the Karamanlis and briefly restore Libya to Ottoman rule, adding to the chaos and ruin of the economy. Finally, Yusuf Karamanli, one of three sons of Ali I, installed himself as pasha in 1795. In a throwback to Ahmad's reign, Yusuf worked to tame the tribes of the interior while defying both Ottoman and British naval power, supporting Napoleon Bonaparte during his 1798–99 Egyptian campaign.

On his way to Egypt, Napoleon liberated Libyan and other prisoners incarcerated on Malta; in response to this magnanimous gesture, Yusuf allowed Napoleon to use Libya as a link between Egypt and France once the British had blockaded the Egyptian coast. Under pressure from the Ottoman sultan to attack Egypt from the west while British and Ottoman forces attacked from the east, Yusuf eventually ended his support for the French expedition but only after the British threatened Tripoli. Yusuf Pasha's support for France exemplifies the policy independence the Karamanlis enjoyed within the Ottoman Empire, particularly in the conduct of foreign relations. The Napoleonic conflict also marked an early recognition by the European powers of the strategic position of Libya on the North African coast.

Heavily dependent on long-distance trade, the income from trans-Saharan caravans and the control of eastern Mediterranean sea lanes combined to allow the Karamanlis to rule, like their predecessors, without heavy dependence on revenues from the countryside. Within a year of seizing power in 1795, Yusuf Pasha moved to solidify Libya's position on the Mediterranean, adopting a maritime policy reminiscent of the days of Ottoman imperial expansion in that it put a premium on naval strength. The Libyan fleet in 1798–1800 numbered no more than eleven ships; however, by 1805, it had grown to twenty-four armed vessels, together with several skiffs.

As Libyan sea power increased, Yusuf Pasha called on the various European powers through their resident consuls in Tripoli to establish appropriate treaty relationships, including the provision of consular presents. Spain was the first to respond, and it was soon followed by others, including France and the Republic of Venice. Some European states, like Denmark, Holland, and Sweden, who refused on the grounds that Libyan demands were excessive, soon found their Mediterranean shipping set upon by Libyan corsairs. With overall expenses relatively low, Libya's new navy became a highly profitable venture in the decade 1795–1805, yielding large surplus revenues for the pasha.

The final years of the Karamanli dynasty were characterized by a severe economic crisis compounded by growing socioeconomic problems and deepening political malaise. In 1806–17, Yusuf Pasha attempted to unify the country politically, including pacification of the interior in the regions of Cyrenaica, Ghadames, and Fezzan, to centralize authority around the nucleus in Tripoli. He had largely achieved this objective by 1818 but was unable to resolve Libya's mounting economic problems.[3]

In the aftermath of the Napoleonic wars, the European powers put an end to Barbary privateering. The end of the corsair system dealt a devastating blow to the economy of Libya and the

Karamanlis. To compensate for the lost revenue, Yusuf Pasha mortgaged the regency's future agricultural produce in a process codified in the *tizkera* system. Tizkeras were promises to settle debts against future income, usually from agriculture, and they soon became objects of speculation, especially in the hands of the growing Maltese community in Tripoli. Additional speculation occurred when the pasha debased the Tripolitanian coinage in a desperate effort to pay his growing debts and satisfy British claims against him. Yusuf Pasha also attempted to develop the Saharan slave trade but proved unable to establish the requisite military and political control of the interior. Attempts in 1817–24 to extend Libya's power south beyond the Fezzan to Bornu failed, largely because Tripoli lacked the economic resources necessary for such a venture. In any case, increased participation in the slave trade risked additional European hostility. The anti-slavery movement in Europe was growing in strength, and the European consuls stationed in Tripoli were increasingly aggressive, intervening directly in the internal affairs of the regency.

After 1825, Yusuf Pasha again tried to make Tripoli a maritime power, hoping to repeat the success of 1795–1805; but after some initial progress, the overall failure of this policy was clear by 1832. Deprived of tribute payments and unable to increase slave trade revenues, the regency of Tripoli could not pay for basic imports or service its foreign debt. The subsequent increase in customs duties, together with the imposition of extraordinary taxes on luxury commodities and consumer goods, provoked considerable domestic opposition which eventually degenerated into civil war.

With opposition mounting for over a decade, the first serious revolt against the economic policies of the Karamanli regime was initiated in the summer of 1831 by Berber tribes dwelling in Fezzan in the south of Libya. Unrest quickly spread to southern and eastern Tripolitania and soon posed a serious threat to the government. At the same time, the accumulated external debt of the regency of Tripoli, estimated at 750,000 francs or $500,000, fell overdue with Yusuf Pasha unable to satisfy his creditors in France and Great Britain. Receiving no satisfaction, overseas creditors pressed their consuls in Tripoli for assistance in receiving their money. Having exhausted all other means to generate the revenues necessary to meet his financial burdens, Yusuf attempted to impose an emergency tax on the khouloughlis. Viewing the imposition of taxes as a threat to their privileged status, this traditionally tax-exempt military contingent began the most serious revolt in the history of the Karamanli dynasty.

When the khouloughlis mounted an attack on Tripoli, Yusuf Pasha realized his hopeless position and abdicated in favor of his son, Ali II, who ruled from 1832 to 1835. At this point, the Ottoman government responded to Ali's calls for assistance by sending troops to Libya to put down the rebellion. An Ottoman fleet of twenty-two ships sailed into Tripoli harbor in May 1835; and when Ali II went on board the flagship to greet the Sultan's representative, Mustafa Najib Pasha, he was detained. Najib landed in his stead to announce to the people of Tripoli that he had come to prepare for the arrival of Mohamed Raif Pasha, who the sultan had nominated as governor general of Libya. As Najib's troops restored Ottoman rule in Tripoli, Ali II was later carried into exile. The Ottoman intervention in 1835, following 124 years of Karamanli rule, was in part a reaction to the French occupation of Algiers in 1830. The Sublime Porte increasingly feared the civil war in Tripoli would lead to European encroachment. Great Britain supported the Ottoman decision to take action in Tripoli because the British saw in the French occupation of Algiers a threat to their interests in the Mediterranean.

BARBARY WARS

When the American colonies were part of the British imperial system, American ships engaged in the Mediterranean trade enjoyed such immunities from Barbary corsairs as the British government bought by payments of tribute to the rulers of Algiers, Morocco, Tripoli, and Tunis. With the American declaration of independence, this protection was immediately withdrawn; and the

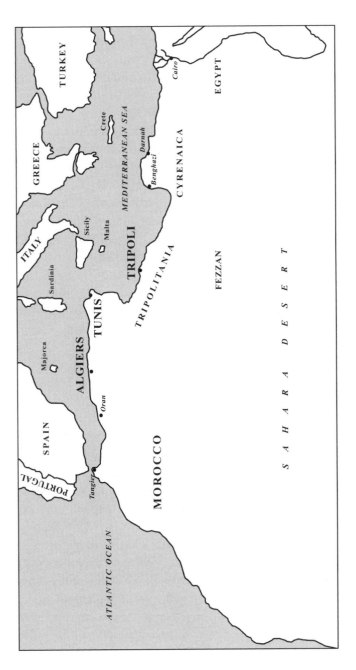

Map 4 Barbary States in 1800: Algiers, Morocco, Tripoli, Tunis

corsairs proved useful to Great Britain in throttling the commerce of its rebellious possessions. After independence was won, the United States continued to face the uncertainties of Mediterranean corsairing. The threat was so severe that some in England argued the nascent economy of the United States would not survive the challenge to commerce posed by the Barbary states.

As early as 1776, the Continental Congress approached France with a proposed treaty, one article of which sought explicit protection from the Barbary states. When the treaty was finally concluded in 1778, France only agreed to employ its good offices and interpose in cases of depredation by Barbary corsairs. The following year, Congress appointed a committee of three to prepare for direct negotiations with the Barbary states; and in 1783 it resolved to send ministers plenipotentiary to the region to conclude treaties of amity and commerce and to procure safe conduct passes. In May 1784, a commission composed of Benjamin Franklin, John Adams, and Thomas Jefferson was established to negotiate treaties of amity and commerce with the principal states of Europe and the Mediterranean, including the Barbary states.

Following the seizure by the regency of Algiers in 1785 of two American schooners, the *Maria* and the *Dauphin*, the United States invoked its 1778 treaty with France; however, the good offices of the latter failed to materialize. In the interim, John Adams and Thomas Jefferson conducted desultory talks, beginning in February 1786, with Sidi Haji Abdul Rahman Adja, the Tripolitanian ambassador in London. In the opening session in which Adams met alone with Adja, Adams was surprised to learn the Tripolitanians considered themselves at war with the United States. These talks eventually floundered on the excessive financial demands of the Libyan emissary, but they remain significant historically, even if there was no direct sequel as far as talks with Tripoli went, as they mark the first direct U.S. diplomatic exchange with the Muslim world. About the same time, Washington dispatched ministers plenipotentiary to Morocco and Algiers. The mission to Morocco soon proved successful as a treaty of peace and friendship was concluded in May 1786.

Backed by Britain, the regency of Algiers proved more intransigent, and a treaty of peace and amity was only concluded in September 1795. Through the terms of the agreement, the United States paid a substantial ransom for the release of American captives and agreed to deliver annual presents to Algiers in the form of naval and military stores. Washington also agreed to give Algiers a thirty-six-gun frigate, appropriately named the *Crescent,* which it delivered in 1798. In the process, American officials opened for the first time the recurring question of whether the United States should supply items of military utility to belligerent states.

The conflict with the regency of Algiers was doubly significant in that it led to the establishment of the U.S. Navy after Congress in early 1794 authorized the building of six frigates. The congressional authorization included a proviso, forced by a determined opposition, that building should cease in the event of peace with the regency of Algiers; however, a compromise bill in April 1796 later provided for completion of three of the six frigates. The remaining three, together with other ships eventually totaling forty-five, were added to the fleet during the undeclared war with France in 1798–1801. The nineteenth century thus opened with a new naval power on the scene, and the United States no longer defenseless against Barbary privateering.

A Treaty of Peace and Friendship between Tripoli and the United States, guaranteed by the dey and regency of Algiers, was signed on 4 November 1796. It promised protection and free passage for the naval vessels of both states and instituted a system of passports to ensure their protection. The treaty recognized money and presents paid to the bey of Tripoli but clearly stated no periodical tributes or further payments would be made by either party. The agreement also incorporated the germs of a serious misunderstanding between the signatories as to the nature of the Algiers–Tripoli relationship, an error that contributed to the outbreak of war in 1801. After 1796, American officials viewed Tripoli as a dependency of Algiers while Yusuf Pasha emphasized repeatedly the need for the United States to treat Tripoli as a sovereign state. American studies of the origins of the war later emphasized the depredations of Libyan corsairing, but Libyan versions more often stressed the failure of the United States to assess correctly the Algiers–Tripoli relationship.

In 1801, Yusuf Pasha demanded better terms from the United States than Tripoli had received in 1796. When the United States refused, he ordered the flagstaff in front of the American consulate in Tripoli chopped down, thereby announcing a breach in diplomatic relations. Bolstered by growing American nationalism and a new fleet of warships, the United States government, headed by newly elected President Thomas Jefferson, decided to pursue a more aggressive policy. Tripoli enjoyed a reputation as a nest of corsairs; however, it was never a major corsairing port. On the contrary, contemporary studies rightly confined Tripoli to a relatively minor role. This relative weakness vis-a-vis other corsairing ports helps explain why the Jefferson administration now chose to make Tripoli an example of its new policy toward corsairing.

In a dramatic expansion of its naval presence in the region, the United States dispatched a naval squadron, consisting of three frigates and a schooner, to the Mediterranean in 1801. When the squadron arrived off Tripoli to learn that war had been declared, it imposed a blockade on the port. The blockade was only partially successful; in October 1803, Tripoli captured the *Philadelphia*, one of America's largest ships with a crew of 307. In one of the most famous exploits in American naval history, the *Philadelphia* subsequently was destroyed in Tripoli harbor in mid-February 1804 by Stephen Decatur and the crew of the *Intrepid*.

In May 1804, Washington appointed William Eaton, a former U.S. consul in Tunis, the navy agent for the Several Barbary Regencies. It also agreed to support an overland expedition by Eaton to overthrow the Tripoli government. The plan was to oust Yusuf Pasha and replace him with a pro-American regime headed by his brother, Ahmad, whom Yusuf had deposed in 1795. In support of this plan, which was the first time the United States government attempted to unseat a head of state, Eaton concluded a treaty with Ahmad in February 1805 in which the latter agreed to guarantee the establishment and paramountcy of American influence in

Tripoli in return for American assistance in helping him regain the Ottoman regency. Commanding a small military force, Eaton departed Egypt in the spring of 1805, seizing the port of Darnah in late April. Still some eight hundred miles east of Tripoli, the gallantry of the U.S. marines at Darnah became the stuff of legend, immortalized in the stanza "to the shores of Tripoli" in the United States Marine Corps Hymn.

As Eaton slowly proceeded westward toward Tripoli, Yusuf Pasha made overtures for peace, which the United States soon accepted; hostilities were terminated on 3 June 1805. In addition to the withdrawal of American forces from Darnah, the terms of the final settlement provided for the release of all prisoners on both sides with the United States giving the regency of Tripoli an *ex gratia* payment of $60,000 because the latter held considerably more prisoners than the United States. It also specified that any Americans or Tripolitanians captured in a future conflict between the two signatories would be treated as prisoners of war, not as slaves. The terms of the agreement were not unfavorable to the United States, but they were criticized at home because they meant the abandonment of Ahmad Karamanli as well as an end to Eaton's plan. Ahmad went into exile and Yusuf remained in power for another twenty-seven years. The Sublime Porte did not participate in the conflict between Tripoli and the United States, and the final agreement between the two parties did not mention the government in Istanbul. Therefore, the bilateral settlement again exemplified Libyan independence from the Ottoman Empire during the Karamanli dynasty.

SECOND OTTOMAN OCCUPATION (1835–1911)

In 1835, the Sublime Porte overthrew the Karamanli dynasty and reestablished direct control over the formerly autonomous province of Tripoli. The restoration of Ottoman rule signaled the end of a long period of decentralized political rule under the Karamanlis and marked a turning point in Libyan history. Under the regime of Mohamed Raif Pasha and his successors, Libya became more closely linked to the Ottoman state. In support of the new Ottoman policy of consolidating power over distant provinces, authorities in Libya were expected to deploy all resources in support of centralization.

When the Ottomans undertook the reoccupation of Libya, they found a war-torn country, undermined by years of strife and neglect. A considerable number of Tripoli's some twelve thousand residents, for example, had fled to the countryside to escape the civil war. The Ottoman reoccupation of Cyrenaica was accomplished with little resistance. A small insurrection near Benghazi was put down without difficulty, and Darnah, the only other Cyrenaican city of any significance, was soon occupied. In western Libya, opposition to direct Ottoman rule was considerably stronger and Ottoman officials spent much of the next fifteen years trying to bribe or coerce local authorities into cooperation. The Ottoman administration did not establish control in Fezzan until 1842 when it installed a governor in Murzuq. Organized resistance to the Ottoman regime did not end in Tripolitania until 1858 when Ghuma, leader of the Mahamid clan and the last holdout against Ottoman rule, was finally captured and killed.

In consolidating Ottoman rule, the power of long influential groups was altered or destroyed, and new relationships developed between the local population and their rulers. Ottoman administrators attacked the entrenched power of Libyan tribes in the firm belief that the traditional decentralization of the Ottoman Empire, largely dependent in the past on local notables for provincial administration, was dangerously outmoded. In its place, the reformers sought to create a more efficient administrative system capable of reviving Ottoman power in the face of European expansion. The implementation of direct control understandably alienated tribal leaders who had enjoyed both autonomous status and socioeconomic privileges under the Karamanlis. Frequent turnover in the Ottoman administration of Libya, a reflection of the rebellious nature of the province and its limited economic importance to the Sublime Porte, complicated efforts at centralization.

Between 1835 and 1911, thirty-two different Ottoman representatives ruled the province with one of those, Ali Rida Pasha, serving twice as governor.

By the mid-1850s, Libya had become fertile ground for the reforms that flowered during the Ottoman reform, or *tanzimat* (reorganization), period. Over the next twenty-five years, the Ottomans proceeded with administrative, economic, and educational reforms as agriculture slowly supplanted the commerce of the dying caravan trade.[4] Two major reforms implemented in the 1860s, land reform and administrative reorganization, reflected the conviction of Ottoman policy makers that fixed settlement was a key to achieving the social and economic development necessary to rejuvenate the empire. Following promulgation of the Ottoman code of land law in 1858, private ownership and registration were introduced to the settled areas of Tripolitania and the urban areas of Cyrenaica. Tribal lands were divided and land ownership was assigned to individuals who paid a small fee for registration. Land reform in Libya was relatively successful in that most of the redistributed land remained in the hands of farmers. In part because agriculture in Libya was a risky business, tribal sheiks did not amass large concentrations of property as happened elsewhere in the Ottoman Empire. Burdensome tax policies also undermined the government's efforts to promote agriculture. Land reform and agricultural development, by encouraging settlement and loosening kinship ties, undermined the tribal organization of nomadic pastoralism.

One casualty of agricultural reform was the commerce of the dying caravan trade. The slave trade was formally abolished in Tripoli in 1853 but continued covertly in the province until the 1890s. After the French successfully suppressed the slave trade first in Algeria and later in Tunisia, trans-Saharan commerce through Libya experienced a mid-century revival, peaking as a major source of income in the decade 1872–81. The reasons for the subsequent decline in the caravan trade included dynastic conflict in the Lake Chad region, French occupation of Kanem, Wadai, and Timbuktu, and the British opening of the Kano–Lagos railway, enabling goods to be shipped from Kano to England.

In the early 1860s, Ottoman administrators also began to implement a variety of political and administrative changes in Libya. New institutional developments included the creation of administrative and village councils together with municipalities and a court system. Criminal and civil courts were established, separating for the first time the duties of administrators and judges. New methods of tax assessment and collection were introduced. The postal system was reorganized, and in 1861 the administration opened a telegraph line between Tripoli and Malta. To encourage commerce between city and countryside, a new gate was opened in the Tripoli city wall in 1865. Further adjustments to the administrative system were made throughout the remainder century as the trend toward settlement and urbanization made municipal government increasingly possible. As a result, Ottoman rule became more centralized, and Libya became more highly integrated within the authority of the Sublime Porte.

The geographical boundaries of Cyrenaica, Fezzan, and Tripolitania were undefined at the outset of the second Ottoman occupation in 1835, and their delineation remained a source of dispute between the Sublime Porte and the European powers for the remainder of the century. Long concerned with French activities in Algeria and Tunisia and British interests in Egypt, the Istanbul government had concluded by the mid-1880s that Italy represented the most serious threat to its African territory. As early as 1883, members of the Italian government and press had urged the occupation of Tripoli, but the new government in Rome refused to embark on an overseas adventure that could endanger its finances and undermine its stability. Thereafter, the Ottoman government in Istanbul pursued a policy intended to mollify the British and French in an effort to gain their support against Italian designs in Libya.

Following the assassination of three French missionaries in Ghadames in 1881, the Ottoman authorities prohibited Europeans from entering the Libyan interior without a visa. Intended to reduce the possibility of future conflict with France or Great Britain, this attempt to isolate Libya from European travelers resulted in a dearth of knowledge about the province. In so doing, the policy of isolation played into the hands of Italian imperialists who later issued exaggerated descriptions of the wealth and promise of Libya. The real limits of the Ottoman policy of appeasement were evident by the turn of the century when the European powers concluded several agreements, dividing Africa into spheres of interests, with little or no consideration for Ottoman claims. For example, France and Italy in December 1902 concluded a treaty recognizing the "special interests" of France in Morocco and Italy in Libya.

SANUSI ORDER

Among the groups granted considerable autonomy by the Ottoman government was a religious order, the *Sanusiyya*. Sayyid Muhammad Bin Ali al-Sanusi (1787–1859) was an Algerian scholar who established the Sanusi Order (*tariqah*) in Cyrenaica in 1842. Born to a distinguished family of sharifs in a village near Mustaghanim in Algeria about 1787, the Grand Sanusi was educated at Mustaghanim, then at Mazun, and later at the famous mosque school at Fez in Morocco. Studying the usual subjects of the time, which included theology, jurisprudence, and the exegesis of the Qur'an, he developed an interest in mysticism, coming under the influence of the Moroccan order of the Tijaniya Darwishes. The Grand Sanusi left Morocco in his thirties and traveled extensively in North Africa and the Middle East before arriving in Cyrenaica in the early 1840s. He founded the first *zawiya* (lodge) of the Sanusi Order at al-Beida, between Benghazi and Darnah near the Mediterranean coast, in 1842; and he later relocated the center in 1856 to Jaghbub, some four hundred miles southeast of Benghazi.

The teachings of Sayyid Muhammad bin Ali al-Sanusi, which advocated a combination of orthodoxy and Sufism, a form of Islamic mysticism, proved well suited to the Bedouins of Cyrenaica. He forbade fanaticism and the use of stimulants and stressed hard work in earning a livelihood. To spread the influence of the Sanusi doctrine, the Grand Sanusi instructed his followers to build rest houses for travelers along the trade and pilgrimage routes. Eventually, these structures became more than rest stops, functioning as religious centers, schools, and social and commercial centers. A strictly orthodox order of Sufis, the Sanusi Order was a revivalist rather than a reformist movement, dedicated to spreading religious enlightenment into areas where Islam was at best only lightly observed. It concentrated its influence away from the main political centers of the Mediterranean Sea and North Africa and among the more inaccessible peoples of the Sahara Desert and Sudan. The Grand Sanusi died at Jaghbub in 1859.

Sayyid Muhammad al-Mahdi al-Sanusi, the eldest son of Sayyid Muhammad bin Ali al-Sanusi, succeeded the Grand Sanusi in 1859. A man with a strong personality and considerable organizational talents, he brought the Sanusi Order to the peak of its influence. During his four decades of leadership, the brothers of the order, known as *Ikhwan*, carried the message to large parts of Islamic and pagan Africa, eventually establishing some 146 *zawaya* throughout the region. Equally important, al-Mahdi succeeded in bringing most of the Bedouins in Cyrenaica under the order's influence. The Sanusiyya brought law and order, curbed raiding, encouraged peaceful trade, and promoted agriculture in a remarkable, civilizing mission amid highly unpromising surroundings. In so doing, the commercial and political activities of the Sanusi Order encouraged educational development and sedentary living, promoting changes similar to those the Ottoman administration was advocating elsewhere in Libya.

Until the 1880s, contacts between the leaders of the Sanusi Order and the Ottoman government in Istanbul were few in number. It was only after Sultan Abdülhamid II recognized the strategic importance of the British occupation of Egypt that the Sublime Porte began to show concern for the future both of the province of Benghazi and the Sanusiyya. There were five high-level exchanges between Ottoman and Sanusi officials in 1886–95. The content of these discussions is not known, but they clearly marked a heightened Ottoman interest in the affairs of the Sanusi Order.

In 1895, Sayyid Muhammad al-Mahdi al-Sanusi moved his headquarters to Kufrah, more than six hundred miles south of Benghazi. The relocation was influenced by Ottoman efforts to extend and assert the provincial government's administrative control over all of Cyrenaica, a move detrimental to the authority of the Sanusi Order and its zawaya. Ottoman taxation efforts may also have played a role in the decision to relocate. Prior to the move to Kufrah, there were armed tax campaigns against Bedouins loyal to the Sanusiyya in 1882–84, 1888–91, and 1891–94. In this context, contemporary research does not support the long-held belief that the Sanusi Order was tax-exempt. There is also little evidence to suggest the Sanusiyya lent Ottoman authorities effective assistance in taxing the Bedouins.[5]

The move south to Kufrah brought al-Mahdi closer to the Sudan and the Sahel. From that location, he could better supervise Sanusi missionary activities under mounting threat from British and French interests who saw the movement as a rival to colonial expansion into Saharan and sub-Saharan Africa. In 1899, the seat of the Sanusi Order was transferred further south to Quru in present-day Chad as growing concern over the British advance from the Sudan rallied local tribesmen around the Sanusiyya. After Sanusi forces suffered their first defeat at the hands of the French in 1902, they abandoned Quru, returning to Kufrah. By this time, Sanusiyya power was on the wane. There were still over sixty zawaya in Cyrenaica and Tripolitania in 1906, but the order appeared to have overextended itself as at least half of these were considered moribund.

With the death of Sayyid Muhammad al-Mahdi al-Sanusi in 1902, his nephew, Sayyid Ahmad al-Sharif, assumed leadership of the Sanusi Order. His leadership fell into three periods, from 1902 to 1912, when he unsuccessfully opposed French expansion in the Sahara; from 1912 to 1918, when he directed the Bedouins of Cyrenaica against the Italians and British; and from 1918, when he went into exile, to 1933 when he died in Saudi Arabia. Al-Sharif lacked the organizational and tactical skills of his uncle, and the fortunes of the Sanusi Order declined as European colonial powers challenged its influence in north-central Africa. As will be seen in the next chapter, with the Italian occupation of Cyrenaica in 1932, the Sanusi Order largely ceased to exist as a religious, political, or social organization in either French or Italian colonial territory.

FOREIGN SCHEMES AND INITIATIVES

American diplomatic and commercial relations with the Ottoman administrators of Libya were minimal throughout the period of the second Ottoman occupation. The one exception surrounded the tenure of Michel Vidal, a former congressman and journalist, who served as U.S. consul in Tripoli from 1870 to 1876. At the time, the consulate was considered a plum assignment for a U.S. diplomat, providing an annual salary of $3,000 plus $800 for expenses. When Vidal arrived in September 1870, there were no Americans resident in Tripoli, and no American merchantman had called for a generation. The formal duties of the incumbent were mostly limited to acknowledging circular instructions from Washington and raising the largest American flag available twice each year to celebrate American independence on the fourth of July and the anniversary of the battle of New Orleans. When he solicited reappointment in 1873, Vidal acknowledged to the State Department that his post could well have been eliminated any time after 1835.

Unwilling simply to enjoy his time and position in Tripoli, Consul Vidal, once granted reassignment, initiated an aggressive, controversial scheme leading to his recall three years later. He had long advocated establishment of a coaling station for American ships on the Cyrenaican coast, involving "colonization by Christians." This was part of a broader strategy aimed at increasing U.S. naval power through creation of a global network of colonies, telegraph lines, and coaling stations similar to that of Great Britain. By 1873, Vidal had linked the question of a Libyan naval base to his personal distaste for the slave trade and his concern for the anomalous position of American diplomats in Tripoli. The latter issue involved Vidal's contention, supported by the State

Department, that the second Ottoman occupation of Tripoli involved a reassertion of suzerainty but had not modified either the legal status of Libya as an entity independent from the Ottoman Empire or American rights under the terms of its 1805 treaty with the Karamanli dynasty. Entwining these issues, Vidal suggested the simplest way to obtain a coaling station would be to return relations to the *status ante pacem* of 1805, dispatch a frigate to Tripoli with instructions to demand an official salute under terms of the 1805 treaty, and, when the pasha refused as Vidal knew he would, seize the desired port.

In August 1875, Vidal was involved in an incident with members of a visiting Ottoman naval squadron which ended with proceedings filed against him in a civil court. When he cabled the State Department requesting protection, he indicated he had been threatened and his home violated, suggesting his opposition to the slave trade was the cause of Ottoman hostility. In support of Vidal, the State Department within two weeks had two warships on station in Tripoli harbor, one of which was the *Congress* whose original namesake had blockaded the port seventy years earlier. Vidal took advantage of the arrival of the *Congress* to remind the pasha, in accordance with the terms of the 1805 treaty, that port fortifications were required to salute the warship. The pasha predictably refused; but under pressure from the Sublime Porte, he eventually visited the U.S. consulate in full uniform to apologize in person. Vidal exulted in this American triumph, but his victory proved bittersweet as he was recalled shortly thereafter at the insistence of the Sublime Porte.

A new consul arrived in October 1876 with explicit instructions from Secretary of State Hamilton Fish, ruling out both an American naval base in Cyrenaica and official support for the emancipation of slaves. Thereafter, the U.S. consulate in Tripoli returned to the *status quo* until 1882 when the U.S. Congress abolished the post. Thus ended a period in American–Libyan relations that began almost a century earlier with the abortive London talks in 1786 between John Adams, Thomas Jefferson, and Sidi Haji Abdul Rahman Adja.

Almost two decades later, the International Territorial Organization (ITO), also known as the Jewish Territorial Organization, was active in Libya as part of an international effort to establish a Jewish national home somewhere besides Palestine. The so-called territorialists sought to direct a part of the Jewish people, in particular emigrants from Europe, to some underdeveloped region where Jews would be a majority, perhaps even with a state of their own. In contrast to the aims of the territorialists, the Zionists thought the problems of modern Jewry would be solved only through the creation of an independent Jewish home in Palestine.

Nahum Slouschz, an active member of the Jewish Territorial Organization, visited a number of ancient Jewish communities in North Africa between 1906 and 1916 in an effort to locate an appropriate site for Jewish emigration. In 1906, he toured Tripoli, the Tripolitanian coast, and the Jebel al-Nefousa; in 1908, he crossed the Jebel al-Akhdar of Cyrenaica, and in 1909, he again visited Tripoli.

Slouschz concluded the prospects for Jewish colonization in Libya were not good, eventually rejecting the idea. In his book *Travels in North Africa*, he explained why he felt Cyrenaica, based on his 1908 visit, would be an especially poor choice for the International Territorial Organization:

> After a three weeks' march across the plateau, we reached Bengazi, richer by the knowledge of a new country and by various scientific discoveries. The plan to colonize Cyrenaica seems to have no future. The lack of water, which could be supplied, as in ancient times, only at great expense and with much persevering effort, daunted the members of the ITO. It was inevitable that a political matter such as this should be liable to change with the political situation: while we were occupied in the interior of Cyrenaica, the Young Turks had been granted a constitution.[6]

YOUNG TURK REVOLUTION

The issues that preoccupied Arabs elsewhere in the Ottoman Empire at the beginning of the twentieth century were also apparent in Libya. While not one of the most cosmopolitan provinces in the empire, Libya and its elite were more closely attuned to events in Istanbul than was immediately apparent. The final decades of the nineteenth century had been a time of relative prosperity in Libya. The province remained the last outpost of the trans-Saharan trade, and Libyan merchants retained widespread commercial ties with the remainder of the empire. Moreover, Sultan Abdülhamid II often used the provinces of North Africa as a form of Saharan Siberia where his more troublesome political opponents could be exiled to prisons or minor posts at the farthest reaches of the empire. One unexpected result of this practice was that the Libyan elite was exposed to much of the intellectual ferment of the time. Turkification policies, the neglect of Arabic in schools, and religious reform were issues of great importance to Libyans as well as to residents of the other provinces of the Ottoman Empire.

At the same time, there was little evidence of separatist sentiment in Libya at this point. Some Europeans, quick to identify local sources of dissatisfaction with the Ottoman administration, thought they had found such a cleavage in Sanusi dissatisfaction with Ottoman policy over French incursions into Chad. Sanusi leaders advocated a policy of direct military confrontation with France while the Ottoman administration preferred to temporize in the vain hope of winning French support against Italian designs on the province. At one point, Sayyid Ahmad al-Sharif even approached the Italian government, via their embassy in Cairo, requesting assistance in combating French influence. Eager to court Sanusi favor and to check French activity in southern Cyrenaica and Chad, the Italians quickly delivered a cache of weapons to the Sanusiyya, weapons the movement later used against the Italians themselves.[7] A difference of opinion between the Ottoman administration and Sanusi leaders thus clearly existed on this issue; however, it was not the genesis of a separatist movement.

Similarly, Sulayman al-Baruni, leader of the Ibadi sect of Berbers in Tripolitania and a deputy in the newly reopened

Ottoman parliament after 1908, was suspected of harboring ambitions for an autonomous Ibadi province in the western mountains. Imprisoned at one point for subversive activity, Baruni appears to have envisioned an Ibadi province within the religious and political sovereignty of the Ottoman Empire as opposed to a fully independent entity.

In 1908, a group of young Turkish army officers joined like-minded civilian revolutionaries in a revolt against the arbitrary rule of the sultan. The Young Turk movement mostly consisted of political reformers, many of whom had traveled in Europe and were influenced by European ideas critical of the Ottoman sultanate. Their immediate interest was a restoration of the constitutional rule suspended by the sultan in 1876. Many Arabs in Istanbul and in Ottoman provinces like Libya welcomed the new era promised by the Young Turks. They hoped the declared spirit of equality would end Turkish domination and increase autonomy for its provinces.

While there was little evidence of separatist activity in Libya, there was clearly dissatisfaction with Ottoman policies. Despite active Young Turk opposition to Italian colonization, local enthusiasm for the Sublime Porte was far from unanimous. Its language policies were not popular while new freedoms were welcomed by only a fraction of the population. Opposition also grew out of more immediate interests, especially a campaign to rid the local administration of reactionary supporters of the sultan. Twice dismissed for political intrigue before the Young Turk revolution, Farhat al-Zawi, for example, eventually joined forces with Suleiman Baruni. By the end of October 1911, both men were traveling their districts preaching resistance and calling for volunteers to oppose the Italian invasion.

TRANSFORMATION

Some 360 years of Ottoman occupation, when the reign of the Karamanli dynasty is included, resulted in a significant social and economic transformation of Libya. The policies of a series of Ottoman governors, most especially during the second Ottoman occupation, combined to establish order, reorganize administration, and increase education. Agriculture and pastoralism, which slowly but surely reduced long-distance trade as primary sources of income, moved from subsistence to revenue-generating activities. While not always evident, the political consequences of this socioeconomic transformation would soon be evidenced in the successful Ottoman mobilization of Libyan popular feeling in defense of the province against Italian encroachment.

In addition to implementing the reforms of the tanzimat period, the Ottoman administrators of Libya in the second half of the nineteenth century sought to centralize power in the province. Successful in part, the Sublime Porte was able to preserve the territorial unity of Cyrenaica, Fezzan, and Tripolitania, no mean achievement in a time when the European powers were carving up much of the rest of Africa. The Ottoman administration was less successful in creating a common identity or a sense of national unity among the people of the province. In consequence, the inhabitants of Cyrenaica, Fezzan, and Tripolitania entered the twentieth century with tribal, local, and occasionally regional identity dominating the political landscape. The failure to develop a broader national identity would also have importance consequences in later struggles, first to challenge the Italian occupation, and then to create a functioning, independent state.

3

ITALIAN COLONIAL ERA, 1911–43

If real violence and murder are to be located in Fascism's international dealings before 1935, they surface in Libya and the so-called pacification being ruthlessly pursued in the empire inherited from the Liberals.

R. J. B. Bosworth, *Mussolini's Italy*, 2006

For Libyans, their perception of their first encounter with the mechanisms of a modern state was that of an authoritarian and domineering [Italian] administration that could be used, seemingly unchecked, to subjugate and often dispossess them.

Dirk Vandewalle, *A History of Modern Libya*, 2006

If it hadn't been for my grandfather [Benito Mussolini], they [the Libyans] would still be riding camels with turbans on their heads.

Alessandra Mussolini, 2006[1]

[Libyan opposition to Italian occupation] was a resistance that was to provide modern independent Libya with the invaluable credentials of battles, national heroes and 'martyrs', and the almost mystical prestige of a prolonged people's 'anti-colonialist struggle' waged against heavy odds.

John Wright, *Libya: A Modern History*, 1982

Italy declared war on the Sublime Porte in late September 1911, seizing Tripoli in October of that year. In November 1911, Rome announced its annexation of the North African province; and the war for control of Libya was joined. In the end, Italy needed more than two decades to subdue Libya; and the cost of that prolonged struggle, in terms of both men and material, far exceeded its most pessimistic expectations. The results of the Italian occupation were even more catastrophic for the population of Libya. Italian colonial policies, which included scorched-earth tactics, concentration camps, deliberate starvation, and mass execution, bordered on genocide, devastating the Libyan people.

MISPLACED OPTIMISM

Italy was one of the last European powers to engage in imperial expansion. The Italian city-states were not united until the second half of the nineteenth century; consequently, Italy was unable to exploit effectively the early colonial opportunities Africa offered other European states. At the turn of the twentieth century, Libya was one of the last African territories not occupied by Europeans; and its proximity to Italy made it a primary objective of Italian colonial policy. Italy saw itself carrying on the traditions of the Roman Empire even though Italian unification had occurred only five decades earlier and Italy was not a leading power at the time.

Visionaries in Rome hoped to return Italy to its former greatness by creating a modern empire. In this regard, many Italians believed it was an historic right, as well as an obligation, to apply Italian sovereignty to those regions once ruled by the Roman Empire. Italy began to penetrate Ethiopia in 1879, but its expansion there suffered a severe blow with the defeat of Italian forces at Adowa in 1896. In part in search of revenge for this humiliating defeat, Italy next turned its attention to Libya which nationalists depicted as a "promised land." Only months before the Italian invasion in 1911, the Italian journalist Domenico Tumiati visited

Ottoman Libya. Standing on the deck of a home-bound steamer, he offered this vision of Libya as an Italian colony:

> The roadsteads of Tripoli, Homs, Misurata and Benghazi, Derna and Bomba, fortified and protected, secure ports, filled with ships loading African riches and bringing in the industrial products of Italy. A network of electric railways branches out from Tripoli to the great plantations of Mesellata, to the mines of Fassato and Yefren, and from there one line extends to Ghadames and another to Murzuk.
>
> In the south, work is being pushed ahead to link Eritrean and Mediterranean Italy, Tripolitania with Ethiopia. The rival of Britain and France, Italy is encamped on two seas, over an expanse of millions of square kilometres, with her own people rapidly increasing alongside the exhausted Arab race. … At Zanzur, Gharian, Mesellata, and Derna, the terraces of Italian villas are surrounded by palms and our lovely women dance away the summer nights amidst a cloud of jasmine near the resurgent remains of Leptis.[2]

In addition to issues of historical right and national pride, many Italians viewed overseas expansion as the best solution to a number of vexing internal problems. At the dawn of the twentieth century, a newly unified Italy still suffered from mutual suspicion and regional conflict. Italian leaders saw a foreign war as a means to divert attention away from internal divisions, unite the population, and increase pride in the homeland. Overseas expansion also offered a means to test the skills and weapons of the armed forces, highly rated at home but held in low regard throughout Europe. In 1913, Italy was able to provide military training for less than twenty-five percent of the available male class compared to seventy-four percent in Germany and eighty-seven percent in France. The shortage of fit potential recruits was one problem, another being the tenuous nature of central government authority over large parts of the national territory. According to historian R. J. B. Bosworth, "In every European chancellery and on every European parade ground, it was assumed that Italians could not fight."[3]

Other Italians believed the colonization of Libya offered an ideal region to settle countrymen wishing to emigrate. Italian emigration to the United States alone exceeded 650,000 people in 1910; and in 1913, the year departures peaked, over 860,000 Italians emigrated to Europe, South America, or the United States. Nevertheless, emigration to many areas, like South America, was becoming more difficult due to the distance and expense involved. In contrast, sparsely populated Libya was close to Italy and reportedly enjoyed a pleasant climate with a favorable coastal terrain. The so-called "agrarian question" in southern Italy and elsewhere, where landless and sharecropping peasants at the end of the nineteenth century were pressuring large landowners for land and voting rights, was also tied to the emigration issue. The ruling classes of Italy hoped to alleviate the problem of land reform by settling peasants in offshore colonies like Libya.

The Banco di Roma was an important component of emigration strategy as it became in the early twentieth century the vehicle in Libya for land purchase, trade investment, and the employment of people to work for the Italian cause. Founded in 1880 by the Vatican with the encouragement of the Italian government, the Bank of Rome opened branches in most major Libyan cities and towns, sponsored factories and mills, controlled maritime transportation between Italy and Libya, and launched an exaggerated propaganda campaign regarding the plentiful raw materials to be found in Libya.

Remote myths regarding the fertility of certain areas of Libya added to the enchantment of this promised land. Enrico Corradini, a nationalist, propagandist, and future minister in the Fascist regime of Benito Mussolini, visited Libya in 1911, only months before the Italian invasion. To convince Italian public opinion of the agricultural potential of the Jabal al-Akhdar region of Cyrenaica, an area the International Territorial Organization had dismissed only three years earlier as unsuitable for large-scale European settlement, he published a highly misleading account of the natural wealth of the region. In so doing, he implied Libya needed only Italian labor and skills to become a flourishing settler-colony:

> Intoxicated with the spirit of felicity that pervades these places where nature has spread out all her bounty, we went on horseback

through wide fields sown with barley and wheat – and I have never seen such wonderful earth, not even in my native Tuscany, nor indeed anywhere else in the world. It is red, stoneless, as fine as powdered tobacco. I rode for hours and hours over the plateau, I went down into the valleys and hollows, I went up again, crossed other plains, found signs of ancient prosperity, of olive trees run wild, a Roman well, cut in the living red rock, which still yielded water.[4]

Italy was also in need of cheap raw materials and markets for the development of its own economy. Based on the limited information available, many Italians assumed the colonization of Libya would address these problems in a positive fashion as well as enable Rome to control the Sahara trade. Little did Italians know that Libya's agriculture was poor, its industry limited, and much of its territory empty.

Ironically, Ottoman authorities contributed to this lack of information, inadvertently encouraging one of the principal arguments for Italian invasion. Afraid that foreign explorers and tourists would be a first step toward occupation, Ottoman officials actively discouraged Westerners in general and Italians in particular from surveying or otherwise touring Libya. In consequence, there was very little reliable, up-to-date information available on Libya with the notable exception of the earlier survey by the International Territorial Organization.

Using real or imagined Ottoman hostility to Italian enterprise in Libya as a *casus belli*, the Italian government sent the sultan an ultimatum on 26 September 1911, demanding the Ottoman Empire agree within twenty-four hours to an Italian occupation of Cyrenaica and Tripolitania. Italian Prime Minister Giovanni Giolitti was determined to annex the entire territory of what became Libya and rejected any counsel to retreat from this course of action. With no interest in a peaceful solution, Italy hurried off to war with the Ottoman Empire in an effort to confront prospective mediators, Austria and Germany, with a *fait accompli*. Italy declared war on 29 September 1911, only four days after its ultimatum to the Ottoman government. With overconfidence and a general lack of Italian preparedness readily apparent, a war between what were, in reality, two third-rate powers quickly developed into a military stalemate. By early 1912, the invasion force was bogged down, signaling the outset of a prolonged conflict.

Despite the relative success of its forces in Libya, the determination of the Sublime Porte, isolated diplomatically and concerned with events in the Balkans, to support resistance in Libya weakened in the first six months of 1912. The Ottoman Empire opened negotiations with the Italian government in July 1912, and a peace treaty was concluded at Lausanne, Switzerland on 18 October 1912, shortly after the outbreak of the first Balkan war. The Ottomans did not cede sovereignty over their North African province; however, the sultan did issue a declaration to his Libyan subjects which granted them full and complete autonomy. At the same time, he reserved the right to appoint an agent charged with protecting Ottoman interests in Libya and agreed to withdraw Ottoman military and civilian personnel. In turn, the Italians reaffirmed their annexation of Cyrenaica and Tripolitania, announced on 5 November 1911, but not recognized by international law until after the Allied peace settlement with Turkey in 1924. Since neither Libyan autonomy nor Italian sovereignty had convincing validity, the status of Libya remained anomalous. A flawed instrument, the ambiguity incorporated in the 1912 peace treaty had a significant impact on future events in Libya as it resulted in the local population continuing to consider the sultan to be both its spiritual and political leader.

EARLY RESISTANCE AND COLLABORATION

The Italian invasion of Libya in 1911 followed on the heels of the Young Turk Revolution; and Young Turk officers, intent on revitalizing the Ottoman Empire, organized resistance to the Italian occupation in 1911–12. The Young Turk movement saw the defense of this Ottoman province as a moral obligation as well as a political necessity and dispatched money, arms, and supplies to

Libya through Egypt and Tunisia. It also encouraged Ottoman officers throughout the empire to converge on Libya to repulse the Italian invaders.

By the end of 1911, an important group of Ottoman officers, known as the Special Organization, had arrived from Istanbul. Functioning as a pan-Islamic secret intelligence unit, the primary objective of the Special Organization was to defeat what the Sublime Porte considered to be the principal dangers to empire – European encroachment and local separatist movements. In taking command of the early military resistance to the Italians, the enthusiasm of these officers for the defense of the territory bolstered Libyan loyalty to pan-Islamic and Ottomanist ideologies. As a result, early Ottoman resistance received growing Libyan support; and after the October 1912 peace treaty abandoned Libya to Italian administration, Libyan forces continued to oppose Italian rule.

In the process, Italy's ruthless treatment of the first Libyan prisoners proved a harbinger of events to come. In October 1911, several hundred Libyan families opposed to the Italian occupation were incarcerated in squalid conditions on the desolate Tremiti islands off the Adriatic coast of Italy. With little available shelter and inadequate food supplies, almost one-third of the internees were dead by June 1912, most of them children and old people.

The 1912 peace treaty incorporated a cessation of hostilities between Italy and the Ottoman Empire with a reestablishment of diplomatic relations; however, it did not end the fighting in Libya. With only a few Ottoman officers left behind, Libyan notables and tribesmen in 1912–15 were left to face the Italians alone. Early resistance proved strongest in Cyrenaica where the Sanusi Order, under the leadership of Sayyid Ahmad al-Sharif, was the focus of military opposition. Supplied with arms and other equipment by Ottoman forces before they departed Libya, Sayyid Ahmad formed a Sanusi state and declared *jihad* (holy war) on the Italian invaders in 1913.

Early Libyan resistance in Tripolitania, in part due to the more open terrain and the absence of organized leadership, was less effective. Sulayman al-Baruni, leader of the Ibadi Berbers in Tripolitania and a deputy to the Ottoman parliament after 1908, attempted to organize Berber resistance but failed. In Fezzan, the withdrawal of Ottoman forces in 1913 produced a power vacuum which France rushed to fill, clashing with Italian interests in the area. In seeking to thwart French incursions, the Italian campaign against local tribes failed, due to a combination of local resistance and the need to divert Italian troops to World War I. Italian forces appeared to have completed the occupation of Tripolitania and Fezzan by August 1914, only to have tribal forces push them north out of Fezzan by the end of the year. Thereafter, the Italian position in Tripolitania steadily deteriorated as Italian forces suffered a string of military defeats.

In April 1915, the battle of Qasr Bu Hadi turned into an Italian rout after Libyans, led by Ramadan al-Suwayhli and thought to be friendly to the Italians, joined the attacking forces against them. As a result, the Italians lost over 500 dead, several thousand rifles, and several million rounds of ammunition. Known also as Gardabiyya, the battle of Qasr Bu Hadi temporarily ended any semblance of Italian control in the hinterlands of Libya. Thereafter, the Italians were forced to withdraw from the interior to the coast. For the duration of World War I, which Italy entered in May 1915, the Italians controlled little more than Tripoli and al-Khums in Tripolitania and Benghazi, Darnah, and Tobruk in Cyrenaica.

In conjunction with the work of various Ottoman elements, internal Libyan resistance to the Italian invasion took many forms. Devout Libyan Muslims generally viewed Italian colonial policies as an attack against Islam and responded by declaring holy war. In this sense, it was religious zeal more than European-style nationalism that provided the motivation to resist Italian occupation, especially in Cyrenaica. Born of the Minifa tribe and educated first at the Sanusi school at Janzur and afterward at Giarabub, Umar al-Mukhtar (c.1862–1931) played a prominent role in the initial and subsequent phases of the Libyan resistance to Italian occupation.

Between 1915 and 1918, during World War I, Ottoman influence reappeared in Libya. While the Ottoman government had formally withdrawn from the province, authorities in Istanbul continued to encourage local Libyan forces in their resistance to the Italians. The high level of support the Sublime Porte provided the Libyan resistance at this point, assistance extended at great expense and at a time when the Ottomans could least afford it, made it all the more notable. World War I, in which the Ottoman Empire confronted major European powers, including Italy, cemented the loyalty of much of the Libyan elite to the impotent empire and its pan-Islamic rationale. Islam later provided the most persuasive and effective ideological foundation to rally Libyan opposition to continued Italian occupation.

When Italy entered the war on the side of the Entente powers, the Ottoman Empire and its Austrian and German allies hoped to use the few remaining troops in Libya to spark a revolt against the British, French, and Italian presence in North Africa. The eventual failure of Ottoman efforts to dislodge the European powers occupying Libya, efforts that revealed the continuing importance of pan-Islamic loyalties in Libya, left the province with leaders more interested in solidifying local authority than in developing wider loyalties. By the end of World War I, these local Libyan leaders had largely given up hope for reincorporation into a wider Ottoman or Islamic political union.

Not all Libyans chose the path of resistance to Italian colonization. Other responses included emigration, negotiation, accommodation, and collaboration. The reaction of disparate classes and factions differed from region to region and within each region. While resistance proved the dominant pattern, at the other end of the scale, local collaboration with the Italian state surfaced in Tripolitania well before the 1911 invasion. Large merchants, like Hassuna Karamanli, mayor of Tripoli; powerful Muslim merchant families often in league with the Bank of Rome, like the Muntasir clan; and Jewish merchants, like the Halfuns family, supported Italian cultural and economic interests in Tripoli and later aided Italian forces in occupying the city. Political ambition motivated Hassuna Karamanli while the Muntasir clan sided with the Italians in an effort to retain their fortune and influence in the region.

Jewish merchants with ties to Italian interests also collaborated with the invaders before, during, and after the occupation. In short, economic self-interest motivated many Libyan merchants in Tripoli and elsewhere in Tripolitania to accommodate or collaborate with the Italian occupation. In the hinterland, the loyalty of tribal leaders in Tripolitania also wavered between collaboration and resistance as they sought to retain status, power, and position in an uncertain, undulating political landscape.[5] Libyan author Bashir al-Hashmi later captured the complexity of these relationships in a poignant short story about a group of Libyan refugees fleeing an Italian military column which is assisted by a Jewish collaborator.[6]

Selected urban notables in Cyrenaica also collaborated with the Italian state, especially those situated along the coast. In the hinterland, decades of education and mobilization in the Sanusi-dominated areas resulted in a notable cohesion among the Cyrenaican tribes along with an anti-colonialist mentality that fostered armed resistance by a volunteer army. Senior tribal leaders, many like Umar al-Mukhtar from lower-status tribal backgrounds, refused to give up their arms, occasioning a social revolution in Cyrenaica when they increasingly opposed a Sanusi leadership inclined to collaborate with the Italians. In the Fezzan, tribes and peasants responded to the occupation in similar ways. Most of the tribes opposed the Italians, seeing them as a threat to tribal autonomy; but a few, due to long-standing tribal feuds, sided with the invaders. Fezzani peasants were mostly too isolated and impoverished to engage in widespread political action.

NASCENT POLITICAL MOVEMENTS

Italy's precipitate withdrawal to the coast, combined with its subsequent preoccupation with World War I, encouraged nascent political activity in Cyrenaica and Tripolitania; and local chiefs or notables created a number of regional governments after 1912. Among the more important examples are Sulayman al-Baruni in western Tripolitania after 1912, Ramadan al-Suwayhli in Misurata and eastern Tripolitania after 1915, Sheik Suf al-Mahamudi in western Tripolitania after 1915, and Khalifa al-Zawi in Fezzan in 1916–26. Although most of these regional governments were short-lived, they highlight the persistent interfactional conflict that plagued Libya in 1910–20. Socioeconomic differences, magnified by struggles over power and revenues, led to frequent hostilities among notables and chiefs, undermining joint resistance to the Italians.

In the wake of the 1912 peace treaty, Sulayman al-Baruni and Farhat al-Zawi, Tripolitanian members of the Ottoman parliament, had organized a meeting of Tripolitanian notables and chiefs to discuss a common response. At the meeting, attendees divided into two camps with one group favoring negotiations with the Italians while Al-Baruni led an opposing group favoring resistance. Unable to compromise, the faction led by Al-Baruni subsequently formed a state in western Tripolitania in 1913. Ironically, the pro-negotiation faction failed to reach an accommodation with the Italian authorities and later joined the resistance forces. When Italian forces defeated the Tripolitanians at the battle of Al-Asabah in March 1913, Al-Baruni and other resistance leaders were forced into exile. Al-Baruni later returned to Libya once Italy entered World War I, rejoining the resistance movement.

Ramadan al-Suwayhli was a prominent Tripolitanian nationalist leader at the outset of the Italian occupation in 1911. He took the field against the Italians during the Turco-Italian war; but after the conclusion of the 1912 peace treaty, he cooperated with the Italians for a short period before leading the revolt against the Italian column at the battle of Qasr Bu Hadi. Like many Libyan notables, Ramadan was probably as interested in extending his own political influence as he was in serving the Ottoman cause. For several years, he succeeded in strengthening Misurata as a safe haven for Ottoman forces as well as an autonomous political district.

Under the leadership of Sayyid Muhammad Idris al-Mahdi al-Sanusi, the Sanusi Order in 1916 opened negotiations with Italy, using the British as intermediaries. These talks resulted in two related agreements, Al-Zuwaytina in April 1916 and Akrama in

April 1917. Among other things, these agreements recognized Italian sovereignty along the coast and Sanusi sovereignty in the hinterland, permitted free trade, and exempted Sanusi and zawaya land from taxes. Most importantly, the agreements gave the people of Cyrenaica a degree of autonomy at a time when the Italian government was responsive to the liberal principles advocated by President Woodrow Wilson. It was an autonomy dependent on Italian financial support and, as it turned out, of short duration as it was soon followed by the brutal policies of the Fascist regime. Relations between the Sanusi Order in Cyrenaica and Ramadan al-Suwayhli in eastern Tripolitania were acrimonious at the time, following a 1916 clash near Bani Walid in which Ramadan's forces engaged Sanusi troops sent to Sirte to collect taxes. In itself, the incident was insignificant. But it made effective cooperation between resistance forces in Cyrenaica and Tripolitania more difficult at a time when a joint response to Italian aggression was desperately needed.

Established in Damascus in the interwar period, the Tripolitanian-Cyrenaican Defense Committee (TCDC) was a Libyan exile organization opposed to Italian rule. Bashir al-Sadawi, a member of the 1922 Tripolitanian delegation to Sayyid Muhammad Idris al-Mahdi al-Sanusi, was its leader. The Tripolitanian-Cyrenaican Defense Committee was only one of several emigré groups formed in Egypt, the Gulf, Saudi Arabia, Syria, and Tunisia in this time frame.

TRIPOLI REPUBLIC, 1918–22

Organized in the fall of 1918, the Tripoli Republic was the first republican government created in the Arab world.[7] Its formation was strongly influenced both by the April 1917 agreement in which Italy granted the Sanusiyya local autonomy as well as by President Woodrow Wilson's January 1918 declaration in support of national self-determination. The name of the new organization was chosen before the form of government was agreed upon and reflected republican sentiment as well as the inability of the founders to agree upon a single individual to act as head of state. For that reason, a Council of Four, supported by a twenty-four-member advisory group, was established to act as a ruling board. The Council of Four consisted of Ramadan al-Suwayhli, Sulayman al-Baruni, Ahmad al-Murayyid of Tarhuna, and Abd al-Nabi Bilkhayr of Warfalla.

The formation of the Tripoli Republic and the proclamation of independence for Tripolitania, together with subsequent efforts by its leadership to plead their case at the Paris Peace Conference, generated little support among the major European powers. Well before the Ottoman Empire signed the Armistice agreements in October 1918, the European powers had promised Italy sovereignty over Libya in the April 1915 Treaty of London. Italy only agreed to meet with representatives of the Republic because Rome hoped to negotiate an accord similar to the 1916–17 agreements with the Sanusi Order. Negotiations opened in April 1919; and from the outset, they were characterized by misunderstanding and misapprehension on both sides. The Tripolitanians saw themselves as negotiating equals to the Italians, in the sense that two independent governments might discuss a dispute. Italian officials viewed the talks with republican leaders as the prelude to a new system of government in which Italy would rule through local chiefs.

While this basic misunderstanding was never resolved, ongoing negotiations did lay the groundwork for the April 1919 Qalat al-Zaytuna Agreement between Italy and the Tripoli Republic and the subsequent promulgation of a *Legge Fondamentale* in June 1919. Initially an agreement between Italy and the Tripoli Republic, the Legge Fondamentale was extended to cover Cyrenaica in October 1919. A liberal document for the time, the Legge Fondamentale provided for a special form of Italian-Libyan citizenship and accorded all such citizens the right to vote in elections for local parliaments. Exempted from military conscription, the taxing power of this new type of citizen rested with the locally elected parliament. The laws also provided for the Italian governor to appoint local administrative positions based on nominations from a ten-man council, eight of whose members would be Libyans selected by the parliament. In Cyrenaica, British intervention forced the Italians to work with the Sanusi Order, and the parliament there met several times before it was abolished in 1923. In contrast, Italian authorities in Tripolitania, under no pressure from external forces, engaged in delaying tactics; and when Giuseppe Volpi was appointed governor in August 1921, he abolished the parliament and assumed a strict, hierarchical approach to the Tripolitanians.

The membership of the council responsible for overseeing administrative appointments under the Legge Fondamentale was nearly identical with that of the founders of the Tripoli Republic; however, the Italians steadfastly refused to recognize the Republic or to acknowledge its authority to administer the hinterlands. Moreover, there was often more competition than cooperation among the Republic's leadership. The factionalism dividing the notables and chiefs of Tripolitania was the product of diverse socio-economic forces, including competition over land, bureaucratic positions, tax collecting, and Ottoman aid, as well as personal rivalry. In late 1919, for example, a quarrel broke out between Ramadan al-Suwayhli and Abd al-Nabi Bilkhayr when the former refused to confirm several of the latter's family members in administrative positions in Warfalla. Abd al-Nabi Bilkhayr also disapproved of Ramadan's animosity toward the Sanusi Order, and both sides traded accusations over accounting for large sums of money sent from Istanbul during World War I. By mid-1920, Ramadan felt sufficiently threatened to launch a campaign against his opponents in which he was defeated and then killed by his captors in August 1920.

On 25 October 1920, Italy reached an agreement with Sayyid Muhammad Idris al-Mahdi al-Sanusi, the Accord of al-Rajma, that granted the latter what the Italians considered to be the ceremonial title of amir of Cyrenaica. He was also given permission to organize the autonomous administration of Ajadabiyyah, Aujila, Giarabub, Jalu, and Al-Kufrah oases with the last becoming his seat of government. In return, Idris agreed to cooperate in applying the Legge Fondamentale to Cyrenaica, to dismantle Cyrenaican military units, and not to tax the local population beyond the religious tithe.

The most important concession, the break-up of military units, was never accomplished.

As part of the Accord of al-Rajma, the Italians granted Idris a personal stipend of 63,000 lire a month with additional monthly payments of 93,000 lire paid to other members of the Sanusi family. In addition, the Italians agreed to cover the costs of administering and policing the areas under Sanusi control, payments that included 2.6 million lire for general expenses. Stipends were also paid to tribal sheiks and administrators of the Sanusi zawaya. Attempts to bribe the Sanusi elite into cooperation proved ineffective; by the end of 1921, diplomatic relations between Italy and the Sanusi Order were again strained. The crisis came to a head at the end of 1922 when Sayyid Idris realized the negotiated peace was breaking down and that Italy and the Sanusi Order could not share Cyrenaica between them. Accordingly, he went into exile in Egypt, leaving more martial members of the Sanusi Order to wage what proved to be an inspiring albeit fruitless guerrilla war against Italy.

In November 1920, shortly after the announcement of the Accord of al-Rajma, the leadership of the Tripoli Republic called a general meeting in Gharyan. With internal dissension destroying any possibility of a united front, participants resolved that a single Muslim leader should be designated to govern the country. The Gharyan conference also established a Council of the Association for National Reform and arranged to send an official delegation to Rome to inform the Italian government of its new organization. Among its stated aims, the association hoped to safeguard Arab rights as expressed in the Legge Fondamentale, to increase understanding between Arabs and Italians, and to spread knowledge in order to bring Western civilization to a country that had preserved the glorious traditions of Islam. The elections called for by the Legge Fondamentale were never held, and the stated aims of the association proved far too ambitious.

Bereft of international support, the increasingly aggressive policies of the Italian government divided the Tripoli Republic and reduced its leadership. By 1923, when the Fascists were consolidating their power at home and beginning the pacification of Libya, the Republic had ceased to exist. In hindsight, the pretensions of the Tripoli Republic proved far too ambitious; however, its creation marked an important early step in the political development of the region as a whole.

RICONQUISTA, 1923–32

In the wake of the Fascist takeover in October 1922, the Mussolini regime soon rejected the Liberal practice of collaboration with local

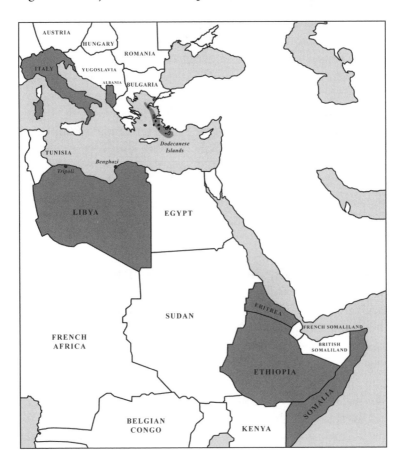

Map 5 The Fascist Empire

Libyan elites in place since 1911. Instead, the Fascists turned to military force to pacify the Libyan population, embarking in early 1923 on a brutal *riconquista* or reconquest of Libya. Enjoying an overwhelming superiority in men and equipment, the Italian army had some twenty-thousand men in the field by 1926 while Libyan guerrilla forces, largely confined to Cyrenaica, seldom numbered more than one thousand. In support of its troops, Italy deployed the most modern weapons available, including airplanes, artillery, and even poison gas. After signing the Geneva Convention in June 1925, which prohibited the use of bacteriological or chemical weapons in battle, the Fascist regime, as early as January 1928, employed poison gas in support of its efforts to pacify Libya.

The military operations undertaken by Fascist Italy to occupy Libya were long, difficult, and costly but eventually successful. Most of the population centers, coastal areas, and countryside of Tripolitania were subdued by the end of 1924; and by the beginning of 1928, the acting head of the Sanusi Order had submitted to the Italian commander in Cyrenaica. With the northern Fezzan already in Italian control, the Italian authorities in January 1929 united Tripolitania and Cyrenaica under a single governor, Marshal Pietro Badoglio, with the capital in Tripoli.

In Cyrenaica, a brief truce was declared in the spring of 1929; however, during the summer, resistance again flared under the leadership of Sidi Umar al-Mukhtar. The Sanusi tribesmen in Cyrenaica effectively employed the type of guerrilla warfare, characterized by raids, ambushes, and sabotage, best suited to their temperament and the countryside. In response, the Italian authorities attempted to isolate the resistance fighters, denying them access to their people. In so doing, the Italians pursued what has been aptly termed a policy of genocide, emphasizing repression and terrorism in which men, women, and children were detained in large concentration camps, wells were blocked, and livestock slaughtered. Exact figures are not available because the Italian colonial archives are still restricted; however, most estimates agree that more than 110,000 people, two-thirds of the population of eastern Libya, were confined to the concentration camps. Of that number, at least forty thousand died from disease, maltreatment, or starvation; and the most recent estimates, based on Libyan archives and oral histories, put the death toll as high as seventy thousand people. Finally, General Rodolfo Graziani, commander of the Italian forces, ordered the construction of a tall barbed-wire fence, four meters thick, from the port of Bardia on the Mediterranean coast to the oasis of Jarabub, to stop supplies from Egypt reaching the guerrillas in Cyrenaica. The distinguished historian, Richard Bosworth, later captured the severity of Italian policy:

> The three cruellest acts in the campaign were the capture and hanging, after a desultory trial, of Arab leader Omar al Mukhtar in September 1931, the bombing of the holy city of Cufra [Al-Kufrah] and other places, including the oasis of Taizerbo, inhabited only by shepherds and peasants, with canisters of poison gas, and the penning of some hundred thousand people from the interior in concentration camps near the coast. These lagers were serviced with such deliberate lack of care that about half of the prisoners – men, women and children – died, while a Fascist expert described events in malignly hackneyed metaphor as a 'cleansing.'[8]

In the face of extreme Italian brutality, Libyan resistance continued until the fall of 1931 when Al-Mukhtar, a highly active and effective guerrilla leader, was finally captured and hanged. Twenty thousand Libyans were brought from confinement to witness his execution in a horrific spectacle staged by the Italians to demonstrate the days of compromise were ended. Acutely aware of the power of imagery, the Mu'ammar al-Qaddafi regime (1969 to present) would later promote the exploits of Sidi Umar al-Mukhtar, including financial support for a feature film about his life entitled *Lion of the Desert* and starring Anthony Quinn, to emphasize the ongoing need to struggle for national liberation. On 24 January 1932, Marshal Badoglio declared the rebellion in Cyrenaica broken, and the war begun more than three decades earlier officially ended.

ITALIAN COLONIAL POLICY

Count Giuseppe Volpi was a financier whose empire was based on electric power in his native Venetia. He was also founder and director of several companies in the Balkans and carried out important diplomatic assignments for the Italian government. He was one of the first of the major industrialists and bankers to join the Fascist Party, and the Fascists celebrated him as one of their own. Appointed governor of Tripolitania in August 1921, more than a year before the Fascist March on Rome, he was the first and only governor of Tripolitania who was not a military officer. Volpi departed Tripolitania in 1925 to become Mussolini's finance minister from 1925 to 1928. In Tripolitania, his consistent, decisive policies contrasted sharply with those of earlier Liberal regimes. First, Volpi resolved the stalemate in the political domain by directing the reconquest of the area. Second, he addressed successfully the problem of creating a public domain for colonization. Volpi felt strongly that policies in these two areas must complement each other. With force alone insufficient to achieve development, he believed the most effective strategy resulted in economics and politics working hand-in-hand.

The Ufficio Fondario (Land Office), founded in 1913 as part of a policy to provide Italian colonists with land in Libya, initially proceeded on the assumption that all uncultivated lands were private property. In the first of a series of decrees, Volpi reversed that assumption on 18 July 1922, declaring that all uncultivated lands were now presumed to belong to the public domain. Additional decrees announced in the following year provided that all uncultivated land would revert to the state after three years and that all land held by rebels or those who aided them would be confiscated by the state. Collectively, these decrees led to a rapid increase (over ten times) in the amount of land made available to Italian colonists in Cyrenaica and Tripolitania. Nevertheless, Italian capital did not move quickly to buy Libyan concessions; and Italian colonists were slow to immigrate to Libya. Laws promulgated in 1928 by Emilio de Bono, who succeeded Volpi as governor of Tripolitania in July

1925, provided additional credits and subsidies to encourage colonists to settle in Libya; but immigration rates remained far below official Italian expectations.

Throughout Volpi's tenure, Cyrenaica and Tripolitania were governed as separate territories with independent governors in the capitals of Benghazi and Tripoli. This dual administration was later consolidated in 1929 under a single governor with the capital in Tripoli. The two territories later merged into the single colony of Libya with the capital continuing in Tripoli. Thereafter, Cyrenaica and Tripolitania, together with a military administration in Fezzan (now referred to as South Tripolitania), were administered by a governor general, a position redesignated first consul in 1937. He was supported by a general consultative council and a council of government made up exclusively of Italians. On 9 January 1939, the colony of Libya was incorporated into metropolitan Italy and thereafter considered an integral part of the Italian state.

The colonization of Libya is closely linked to the name of Air Marshal Italo Balbo, Italian governor from 1934 until his death in a plane crash over Tobruk in 1940 when nervous Italian anti-air-craft gunners shot down his plane. Successor to Pietro Badoglio, Balbo was an enthusiastic, early supporter of Fascism in his native Ferrara in northeast Italy, organizer of the March on Rome that brought the Fascists to power in October 1922, and a renowned aviator. Owing much to the work of his predecessors, Balbo was fortunate to become governor at an opportune moment for the colony's development in that he assumed office after the destruc-tion of the Sanusiyya resistance. For the first time in more than two decades, Libya was at peace and the Italians could concentrate on its economic development. A cluster of economic and social issues in Italy in the early 1930s also encouraged the colonization of Libya. Most important, a negative balance of trade, combined with a strong lira, aggravated the chronic unemployment problem, boosting emigration.

Balbo was also fortunate in that his governorship coincided with a period in which the Mussolini regime was less interested in the costs of colonization than in the prestige the projects might reflect. A modern, highly colonized Libya promised a strong card in Italy's bid for Mediterranean hegemony and African empire. On a less belligerent note, the Libyan example, with its emphasis on large-scale public works and resettlement projects, also seemed to offer new answers to a world troubled by depression and unemployment. Finally, the colonization of Libya struck a responsive chord in the hearts of patriotic Italians, many of whom dreamed of creating population outlets under the Italian flag in Africa.

Fascist dictator Mussolini, imprisoned in 1911 for protesting the Italian invasion of Libya, later visited the colony three times, in 1926, 1937, and 1942. His 1937 tour, in particular his inspection of Fascist public works, amounted to a public endorsement of the three-year-old governorship of Italo Balbo, himself no particular friend of the Duce. Mussolini had shunted Balbo off to Libya in 1934 out of fear his expoits as an air ace would rival Mussolini's own glory. Indeed, it was suggested Mussolini visited Libya, not to flatter Balbo, but to deprive the latter of the satisfaction of opening the colony's single largest public work, the *strada litoranea* or "coastal highway," running from the Tunisian border to the frontier with Egypt. The Italians insisted the road was built to promote tourism; however, contemporary observers recognized its military value. During World War II, the road became a two-way invasion route, carrying Italian or Italian-German armies into Egypt in 1940, 1941, and 1942 and British armies into Libya in 1940–41, 1941–42, and 1942–43. In touting the strada litoranea as a prominent example of the modernization program being implemented in Libya, Italian publicists also failed to note that it was built largely on the backs of Libyan laborers.

In the course of his 1937 visit, the Duce received the "Sword of Islam" (which had been fabricated in Florence for the occasion). His pretension to be seen as the "Protector of Islam" was never fulfilled, but Mussolini's 1937 visit did ratify Libya's newfound place in Italian strategic and imperial thinking. Libyan author Ali M. Almisrati later penned a wonderfully evocative short story about the Duce's visit to Libya. In 'An Extract from Mussolini's Nail', he tells the story of Fara'as, a former freedom fighter reduced to making ornamental saddles for a livelihood. When forced by the Italian authorities to make a saddle for Mussolini, he retaliates by inserting a sharp nail in the seat of the saddle which later penetrates Mussolini's backside in a most painful manner. Hours later, Fara'as is taken to jail:

> No one inquired about his fate, whether it was deep in the sea or sealed by the noose … But Fara'as in any case was happy with his revenge, for as they were coming to take him to prison for interrogation, he was hugging his father's saddle and kissing the bloodstains on it.[9]

Balbo assumed a position of total authority over administrative, financial, legislative, military, and political matters in Libya; and under his tutelage, the Italian state was extended across the Mediterranean, incorporating the two coastal provinces of Cyrenaica and Tripolitania into metropolitan Italy proper with the Fezzan accorded the status of a colonial province. Known as the *quarta sponda* or "fourth shore" when added to the peninsula's Tyrrhenian, Adriatic, and Ionian coasts, Libya became an integral part of Italy, enclosing the Mediterranean and rendering it a genuine *mare nostrum*. In the process, the Italian colony of *Libia* was defined and delineated, for the first time, in legalistic European terms.

If one moment epitomized the Balbo era, it was the so-called *ventimila*, or twenty thousand, in which twenty thousand (really about ten thousand) colonists were transported to Libya in a single mass convoy in October 1938. The plan was to settle twenty thousand colonists annually for five years, beginning in 1938, with a longer-term goal of 500,000 Italian colonists in Libya by 1950. While Balbo led a second emigration of about ten thousand people in 1939, the ventimila in 1938 was his most spectacular and last great public triumph. The parade and carnival aspects of mass emigration subsequently came under increasing criticism in Italy. Mass emigration was also poorly received in Libya and throughout the Arab world, provoking violent demonstrations in Baghdad and elsewhere.

Balbo's blueprint for Libya's future prosperity faded with the outbreak of World War II. As the North African campaign see-sawed across Cyrenaica, many Italian colonists were eventually evacuated. By the end of 1941, only 8,426 colonists remained and that number was halved the following year when the fighting raged over the very areas Balbo had chosen for large farms. With the end of the war, and the end of Italian subsidies for colonization, the remaining settlement schemes in Tripolitania also faltered.

Largely unsuccessful in developing Libya, the Fascist regime proved equally incapable of defending it. Approximately two-thirds of the Italian troops transported to Libya were lost to the British between December 1940 and February 1941, with 130,000 Italian POWs taken while the British suffered only 550 deaths. The North African campaign of 1940–43 ended in February 1943 after the British Eighth Army occupied Tripoli, the undefended capital of Italian *Libia*, on 23 January 1943. Under the British, as historian John Wright aptly recognized, a new era had begun in Libya:

> By 1943 it should have become clear to Italians in Libya that under the British their interests were to be subordinated to those of the native Libyans. As long ago as January 1942 the British Foreign Secretary, Anthony Eden, had made a statement in the House of Commons pledging that the Sanusi of Cyrenaica would under no circumstances again fall under Italian domination. Although there was no similar pledge covering Tripolitania, the Italians had little reason to suppose that the British would take a markedly more sympathetic view of their record and status, at least as colonialists, if not as colonists.[10]

With the end of fighting, Great Britain occupied Cyrenaica and Tripolitania, and France gained control over Fezzan. The division of Libya between two new colonial masters appeared to some to augur ill for the future, but it eventually led to a declaration of independence in December 1951.

JEWISH COMMUNITY

Among the Fascist leadership, the small but highly patriotic Jewish community in Libya enjoyed an anomalous position. Italo Balbo was pro-Jewish, stating openly in 1937 that his three best friends were Jewish. While he viewed local Jews as natural allies in his plans to develop and modernize Libya, legislation that closed shops on Sunday but enforced their opening on Saturday ignored Jewish susceptibilities. Laws enacted in 1938 later placed Libyan Jews below their Muslim neighbors whom the former had previously regarded as inferiors. At the same time, Balbo did his best to temper the most severe provisions of the racial laws implemented in Fascist Italy and Nazi Germany. Therefore, the relative plight of Libyan Jews up to the outbreak of World War II was not too bad.

The period immediately following the end of World War II was characterized by a state of euphoria in which Jewish–Muslim relations, especially in smaller towns and rural areas, seemed to settle down as both groups evidenced a sincere desire to work peacefully together. In the prevailing milieu, the anti-Jewish riots that broke out in Tripoli on Sunday, 4 November 1945, were almost totally unexpected.[11] The immediate cause of the riots remained unclear with official British inquiries mentioning a fight that took place between a Jew and a Muslim as well as sporadic brawling between the youth of the two communities, a common Sunday evening event. In turn, a Jewish community report stressed the initial rioting occurred simultaneously in several different places, implying some planning and coordination had been involved.

The anti-Jewish rioting, which involved shop looting, arson, and physical attacks, quickly grew in intensity. In Tripoli, Jews living outside the Jewish quarter suffered the most while those residing inside were able to isolate themselves in the old Jewish section. The only official response to the riots was a curfew announcement on 5 November 1945, accompanied by the appearance of a few troops in the streets who failed to react against the mobs. In fact, firm and effective government action to stop the rioting did not occur until the evening of 6 November. During this period, thirty-eight Jews and one Muslim were killed in the city of Tripoli alone. The riots spread from Tripoli to other towns with attacks on Jewish populations in outlying areas occasionally beginning several days after the outbreak of violence in Tripoli. The dead in the villages, all of whom were Jews, totaled almost one hundred. In addition to the loss of lives, there was a heavy loss of property from burning and looting.

The anti-Jewish riots of 1945 were a turning point in Jewish–Muslim relations in Libya as well as in the relationship of Jews to Libya itself. Dealing a severe blow to any Jewish sense of security, the pogrom challenged, if not destroyed, any illusions Libyan Jews held for taking initiatives in Libya. Almost three years of political upheaval were to pass before the state of Israel emerged as a reality in May 1948; nevertheless, the 1945 riots became an important factor in bringing about mass emigration to Israel after 1948. Many Jews would probably have emigrated eventually from an independent Libya, as they did from other North Africa states under different circumstances; however, the emigration would almost surely have been more gradual if the riots had not occurred.

IMPACT OF ITALIAN OCCUPATION

Once the Italian government had put down the Libyan resistance, it faced a new challenge in carrying out its ambitious plans for the colonization of the territory. Italian officials found it difficult to attract private capital to colonial agriculture; and those entrepreneurs who did invest found the settlement of colonist families to be a financial burden, attractive only if the government provided handsome subsidies. Italian emigrants were also a problem as they generally preferred to follow their relatives to the United States or South America as opposed to beginning a new life alone in North Africa. Moreover, Italian emigrants often did not make good colonists because even those with a rural background seldom had experience in farm management, preferring instead to settle in urban areas. In addressing these problems, the Fascist regime invariably came up with the same solution – more financial and technical aid. The colonization of Libya thus did little or nothing to resolve Italy's pressing economic and social problems while Libyans faced a future in which they would always be second-class citizens in their own country.

Three decades of Italian rule left Libya with a considerable infrastructure of roads, agricultural villages, and other public works but a poor legacy in terms of a skilled, informed, and politically active citizenry. Italian colonial policy left a devastated population, largely uneducated, and outside the mainstream Libyan economy. The Italian government failed to encourage political participation or to develop political institutions. On the contrary, it actively discouraged indigenous political activity. Fascist policy in Cyrenaica, for example, aimed to destroy the power of the Sanusi Order, abolishing traditional tribal assemblies and weakening the authority of established leaders. In so doing, the Italians effectively disrupted the delicate balance that had emerged between enduring tribal alliances and emerging class and economic formations.

The political turbulence that began in Libya shortly after the Young Turk revolution in 1908 and accelerated with the Italian occupation in 1911 had other important consequences for the political development of Libya. As Lisa Anderson later pointed out, the unique nature of the upheaval, including the timing of events and the character of the participants, strongly influenced subsequent Libyan conceptions of the nation's place in modern Arab and Islamic identities. Between the Young Turk revolution and the end of World War I, Libya remained loyal to pan-Islamic aspirations instead of turning to Arab nationalism. While a segment of the Libyan elite attempted to develop a political organization in Tripolitania based on secular, republican grounds, internecine disputes doomed their efforts to failure, and they were destined to turn again to religiously inspired leadership in Cyrenaica to continue the fight against Italian rule. The most widely embraced political identity in Libya throughout this period, both in terms of a wider loyalty to the Ottoman Empire and a narrower form of provincial patriotism, was provided by Islamic as opposed to Arabic symbols and attachments. As a result, an important legacy of the Italian colonial era was the close association of nationalism, anti-imperialism, and pan-Islamic loyalties with Libya after this period.[12]

Italian educational policy, as embodied in a June 1928 decree, effectively confined educational opportunities for Libyans to the elementary level, together with the learning of traditional arts and crafts, in effect sanctioning educational and economic apartheid. Libyan children were taught to read by parroting phrases such as: "I am happy to be subject to the Italian government," or "The Duce loves children very much, even Arab children." Italian apologists attempted to justify the system by pointing out that Libyans could apply both to become *cittadini italiani speciali* or "special citizens" and for places in Italian secondary schools. But they failed to mention that embracing either of these privileges would have implied support for regime policies the vast majority of Libyans deplored.

A measure of the effect of Italian educational policies is the knowledge that Libya at independence in 1951 boasted only five graduates of Italian universities and ten from the Islamic University of Al-Azhar in Cairo. There were no qualified Libyan directors of elementary or secondary schools and no people qualified for non-Islamic professions or trained as agricultural experts. The shortage of trained teachers later forced the United Kingdom of Libya to import teachers from Egypt and elsewhere, many of whom did not share the monarchy's traditional values, contributing to its overthrow in 1969.

A promising cultural and literary revival, which began in Libya in the second half of the nineteenth century, was also stifled by the Italians after 1911. Sixteen periodicals and journals that appeared regularly in the years before the Italian invasion were quickly suppressed by the new regime. Over the next three decades, the Italian administration conducted what Ahmed Fagih, a distinguished Libyan writer, has described as "a racist physical and cultural war of extermination" in which few Libyan newspapers or journals survived beyond the first issue.[13] In a highly innovative study of colonial architecture in Libya, Brian L. McLaren later characterized the Italian approach to Libyan culture:

> While their land was embraced as part of the metropole – and in
> that sense it was continuous with the political and economic sys-

tems of modern Italy – their culture was always considered primitive and backward in relation to the West.[14]

It would be 1950 before the indigenous population of Libya returned to the level it enjoyed at the outset of the Italian occupation. According to one tabulation, the native population dropped from 1.4 million in 1907 to 1.2 million in 1912 to 825,000 in 1933. Some of this decline could be attributed to internecine fighting and nomads migrating to bordering states in search of shelter. That said, a population drop of this magnitude would indicate any suggestion that Italian rule was benign as misleading at best. The Italians sacrificed both treasure and lives in their subjugation of Libya; and their reputation in Libya and the wider Islamic world suffered greatly, and for good reason, as a result.

4

STRUGGLE FOR INDEPENDENCE, 1943–51

Before Libya achieved independence, its name was merely a geographical expression, for its people preferred to be called Tripolitanians, Cyrenaicans, and Fazzanese rather than to be identified by the geographical name of the country.

Majid Khadduri, *Modern Libya*, 1963

If there was discord in Libya, there was more of it in the world outside. And, paradoxically, Libya was put on the road to independence because international disagreement was greater than her own national disunity.

John Wright, *Libya*, 1969

My terms of reference are clear: they lay down that the United Nations Commissioner will assist the people of Libya in the formulation of their constitution and in the establishment of an independent government.

UN Commissioner Adrian Pelt, 1950

More than Iran or other rimland controversies, Libya was center stage in the East–West conflict in the immediate postwar period, and it would remain so for many years to come.

Ronald Bruce St John, *Libya and the United States*, 2002

Libya was the first African state to achieve independence from European rule, and the first and only state to be created by the

United Nations General Assembly. It became an arena for the interplay of great power rivalry before World War II ended, and it remained in a highly dependent position for years to come. In the process, the role of the Four Powers (France, Great Britain, the Soviet Union, and the United States) in the decision to grant Libya independence was dictated largely by the exigencies of the Cold War.

LIBERATION AND OCCUPATION

With the surrender of the Axis forces in Tunisia in May 1943, the British government established a British Military Administration to administer Cyrenaica and Tripolitania. Free French troops from their garrison on Lake Chad had earlier occupied Fezzan in January 1943, and the French government, in turn, established a French Military Administration to administer Fezzan. The occupation of Cyrenaica and Tripolitania by British forces, preceded as it was by British Foreign Secretary Anthony Eden's statement to the House of Commons on 8 January 1942 that the Sanusiyya would not again fall under Italian domination, raised the issue of the future disposition of the former Italian colonies. The Sanusi Order, which had long resisted Italian domination, had allied itself with the British during World War II, forming the core of a small but symbolically important contingent known as the Libyan Arab Force. Consisting of five battalions, the Libyan Arab Force wore the Sanusi emblem, a white crescent and star on a black field, as a badge. The full implication of Eden's statement in 1942 was unclear at the time, but his remarks suggested there might be separate arrangements in the postwar era for the different Libyan territories.[1]

Sayyid Muhammad Idris al-Mahdi al-Sanusi and his followers found Eden's statement especially disappointing because it made no definite pledge that Cyrenaica would be independent after the war. As he made abundantly clear at the time, the Sanusi leader objected to either the Italians or the Soviets playing a postwar role in Cyrenaica, preferring independence for the province together with a close alliance with the British government. When Sayyid Idris pressed British officials for an explicit statement of complete independence, he was told no specific promises could be made before the end of the war; but he was reassured that Libya would be given its freedom at that time. British initiative in this regard was constrained by its adherence to the 1907 Hague Convention which limited a military occupation to a holding operation until an international body determined the future of the occupied territory. British forces would continue to administer Cyrenaica and Tripolitania in a "care and maintenance" status until 1949.

The notables of Tripolitania, who professed no less hatred for Italian domination and an even greater fear of Soviet occupation, shared the sentiments of Sayyid Idris, if not all his plans. Tripolitanian leaders criticized the Eden statement on the grounds that it failed to include a promise that Tripolitania as well as Cyrenaica would not again fall under Italian domination and because its explicit reference to the Sanusiyya implied prior British recognition of Sanusi leadership over all Libya. Fearing their prospects for independence were not as certain as those of Cyrenaica, the people of Tripolitania, viewing Libya as one country with no reason to differentiate between provinces, became increasingly restless. In August 1943, for example, the citizens of Tripoli presented British authorities with a petition, voicing grievances and requesting the employment of more local officials and the opening of primary schools for Muslim students.

To the south, France administered the Fezzan through a combination of French military authorities, the House of Sayf al-Nasra, a local ruling family, and Fezzanese officials. From the beginning, the French made clear their desire to retain permanent control of the province to link their colonies in Equatorial and North Africa and to serve as a buffer to protect those colonies from outside influence and infiltration. The French Military Administration would remain in place in Fezzan until independence in 1951.

WARTIME DISCUSSIONS

In Washington, the Atlantic Charter, an August 1941 declaration by President Franklin D. Roosevelt and Prime Minister Winston Churchill, provided the clearest definition of early American intent in Libya. In the charter, the United States pledged respect for the self-determination of peoples as well as progress toward global economic justice. In the new world order, the major powers would promote freer channels of commerce and fuller access to sources of raw materials but would not seek territorial changes that did not accord with the freely expressed wishes of the peoples concerned. Beginning in 1942, President Roosevelt and other American officials routinely referred to the Atlantic Charter as a global commitment. For this reason, colonial subjects in Libya and elsewhere viewed the moment as highly propitious to press for autonomy or even independence. The practical implementation of the ideals contained in the Atlantic Charter would later leave many of these early enthusiasts very disappointed.[2]

The U.S. Department of State, in a memorandum prepared for the First Quebec Conference in August 1943, outlined four alternative approaches to the question of Libya. The preferred solution was the creation of an international trusteeship to govern Libya as part of a wider North African region. This proposal, put forward by a special subcommittee as early as 26 September 1942, was modified several times over the next eight months. The idea was to place the administration of Libya in the hands of an international trusteeship with the governing council composed of Great Britain, France, and Egypt. Given the rapid development of air power, the document suggested it was unimportant, from the standpoint of security, which states controlled Libya. In contrast, Great Britain recognized early on the strategic importance of Cyrenaica although London felt it had no strategic interest in Tripolitania beyond denying it to a hostile power. The American position on the strategic importance of Libya would change dramatically in a very short time.

The second alternative explored in the 1943 memorandum was to divide Libya with Cyrenaica going to Egypt and Tripolitania to

Tunisia. This proposal was opposed on the grounds that the poor administration of Egypt should not be extended to Cyrenaica while adding the Italians in Tripolitania to those already in Tunisia would further disturb the delicate balance between French and Italians in Tunisia. The third alternative was the return of Libya to Italy. While there was little support for this approach, there was general agreement that any course of action adopted should not preclude Italian migration into Libya or the enjoyment of equal opportunities by Italians in Libya. The final alternative discussed was the establishment of a Jewish refuge in Libya. This solution included the creation of a Jewish state in Cyrenaica and the settlement of Jewish refugees in the villages and farms vacated by Italians as well as on additional land. One obstacle to this alternative was the limited arable land available in Libya. In addition, the U.S. Department of State rightly acknowledged it would be extremely difficult to persuade Libyan Arabs to accept Jewish settlement. With Arab nationalism on the increase in Libya, the memorandum recognized that any attempt to foster Jewish settlement would likely extend the arena of Arab–Jewish conflict without offering substantial relief to the Jewish refugee problem.

The British Chiefs of Staff in the spring of 1944 advanced a variation of alternative two, the division of Libya. Under the British proposal, Cyrenaica would become an autonomous principality under Egyptian suzerainty with adequate safeguards for United Nations military requirements, including air and naval facilities in the Benghazi area. Tripolitania would be restored to Italy subject to a guarantee of demilitarization and British retention of the right to use the Castel Benito Airfield as a staging point. Secretary of State Cordell Hull responded to this proposal in a memorandum to President Roosevelt, arguing the preferred disposition of Libya would be an international trusteeship over both Cyrenaica and Tripolitania administered by a commission of experts responsible to the United Nations. This approach, he added, would not preclude the establishment of an autonomous Sanusi Amirate. If the British rejected this proposal, Hull suggested to Roosevelt a feasible if less desirable arrangement would be to establish Cyrenaica as an autonomous Sanusi Amirate under Egyptian (or possibly British) trusteeship along the lines of the British proposal. Tripolitania could then be placed under an international trusteeship to be exercised by Italy.

At the Moscow Conference of Foreign Ministers in December 1945, the Soviet Union complicated the Libya question by pressing for a Soviet trusteeship over Tripolitania. The Soviets argued Great Britain and the United States had plenty of bases around the world; therefore, they surely could take Soviet interests in North Africa into account. When Stalin later suggested the British appeared unprepared to trust the Soviets in Tripolitania, British Foreign Secretary Ernest Bevin tactfully responded the issue was not one of trust but rather a desire on the part of his government to avoid competition in the region.

In a briefing book for the 1945 Potsdam Conference, the Truman administration, which took over with the death of President Roosevelt in April 1945, indicated it would support one of three solutions, if proposed by another government. First, in a reversal of policy, Washington now supported a return of Libya to Italian sovereignty, subject to any demilitarization measures devised for Italy. As a secondary preference, it supported the partition of Libya into its historic parts with Cyrenaica established as an autonomous Sanusi Amirate under British or Egyptian trusteeship and Tripolitania retained under Italian sovereignty. Failing either of these solutions, the Truman administration would support the partition of Libya with Cyrenaica established as an autonomous Sanusi Amirate under Egyptian or British trusteeship and Tripolitania placed under international trusteeship exercised by Italy. The 1945 briefing book also evidenced a newfound American appreciation for the strategic position of Libya, recognizing its ports and air fields made the country important to the control of the central Mediterranean.

At the close of the Potsdam Conference, the respective positions of the major powers on the disposition of the Italian colonies in Libya were relatively close. The British favored sovereignty over the territories placed collectively in four powers; the Soviets

favored three powers; and the Americans appeared willing to follow the British lead. Everyone talked of international trusteeships,
but the Europeans in reality had old-fashioned, big-power man-
dates in mind. The Soviets had picked Tripolitania for their postwar experiment in tending a Mediterranean outpost, but this was
totally unacceptable to the British as well as to a Eurocentric State
Department bombarding its new president with dire warnings
about the resurgence of Communism in Europe. On the issue of
Jewish settlement, Prime Minister Churchill rightly suggested
there was little enthusiasm among European Jews for resettlement
in Libya. Four months later in November 1945, the violent Muslim
attacks on the Jewish minority discussed in the previous chapter
dashed any remaining hopes for the creation of a Jewish refuge
in Libya.

GREAT POWER GRIDLOCK

Established at the 1945 Potsdam Conference, the Council of
Foreign Ministers met from 1945 to 1948 in a series of long, spir-
ited, and largely unproductive sessions. Coexisting with the United
Nations, widely viewed as a promising new path for international
planning, the Council of Foreign Ministers was a throwback to
older patterns, reflecting the disarray among the Four Powers. In
regards to the disposition of the Italian colonies, Council discussions occasionally offered tantalizing possibilities for compromise
and accord; but they more regularly mirrored the bipolar character
of the new world order that defined the postwar era.

    United States policy at the time was torn by divided counsel as
was evident when the Council of Foreign Ministers met in London
in September 1945. The issue of the Italian colonies was not, and
had never been, a vital one for U.S. policy makers except in so far as
American security might be involved. While Europe was the priority, Italy was not a priority even in Europe. The U.S. Office of
European Affairs, concerned about the future role of the Soviet
Union in the Mediterranean, recommended the Italian colonies,

including Libya, be returned to Italy in the form of trusteeships. The U.S. Office of Near Eastern and African Affairs, on the other hand, was inclined to give free rein to the United Nations and to implement principles of international administration.

Secretary of State Byrnes eventually offered in mid-September 1945 a plan for establishing UN trusteeships in all former Italian territories. The proposal included a ten-year administration over a unified Libya after which time the territory would become independent. In a private meeting with his Soviet counterpart, Byrnes reiterated many of the policy themes found in the Atlantic Charter, arguing the Arabs expected the Allies to honor wartime statements favoring self-determination. He emphasized the creation of UN trusteeships would demonstrate to the world the big powers were not seeking to exploit their victory. Foreign Secretary Bevin accepted the U.S. proposal, but the Soviets continued to press their claim to Tripolitania.

As the Council of Foreign Ministers continued its deliberations in London, on 2 September 1945 *New York Times* columnist James Reston published what became a famous article, in which he outlined the State Department's internal dialogue over the colonial issue. Reston viewed the dispute as one involving great power relationships and the reorganization of Europe. He portrayed the wrangling over African colonies as a struggle for the mastery of Europe with fundamental issues at stake over the character of the postwar world.[3] The Reston column later proved highly influential as it became a common reference point for analysts arguing the disposition of the Italian colonies was a test case of Allied resolve to confront the new world order. From this viewpoint, the chief roadblock to international trusteeship was not the question of revived Italian rule but instead Western fears of Soviet involvement.

The Italian peace treaty, signed on 10 February 1947, required Italy to renounce all right and title to its former African possessions of Eritrea, Libya, and Somaliland, leaving the respective British and French military administrations in power. Annex XI of the treaty stipulated that future arrangements regarding the former Italian colonies would be determined by the joint decision of the United

States, Great Britain, the Soviet Union, and France. The Four Powers were obliged to arrive at a settlement within a year of the agreement coming into force which occurred on 15 September 1947. Failing that, they were to submit the question to the UN General Assembly. In the interim, the Council of Foreign Ministers was authorized to continue study of the issue, using such investigative commissions as might be required.

REGIONAL AND DOMESTIC POLITICS COLLIDE

Sayyid Idris remained in Egypt in the years immediately following the end of World War II, preferring to reside outside Cyrenaica as long as it remained under British military administration. With the end of foreign administration, he was confident he would be entrusted with civil responsibility; but he did not want that responsibility as long as the military authorities were governing. In June 1945, before the Council of Foreign Ministers had begun its deliberations, his supporters addressed a letter to the British Minister of State in Cairo, outlining a plan for an independent Cyrenaican government under the leadership of Sayyid Idris. In July 1946, tribal chiefs issued a manifesto which demanded, among other things, British recognition of a Sanusi Amirate under Sayyid Idris and the formation of an independent, constitutional government in Cyrenaica. Sayyid Idris finally took up permanent residence in Cyrenaica in November 1947. Alarmed at the political factionalism that had developed, primarily between the younger generation members of the Umar al-Mukhtar Club and the older notables and tribal leaders in the National Front, he soon dissolved all political organizations in December 1947 in favor of a new united front which took the form of a National Congress.

In Tripolitania, the end of the war sparked a burst of political activity. Long oppressed under Italian rule, which prohibited political associations, Tripolitanian leaders took advantage of newfound freedoms to organize numerous political parties, including the Nationalist Party, United National Front, and Free National

Bloc. The province had suffered in the past from factional differences and an absence of organized leadership, and family and feudal loyalties continued to play a major role in the creation of these political groups. That said, apart from the Sanusi Amirate and selected constitutional issues, virtually all parties in Tripolitania reflected the republican experience in 1918–22 in that they agreed on the fundamental principles of unity and independence. Specific demands included complete independence, a united Libya composed of Cyrenaica, Fezzan, and Tripolitania, and membership in the Arab League.

In Fezzan, French administrators continued to hope the province might be united with other French colonies in Africa. Having already tied the administration of the province to southern Algeria, they further discouraged Fezzanese relations with Cyrenaica and Tripolitania by diverting Fezzan's trade relations to Algeria. When local leaders expressed a desire to establish an autonomous regime, French authorities tightened their control over the territory, prompting the former in late 1946 to organize a secret opposition society. The French later discovered the existence of the society and arrested some of its members in 1947; nevertheless, the group continued to oppose French administration.

In early 1947, Libya thus remained divided into three zones, consisting of a nascent Sanusi Amirate in Cyrenaica, a volatile mix of ethnic groups together with a more urbanized culture in Tripolitania, and the French-controlled oases in the Fezzan. In spite of the plethora of proposals made during Council of Foreign Minister sessions, there was little reason at this time to believe a unified Libya would emerge in the foreseeable future. Great Britain planned to continue its close ties with Cyrenaica but was not interested in overseeing Tripolitania and could see little chance of dislodging the French from Fezzan. The United States, with no interest in assuming trusteeship responsibilities in Africa, promoted a collective trusteeship plan that had some ideological appeal but generated little real support. France appeared determined to retain control in Fezzan and to see Italy restored in Tripolitania. The Soviet Union hoped to use the colonial issue to improve its bargaining position in Europe and to increase its appeal to the Italian electorate by sponsoring the restoration of Italian rule in their former colonies.

The run-up to the Italian general elections in 1948 impacted heavily on events in Libya as the United States and its allies worried that a sizeable number of Italian voters could be swayed by the colonial issue. The Soviets weighed in early, in an effort to influence Italian voters, announcing in mid-February 1948 their support for an Italian trusteeship over all former colonies. American and British policy makers took a more cautious approach, favoring the postponement of a decision until after the elections. In the end, the Italian elections came and went with the Gasperi-Sforza regime in Rome demonstrating it could withstand a Communist challenge when sufficiently bolstered by external aid. The lesson learned in Washington was that there was no need to accept Italian demands for trusteeships over former colonies.

Even though strategic considerations had been central to the question of Libya since the end of World War II, it was the crisis in Italy in early 1948 that galvanized Anglo-American defense plans. Following the Italian elections, the State Department and the Foreign Office pledged not to make public statements about the colonies without first consulting each other. And the State Department later instructed the American delegation to coordinate its strategy with the French as well as the British.

Throughout this period, Libya remained the key to the preservation of Anglo-American strategic interests in the eastern Mediterranean. Sir Orme Sargent, British Permanent Under Secretary, in January 1948 described Cyrenaica as the best aircraft carrier in Africa albeit one lacking resources. Largely demobilized in 1947, the American base at Mallaha in Tripolitania, generally known as Wheelus Field, also took on new life. The United States by early 1948 had committed itself fully to British interests in Cyrenaica, and by the summer of 1948 to the development of a major postwar base at Mallaha. With the European crisis of 1948 serving as a catalyst, the strategic interests of Great Britain and the United States were now intertwined.[4]

In accordance with the provisions of the Italian peace treaty, the Council of Foreign Ministers in early 1948 dispatched a Commission of Investigation to Libya to report on internal conditions and to ascertain the wishes of the people. Consisting of one representative from each of the Four Powers, the Commission was instructed to gather facts but to refrain from making recommendations on the final disposition of the territories. Arriving in Libya on 6 March 1948, the Commission spent forty days in Tripolitania, twenty-five in Cyrenaica, and ten in Fezzan. When the Commission visited Cyrenaica, the National Congress submitted a proposal that called for complete and immediate independence for Cyrenaica and the recognition of Amir Idris as King of a constitutional Cyrenaican state. With regards to Tripolitania, the National Congress took an equivocal position, stating that Tripolitania could unite with Cyrenaica under the Sanusi crown; otherwise, Cyrenaica would retain its own full independence. During the Commission visit to Fezzan, members of the secret opposition society openly denounced the French administration, demanding the union of Fezzan with Cyrenaica and Tripolitania under Sanusi leadership. Once the Commission had departed, French authorities arrested and jailed at least one member of the society, Muhammad Bin Uthman al-Sayd, for a period of six months.

Torn by conflicting interests, the members of the Commission eventually agreed only on a few fundamentals. Recognizing the people of Libya were virtually unanimous in their desire for freedom from foreign rule, Commission members acknowledged a widespread lack of sentiment for a return to Italian rule but reported a mature understanding of the responsibilities of independence was clearly lacking. Due to the low level of economic development, the Commission concluded Libya was not ready for independence, a decision that caused bitter resentment throughout Libya.[5]

At the final session of the Council of Foreign Ministers, which opened in Paris on 13 September 1948, the Soviet delegate, in an astonishing policy shift, proposed placing the colonies under a UN trusteeship. Administration of the trusteeship, according to the Soviet plan, would be the responsibility of a Trusteeship Council assisted by an advisory board that included members of the Council. The Soviet initiative reproduced almost verbatim the 15 September 1945 proposal of Secretary of State Byrnes and thus returned the Council to its starting point. Rejecting the Soviet plan as no longer practical, the American, British, and French representatives joined together to transfer responsibility for the Italian colonies to the United Nations; and the Council of Foreign Ministers ceased to function.

AMERICAN STRATEGIC INTERESTS

The United States in the aftermath of World War II worked to clarify its strategic position in the eastern Mediterranean and Middle East, a region now considered to be of critical importance to American security. Recognizing the important role Arab–Israeli relations would play in the achievement of American objectives, Washington developed a number of propositions to guide its policy towards the region. First, it recognized the political and economic stability of the region was crucial to U.S. security. It then concluded it was in the national interest to enjoy the goodwill and respect of all peoples of the region, Arab and Jew alike, and to orient those peoples away from the Soviet Union. Third, the differences between Israel and its Arab neighbors should be reconciled, at least to the extent the Arab states and Israel would act in concert to oppose Soviet aggression. Finally, the close collaboration between the United States and Great Britain, in evidence throughout the postwar period, should continue wherever possible to achieve these core objectives.

The above appraisal of American security interests in the eastern Mediterranean and Middle East suggested the following strategic requirements. First, Washington must deny a foothold in the region to a hostile power. It must also maintain friendly relations with the countries involved, promoting and cultivating relationships with economic and social assistance, together with military aid as might be practical. Third, the United States and its allies must develop the oil resources of the area. Finally, the United States must take the steps necessary to ensure the right of its military forces to enter essential areas upon threat of war.

In support of these four strategic requirements, the Department of State on 28 August 1947 recommended the United States secure a series of air base facilities in the region anchored in the east by the base at Dhahran in Saudi Arabia and in the west by the facility at Wheelus Field outside Tripoli. Regarding Wheelus Field, the State Department memorandum emphasized it was very important to work out a satisfactory arrangement for the continuation of American base rights even as a solution was reached in the United Nations regarding disposition of the Italian colonies. The same communication reiterated the importance of British policy to American strategic interests in the region. While the British bases in Cyrenaica were not specifically mentioned, they had been the subject of earlier State Department memos and were clearly considered by Washington to be crucial to American interests in the region.

The strategic interests of the United States remained largely unchanged as Libyan independence approached. If there was a change, it was a growing recognition that British defense potential might prove inadequate to the needs of a region threatened by an adversary as formidable as the Soviet Union. Washington eventually concluded American actions in the long run would likely be decisive here as well as elsewhere in the world. The United States joined Great Britain, France, and Turkey in proposing a Middle East Command whose principal efforts focused on bringing Greece and Turkey into the North Atlantic Treaty Alliance (NATO) and developing a chain of strategic air bases under American control. Washington even considered including Libya in NATO on the grounds that it might prove easier to address defense requirements through a multilateral arrangement; however, the idea was quickly disgarded as impractical.[6]

UNITED NATIONS DECIDES

The transfer of the Libyan question from the Council of Foreign Ministers to the UN General Assembly proved to be of decisive importance to the future of Libya. No veto could prevail in the General Assembly as it was composed of fifty-eight members voting on the basis of equality and deciding important issues by a two-thirds majority. Resolution of the issue might not be made easier by the change in milieu, but the question in this forum would be addressed under very different rules. Unanimity was no longer a prerequisite, and all debates were public with the exception of those in subcommittee. The transfer of proceedings to the United Nations thus gave all involved parties a larger and more accessible forum in which to plead their case.[7]

Adopting an equivocal position from the outset, the American delegation emphasized that a decision on the future of Libya should consider the interests of the inhabitants as paramount but also take into account concerns for international peace and security. The inhabitants of Libya seemed well advanced toward self-government and independence, according to the United States; nevertheless, the relevance of the area to international peace and security could not be ignored. In contrast, the Egyptian delegate took the view that Libya was ready for immediate independence. Other delegates questioned the preparedness of Libya for such a decisive step. When a prolonged discussion identified no consensus for action, a subcommittee was appointed to study and propose a resolution to the opposing viewpoints on Libya.

The principal reason the United States remained reluctant as late as 1949 to see a UN trusteeship in the area was that such a step threatened Washington's plan to develop Wheelus Field into a strategic air base. The administrator of a trust territory, under the UN trusteeship system, could not establish military bases except in the case of a strategic trusteeship, such as that enjoyed by the United States in the former Japanese islands of the Pacific. However, strategic trusteeships were subject to veto in the UN Security Council of which the Soviet Union was a member. If Libya passed under any form of UN trusteeship, it would thus become virtually impossible for it to play a role in the defense arrangements of the Free World.[8]

Following formation of the UN subcommittee, the British and Italian foreign ministers proposed a compromise, known as the Bevin–Sforza plan, which gave ten-year trusteeships to Britain in Cyrenaica, Italy in Tripolitania, and France in Fezzan. At the end of this period, Libya would be established as an independent state if the UN General Assembly decided such a step was appropriate. Acknowledging Libyan aspirations for independence, the proposal safeguarded, at least temporarily, American and British strategic interests in the region. France, Great Britain, the United States, and the Latin American states supported the Bevin–Sforza plan; but it was opposed by the Arab, Asian, and Soviet blocs on the grounds it ignored the national aspirations of the Libyan people. Less than six weeks after declaring the interests of the Libyan people to be paramount, the American delegation justified its support for the Bevin–Sforza plan on the grounds that it offered a path both to independence and unity. In reality, American support for the plan was simply another example of U.S. strategic concerns outweighing the articulated and recognized interests of the Libyan people. The Bevin–Sforza plan generated widespread, intense protests in Tripoli and elsewhere in Libya before it was finally defeated in a May 1949 General Assembly vote.

With the rejection of the trusteeship proposal, some agreement on independence for Libya appeared to be a foregone conclusion. The American and British delegations now declared themselves in favor of independence, despite what they considered to be the backwardness of Libya; but they also argued that a preparatory period of three to five years was necessary to lay the groundwork for self-government. Championing the cause of colonial areas, the Soviet Union called for immediate independence, together with the early withdrawal of foreign forces and the liquidation of military bases. The Arab and Asian representatives, along with Italy, joined the Soviet Union in advocating immediate independence. After considerable debate, the General Assembly on 21 November 1949, by the narrow margin of a single vote, called for Libya to become an independent and sovereign state no later than 1 January 1952.

The UN General Assembly in December 1949 appointed Adrian Pelt, Assistant Secretary-General of the United Nations, as the UN Commissioner for Libya with a charter to assist its inhabitants to draw up a constitution and to establish an independent state. The General Assembly also approved a ten-member Advisory Council consisting of representatives of Egypt, France, Italy, Pakistan, Great Britain, and the United States, together with four Libyan leaders appointed by Pelt, to assist the Commissioner to accomplish his tasks. The Egyptian and Pakistani members, on what came to be known as the Council of Ten, would later express dissenting opinions on several administrative and constitutional issues. The Egyptian delegate was especially forceful on the question of federalism versus unity, advocating a unified form of government for Libya. In turn, the United States delegation argued consistently, and in the end successfully, that federation was the optimum form of government for Libya.

In July 1950, Commissioner Pelt invited twenty-one prominent Libyans, seven each from Cyrenaica, Fezzan, and Tripolitania, to form a Preparatory Committee to discuss the composition and means to select a provisional National Assembly. The so-called Committee of Twenty-One subsequently decided the Assembly should consist of twenty members each from the three constituent provinces, to be appointed by province chiefs. With two-thirds of the Libyan population resident in Tripolitania, the Tripolitanian members of the committee argued unsuccessfully that a truly democratic Assembly would be based on proportional representation. This first decision of the committee was thus of enormous importance, effectively determining the future form of the Libyan state, since both Cyrenaica and Fezzan favored a federal form of government. Once established the Assembly passed a resolution proposing the state of Libya be a federal monarchy, under the crown of Sayyid Idris of Cyrenaica, and a law to that effect was unanimously adopted by the National Assembly on 2 December 1950.

The National Assembly on 7 October 1951 approved a constitution, consisting of 213 articles. Declaring the United Kingdom of Libya to be a hereditary monarchy, the constitution provided for a federal form of government. Cyrenaica, Fezzan, and Tripolitania were described as provinces, not states, to emphasize national unity. The parliament consisted of a senate of twenty-four members, eight from each province, and a house of representatives based on proportional representation with adult male voters electing deputies in a ratio of one per twenty thousand inhabitants. Islam was the declared religion of the new state. Unable to agree on a location for the national capital, Benghazi and Tripoli were named as joint capitals. In an arrangement that was to cause considerable inconvenience, expense, and inefficiency in coming years, the capital was to alternate year by year (later every two years) between Benghazi and Tripoli.

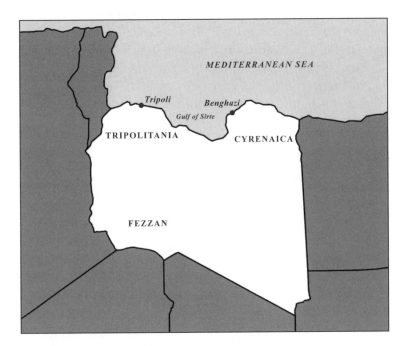

Map 6 Libya at Independence

To the surprise of most observers, the Soviet Union largely disengaged from the Libyan issue in the years immediately after 1949. Intensely involved in the earlier Council of Foreign Ministers discussions, Soviet interest waned after the question passed to the United Nations and debate moved outside Moscow's central concern, a military base in North Africa. If Soviet involvement had continued in 1949–51 at previous levels, the outcome of the UN mission might have been different. Effective Soviet support for Arab League and Egyptian demands for a unitary Libyan state dominated by Tripolitania, for example, could have affected political attitudes in Cyrenaica and Fezzan and possibly blocked the creation of a unified Libya.

The Western governments, on the other hand, continued to view Libya within the context of the Cold War and related global strategies. The British worked to consolidate diplomatic and political relations in Cyrenaica in an effort to establish a sound foundation for their military bases. The French repeatedly expressed concern that independence for Libya could destabilize the region by encouraging similar movements elsewhere in North Africa. For strategic purposes, France hoped to retain and strengthen its position in Fezzan to slow the westward spread of Arab nationalism. Even as it supported independence for Libya, the United States worked to solidify its strategic position at Wheelus Field before independence took place. American diplomats also worried about the level of Communist activity in Libya, a concern in retrospect more a reflection of American xenophobia than an accurate recognition of a realistic threat. Finally, the Italians, reconciled to independence for their former colony, now waited impatiently for the opportunity to forge new agreements to protect their economic interests in Tripolitania.

ARAB NATIONALISM, AID, AND BASE RIGHTS

Concerned American intentions in Libya might be misinterpreted, Secretary of State Dean Acheson summarized U.S. policy in a May

1950 telegram to the American consulate in Tripoli. He emphasized the United States had two central objectives in Libya. First, in conjunction with London, Washington sought to obtain the right to use American and British military facilities in the area. Second, the United States looked forward to establishing an independent and sovereign Libya no later than 1 January 1952. In working toward these objectives, Acheson expressed a desire to enjoy the friendship, understanding, and respect of the Libyan people, Arab states interested in the issue, and other UN members.

Arab nationalism, following the creation of Israel in mid-1948, was recognized by the United States as a potent force as well as a future threat to security interests. According to American officials, Arab nationalism was an important factor in North Africa albeit one that had been exploited by political opportunists and the Arab League; nevertheless, they realized it constituted the force of the future in the region. Moreover, because these nationalist elements tended to be strongly anti-France, and U.S. policies were often similar to those of the French, Arab nationalists frequently opposed American policies as well. The reservoir of goodwill the United States had enjoyed in Libya and elsewhere in North Africa as a result of World War II was thus receding because America was not assisting the Arab nationalists to achieve their goals.

Misreading the intent of many Arab nationalists, American policy statements often expressed undue concern over the potential for Communist infiltration of the region, especially in the wake of Arab nationalist activities. Washington continued to take a jaundiced view of nationalist movements in Libya for much of the next two decades out of fear such movements would encourage and facilitate the spread of Communism. With the advantage of hindsight, this policy was doomed to failure from the outset. A policy of opposition to Arab nationalist movements, especially when coupled to support for unpopular French policies in neighboring states, actually facilitated the spread of the very movements it hoped to contain.

The core objectives of the United States government, as outlined by Secretary of State Acheson in May 1950, led the United States to take three important, interrelated decisions at the beginning of the decade. First, Washington recognized it must continue to coordinate its policies with Great Britain if it was to maximize its strategic position in the region. Second, Libya clearly required ongoing support from the United States if it was to maintain its independence. Finally, American policy makers agreed it would be wise to negotiate a military base agreement in Libya before independence because independence would both strengthen the negotiating position of the Libyan government and embolden the opposition.

In advancing these objectives, American reluctance to negotiate base rights agreements on a *quid pro quo* basis in return for economic assistance was a difficult obstacle. The United States recognized that one of Libya's few assets was its strategic location and that Washington would have to make some contribution to the Libyan economy in return for the use of its bases. At the same time, American officials argued there should be no formal connection between base rights and financial aid because any linkage of the two issues threatened to open the United States to blackmail on the part of any new state. It could also introduce a source of constant friction, especially in situations where circumstances forced fluctuations in aid levels.

Washington's ongoing desire to coordinate its policies with London further complicated the question. Anglo-American consultation and cooperation in the Middle East and North Africa had worked well in the immediate postwar years; however, American policy makers in the early 1950s began to voice concern about long-term British resources and capabilities in the region. In December 1950, the State Department partially justified a top secret review of Middle East policy on the grounds that the United Kingdom lacked both the manpower and resources required to defend the area and had no plans for the defense of the Saudi Arabian oil fields and the Dhahran base. The review described as wishful thinking any assumption that the United States could rely on Great Britain to defend the Middle East because the capabilities of the latter were simply too small to provide a sound basis for defense of American interests in the area.

In mid-1951, France and the United States reached an agreement through which the United States would operate five air bases in Morocco. About the same time, agreements with Saudi Arabia ensured continued use of the Dhahran base for a five-year period. Other bases were under construction or planned in Crete, Cyprus, and Rhodes. In December 1951, the United States disclosed that it had secured permission from Libyan authorities to retain Wheelus Field, as well as other facilities throughout the country, in advance of the formal proclamation of Libyan independence. The terms of the agreement included payment by the United States to Libya of $1 million annually for twenty years in addition to reimbursing Libya with equitable rents for land use. When the United Kingdom of Libya proclaimed its independence on 24 December 1951, the United States extended full recognition and elevated the American Consulate General to the status of a Legation.

CONFLICTING INTERESTS

Postwar negotiations regarding the disposition of the Italian colonies in general, and Libya in particular, were prolonged and often heated. A myriad of aims and interests were at stake in the decisions to be made. Military and strategic considerations included American and British plans to maintain Libya as a Western base area as well as to keep it out of Soviet hands. The French government rightly worried that any decision taken on Libya could generate strong nationalist sentiment and unrest in neighboring French territories. The Soviet Union desired access to the Mediterranean shore. Other considerations included Italian prestige, the British pledge not to return the Sanusiyya to Italian rule, and Arab concerns for the future of the Muslim population of Libya. Of course, there were also the expressed interests of the Libyan people themselves, interests accorded growing weight as the dialogue progressed. And even this list of interests and objectives is by no means exhaustive of the multitude of crosscurrents and ramifications concerned with the final disposition of Libya.

The defeat of the Bevin–Sforza plan, which would have given ten-year trusteeships to Britain in Cyrenaica, Italy in Tripolitania, and France in Fezzan, marked a turning point in the debate. With the defeat of the trusteeship proposal in May 1949, all sides reluctantly and belatedly declared themselves in favor of independence. When the UN General Assembly met in September 1949, they found Sayyid Idris had proclaimed the independence of Cyrenaica at a 1 June 1949 meeting of the National Congress. In response, the British Chief Administrator formally recognized both the Amir as head of the Cyrenaican government and the desire of Cyrenaicans for self-government. Knowing Tripolitanians could view this unilateral decision as threatening, Sayyid Idris directed the National Congress to dispatch a cable, assuring them he was still working for the unity of Cyrenaica and Tripolitania. In response, the Tripolitanian National Front dispatched a delegation to Cyrenaica to congratulate the Amir and to request his support in achieving the unity of the sister provinces. The French government followed suit in February 1950, establishing a transitional government and representative assembly in Fezzan.

The question of the Italian colonies was never a vital one for the United States, but Soviet interest in Tripolitania eventually made the disposition of Libya an important issue. As the future of Cyrenaica and Tripolitania assumed an exaggerated strategic importance in the immediate postwar world, the conflicting policies of the Four Powers became Libya's strongest ally in achieving unity and independence. In the process, Washington shifted policy positions frequently in an effort to surface solutions that would guarantee the security of the region and also protect American interests. The short-term, tactical need to employ Wheelus Field near Tripoli as a link in the supply chain for American occupation troops in Europe was a primary concern together with the longer-term, strategic requirement to maintain a position on the Mediterranean coast. Washington viewed Wheelus Field as the essential western anchor in an arc of strategic bases stretching from Libya to Saudi Arabia. With these objectives in mind, the fundamental aim of American policy in Libya became an agreement, any agreement, that served and supported core American interests. In brokering such a settlement, the United States, less than a decade after the issuance of the Atlantic Charter in August 1941, compromised and very nearly abandoned its pledged respect for the self-determination of peoples, despite a clear understanding in Washington as to the interests and wishes of the Libyan people.

In Libya, the composition of the political groups opposed to a return to Italian rule and in support of independence differed from Cyrenaica to Tripolitania to Fezzan; but in all three areas, they mostly remained centered on local, provincial interests. Most Libyans still drew their identity from family, tribe, or region; or in the largest sense, as members of the broader Islamic community. Given the Libyan experience under first Ottoman and then Italian rule, this was perfectly understandable; however, this largely provincial focus prevented the galvanizing of a nationalist ideology that could be harnessed after independence in support of wider socioeconomic and political goals. In addition, a growing number of Libyans, especially after Israel was created, were attracted to the the nascent forces of Arab nationalism, forces that would grow in strength and importance in the coming decade. Journalist Ann Dearden in October 1950 captured the intensity of the growing ideological divide:

> The Libyans themselves are torn between these two imperialisms – that of the West, which offers material aid in return for bases, and that of the Arab East, which offers the emotional satisfaction of Islamic isolationism in return for becoming the tools of Egyptian expansionism. And there is no doubt that in 1950 the Eastern ideas have gained on those of the West.[9]

The forces of Arab nationalism would later prove a formidable challenge for an independent Libya ruled by a conservative monarchy.

Once the question of Libya was placed before the United Nations, which called for the establishment of a sovereign state by January 1952, the subsequent transition period was not without its problems. However, a national constituent assembly was eventually created, meeting for the first time in November 1950. It authorized a federal system of government with a monarch as head of state, designating Sayyid Muhammad Idris al-Mahdi al-Sanusi as king. Committees formed by the constituent assembly then drafted a constitution which was adopted in October 1951. On 24 December 1951, King Idris I proclaimed the United Kingdom of Libya as a sovereign and independent state. Libya thus became the first African state to achieve independence from European rule and the first and only state created by the General Assembly of the United Nations.

5

UNITED KINGDOM OF LIBYA, 1951–69

At independence, a low level of national consciousness or national identity had existed in Libya.

Ronald Bruce St John, *Qaddafi's World Design*, 1987

In short, to the thinkers and activists who made up the nationalist generation, Arab nationalism would be a hollow and meaningless concept if it did not strive to gather its children under one roof in one unified and sovereign Arab state.

Adeed Dawisha, *Arab Nationalism*, 2003

We cannot afford to lose Libya.

Vice President Richard M. Nixon, 1957

I could see the beginnings of the deterioration of the monarchical system, and the spread of corruption which was becoming so overwhelming [in the mid-sixties] that it was damaging the props of constitutional rule and the integrity of public servants.

Mustafa Ahmed Ben-Halim, *Libya*, 1998

The United Kingdom of Libya was a fragile product of agreements, deals, and compromises, driven by a complex multitude of interests and pressures. Consequently, it was a surprise to most observers that it lasted almost eighteen years. From 1951 to 1969, eleven prime ministers and over forty cabinets displayed an unexpected resilience in dealing with a succession of internal and external crises. During this period, Libya experienced dramatic socioeconomic change even as it brought a certain precarious stability to the central Mediterranean.

SOCIOECONOMIC INHERITANCE

The Libyan economy at independence faced serious challenges. Approximately eighty percent of the population was engaged in an agriculture that yielded a pitifully small return owing to a combination of poor rainfall, tired soil, destructive desert winds, primitive farming methods, and occasional locust swarms. The depressed state of the agricultural sector led to a heated debate as to whether it was underdeveloped or overdeveloped. The UN Food and Agriculture Organization took the position it was overdeveloped because climate, erosion, and poor land use in the past made it impossible to work agricultural miracles in the present.[1] The industrial sector offered even less potential than agriculture. Libya lacked raw materials, capital, and skilled manpower, the factors necessary for a successful industrial base, together with a known power source. In the early years of independence, the formal economy relied mainly on the export of castor seeds, esparto grass (used in making paper), and scrap metal scavenged from World War II vehicles damaged in the fighting, together with aid from friendly countries and international bodies.

The effects of World War II visited additional problems on the Libyan economy. The Italian banks closed all their Libyan branches in 1942 and did not reopen them until 1951. During the period of the British Military Administration, Barclay's was the only functioning bank; and it played a limited role, functioning mainly as a central bank for the military administration. With all banks effectively closed and credit thus nonexistent, commerce was largely paralyzed. Moreover, the widespread use of land mines during the war, estimates reach as high as twelve million mines planted, hampered not only agriculture development but also air, land, and sea transport in the postwar period. As a result, imports exceeded exports throughout the period of British administration, and the balance of trade remained in continuous and increasing deficit. Libya began the independence era with no outstanding public debt but only because American, British, and French largesse covered the trade deficit in the years prior to independence.

The available human resources in Libya also suffered distinct quantitative and qualitative limitations. A population of a little more than one million people enjoyed a relatively high birth rate, estimated at four percent a year; but primitive conditions and poor health care facilities resulted in a similar death rate with the result annual population growth did not exceed one percent. Qualitative shortcomings were principally the product of extremely limited educational and vocational training facilities which left ninety percent of the population illiterate at independence. During the Italian occupation, educational facilities largely targeted Italian children; and during much of World War II, the schools were closed. The British Military Administration later opened eighty-one primary schools; and by 1950, more than two hundred primary schools with more than thirty thousand students were in operation with two-thirds of them located in Tripoli. Three secondary schools had also opened as well as two teacher training centers and a center for training government employees. Nevertheless, the United Nations in 1950 estimated only twenty percent of those eligible for schooling were actually in school.[2]

PALACE SYSTEM OF POWER

The 1951 constitution established an hereditary monarchy based on Sayyid Muhammad Idris al-Mahdi al-Sanusi and his male successors, descendants of a distinguished North African family which traced its ancestry from the Prophet Muhammad through the Prophet's daughter, Fatima. Throughout much of the 1950s, the governments formed under the constitutional monarchy were too weak, poor, and inexperienced to have much choice in either domestic or foreign policy. As a result, the Idris regime mostly sought to balance the interests of the Western powers, upon whose support the Libyan economy depended, against the growing claims of Arab nationalism.

The independence era began inauspiciously enough with parliamentary elections in February 1952. While details remain unclear, the elections were likely manipulated by the government to ensure the defeat of the National Congress Party which advocated abandonment of the federal system in favor of a unitary state. The change would have transferred the power center from Cyrenaica, the base of the Sanusi Order, the principal interest of King Idris, and the probable limits of his sense of political community, to Tripolitania where two-thirds of the population lived in a more urban setting. In any case, allegations of electoral fraud by National Congress members, accurate or not, led to rioting in Tripolitania. When the disorder threatened to mushroom into a full-scale uprising, the government arrested a number of party leaders and expelled the head of the party.[3] Contained by the government, the 1952 electoral crisis had the unfortunate effect of destroying legitimate, effective political opposition just as a democratic parliamentary system was emerging. It also had a deeper, more sustained impact in that multi-party elections were never again held in Libya from 1952 to the present.

Following dissolution of the National Congress Party, all political parties in Libya were banned and publicly responsible political opposition to the government ended. Thereafter, politics in Libya became largely a contest of family, tribal, and parochial interests as networks of kinship and clan provided the organizational structure for political competition. Rather than rely on ideological loyalty or administrative competence, the monarchy delegated authority to powerful local families who consolidated their economic and political positions through intermarriage. With the tribal element constituting a core aspect of political leadership, many Libyans rightly concluded only a few families controlled the country and determined its destiny. Historian John Wright captured the essence of the autocratic system that developed:

Yet the Libyan people as a whole had small reason for confidence in their post-independence governments, and little opportunity for understanding their policies. For despite careful United Nations supervision of its independence and its nicely composed constitutional arrangements, the Libyan kingdom was from the outset little more than a benign despotism administered by an oligarchy of leading families and tribal and commercial interests.[4]

Since local notables and tribal leaders often owed little to the central government, their legitimacy in the eyes of their people was based on family status, wealth, and symbols of religious piety. Reflecting facts on the ground, the boundaries of local administrative units were mostly the *de facto* boundaries of Libya's major tribes. This system of government was largely immune to challenge from the base because the general ignorance of the masses, coupled with their passivity, conformity, and pervasive sense of fatalism, made it very difficult for them to question the traditional system. The limited political participation allowed at the local level also hampered central government efforts to accomplish much-needed socioeconomic development programs.

At the top, King Idris ruled Libya from what has been termed a "palace system of power."[5] The foundation of the system rested on both religious and secular bases. As head of the Sanusi movement, Sayyid Idris had a strong claim to religious legitimacy. A descendant of the Prophet Muhammad, his position in this regard was similar to that of the Alawite monarchy in Morocco and the Hashemite Kingdom in Jordan. His secular strength rested on a tribal constituency whose fortunes he worked to tie to the monarchical regime. Political authority was exercised through local notables and tribal leaders who served as the link between the head of the system and the tribal clans.

In Cyrenaica, the system was reinforced by a parallel administration controlled by the Sanusi hierarchy through its system of religious lodges and schools. In Tripolitania, where the personal characteristics of the king were widely respected, nationalists and republicans accepted the monarchy as a necessary condition to independence. In Fezzan, the local tribes were not members of the

Sanusi Order but agreed to trade personal loyalties for local administrative power within a national body. The same was true of tribal areas in Tripolitania. Throughout Libya, it was also true that loyalty to Idris was stronger among the older generation than among Libyan youth, an increasingly important issue in the decade to come.

Theoretically a constitutional monarch, the king enjoyed remarkably broad powers as "supreme head of state" and "supreme commander" of the armed forces. "Inviolable" and "exempt from all responsibility," his constitutional right to issue decrees with the force of law, appoint and remove all senior officials, and exercise legislative power in conjunction with the parliament resulted in a system of government dominated by his nominees. Prime ministers were generally selected based on regional considerations and loyalties, and cabinet appointments reflected the principle of tribal balance. In theory and practice, the king was the supreme arbiter in national affairs with no one in or out of government in a position to challenge his ultimate authority.

Yet, it was an absolutist system with a difference in that the king's exercise of authority was seldom obvious. He made no important policy statements and seldom made public comment on affairs of state. And he preferred to reside outside Benghazi and Tripoli, remaining aloof from the political pressures and machinations of the capitals. Seemingly remote from the workings of government, he remained above the political fray, effectively employing a system of palace power and patronage, centered on personal advisers known as the royal *diwan*, to dissociate himself from direct decision-making.

To preserve unity, the United Kingdom of Libya emerged as a federal state in 1951 on the basis of bargains and compromises, papering over differences instead of resolving them. With the deficiencies of the federal system increasingly obvious, it was abandoned in 1962–63 in favor of a unitary state. Provincial administrators were subordinated to the federal government in December 1962; and in April 1963, both federal and provincial administrations were abolished with their powers combined into one central government. At the lower level, ten administrative districts replaced the three provinces of Cyrenaica, Fezzan, and Tripolitania. Reflecting the change to a unitary state, the United Kingdom of Libya was renamed the Kingdom of Libya.

For the previous twelve years, four governments sitting in two national and three provincial capitals had ruled Libya. There had been fifteen federal ministries with an average of eight in each of the provinces, and both Cyrenaica and Tripolitania had employed more civil servants than the federal government. Liaison between the federal and provincial governments and between the three provincial governments had been poor, often resulting in conflicting policies or a duplication of services.

The move to a unitary state thus appeared to mark a vast improvement in governance, streamlining a cumbersome system, cutting administrative costs, and reducing if not eliminating a bureaucratic nightmare. On the other hand, the unitary system, in creating the essential machinery of a centralized state, increased power in the hands of the king and the royal diwan. After 1963, a small group of people, driven by self-interest, continued to make all important decisions, and selection and advancement in government service continued to depend largely on background and connections.

ALLIANCE POLITICS

In the aftermath of World War II, two rival alliance systems, the Arab and the Middle Eastern, struggled for predominance in North Africa and the Middle East. The United States, backed by its North Atlantic Treaty Organization (NATO) allies, was the architect of the Middle Eastern system. Viewing the region in geographical terms, as a land mass vulnerable to the Soviet Union, the Middle Eastern system expected the Arab states to ally with it to guarantee the region's security. In contrast, the Arab system viewed the region, not as a geographical expansion between Europe and Asia, but as a single Arab nation with common interests and security priorities distinct from those of the West. From this viewpoint, the states constituting North Africa and the Middle East should take advantage of a unity of history, culture, language, and religion to create their own system to counter outside threats. Instead of the Soviet Union, the Arab system saw the recently declared state of Israel as its main threat.

In a policy that was controversial from the start, King Idris accommodated to and cooperated with the Middle Eastern system while limiting his participation in the Arab system. During the first decade of independence, the monarchy maintained a generally Western orientation; and Libya was universally regarded as one of the more conservative, traditional states of the Arab world. Thought to lack any natural resources, Libya's diplomatic orientation rested heavily on the assistance and income generated by American and British military bases.

The United Kingdom concluded a twenty-year treaty of friendship and alliance with Libya on 29 July 1953 in which the former received extensive extraterritorial and jurisdictional rights in return for financial assistance and military training. One year later, the United States concluded on 9 September 1954 a treaty of friendship and mutual support with Libya scheduled to last until 24 December 1970. Under the terms of this agreement, the United States secured military base rights, most especially Wheelus Field outside Tripoli, in return for economic, technical, and military assistance. Henry Serrano Villard, appointed the U.S. Minister to Libya at independence, the senior American diplomat in the country at the time, later emphasized the central role Wheelus Field played from the beginning in American–Libyan relations:

> From our first glimpse of Wheelus to the last, the American stake in this fragment of foreign territory was to be a paramount concern of the Legation and one of the principal subjects of discussion in my daily dealings with the Libyan government.[6]

The United States by the end of 1959 would extend over $100 million in financial assistance to Libya, making it the largest per capita recipient of U.S. aid in the world.

With the conclusion of these base agreements, the United Kingdom and the United States occupied paradoxical positions in Libya for much of the next decade. The monarchy embraced the Eisenhower Doctrine, through which the United States sought to build anti-Communist alliances; nevertheless, official opinion toward Washington was not as warm as it was toward London, in large part due to the longer relationship the Sanusi Order had enjoyed with the latter. On the other hand, public opinion in Libya and elsewhere in the Arab world was not yet as hostile to the United States as it was toward the United Kingdom. In the coming decade, the United States would squander the privileged position it enjoyed in Libya throughout the 1950s.

The French government hoped to negotiate a base agreement with Libya similar to those negotiated by the United Kingdom and United States, but events in neighboring Algeria soon frustrated its desires in this regard. In late 1954, Prime Minister Mustafa Ahmed Ben Halim agreed to allow Egypt to ship supplies through Libya to Algeria where the war of independence had just begun. At the same time, the Libyan parliament was pressuring the government to force the French to evacuate garrisons, totaling some four hundred soldiers, stationed in the south at Sebha, Ghat, and Ghadames. Invaluable to France, these troops were well placed to intercept the flow of men and material from Egypt to Algeria. The Libyan government was wary of the French role in Fezzan, as Prime Minister Ben Halim subsequently confirmed in his memoirs, and was willing to negotiate only on the basis of a total withdrawal of French forces:

> French declassified documents make it clear that France actually wanted to annex either the whole of the Fezzan or the oases of Gat [Ghat] and Ghadames. This is the distinguishing mark of French policy: an attitude of expansionist imperialism. And this is why I [Ben Halim] consider it one of my most significant political achievements to have got the French military out of the Fezzan and without conceding one inch of Libyan territory.[7]

A Franco-Libyan agreement reached in August 1955 provided for the evacuation of French forces from Fezzan by late 1956. In return for air and ground transit rights, together with minor modifications to the Libya border with French territories, France promised some $1 million in development aid to Libya. Other points of contention with France included the hospitality Libya occasionally showed to Algerian exiles and the nuclear tests France conducted in the Sahara Desert. A battle in October 1957 between Algerian and French forces on the Libyan border, followed by similar incidents in the coming year, resulted in the creation in 1958 of a Franco-Libyan commission to investigate future violations. Libyan relations with France did not begin to improve until after Algeria won its independence in 1962.

Diplomatic and commercial relations with Italy improved following the conclusion in October 1956 of a bilateral agreement that confirmed the earlier transfer of most Italian public property to Libya and brought $7.7 million in aid to Libya in return for the recognition of certain Italian commercial rights. In addition, the agreement provided for Italy to spend approximately $3.7 million to complete by 1960 certain colonization schemes in Tripolitania. As part of this deal, Italian colonists became outright owners of the land, regardless of how it had been acquired; and they were free to sell it to Libyans and to transfer the capital if they so desired. By the end of October 1961, almost two-thirds of the Italians in the settlement projects had sold their land to Libyans; by 1964, only some 120 colonist families remained in Tripolitania.

In contrast to the United Kingdom and the United States, commercial and diplomatic exchanges between Libya and the Soviet Union were minimal throughout the period of monarchical rule. The Soviet Union vetoed Libyan membership in the United Nations from independence in 1951 until 1955 when Libya established diplomatic relations with the Soviet Union, paving the way for Libyan admission as part of a package deal that included fifteen other new UN members. Conservative Libyans were uncomfortable with a Soviet embassy in their midst, and Prime Minister Bin Halim made it clear to the incoming Soviet ambassador that Communist activities would not be tolerated. Despite its economic difficulties at the time, Libya also refrained from accepting economic aid from the Soviet Union. In 1958, a rumored Soviet offer of $28 million in assistance did not materialize; coincidentally, U.S. payments to Libya doubled at about the same time. Some observers suggested the increase in American aid was designed to counter the Soviet offer or to support promising oil prospects in Libya. But it is more accurate to view it as a consequence of the Eisenhower Doctrine and other American policies intended to buttress pro-Western regimes in the Middle East.

As expanding oil revenues decreased Libyan dependence on income from the American and British bases and Arab nationalists increased their criticism of Libyan dependence on the West, Soviet links with Libya expanded modestly in the coming decade. The Soviet Union began to participate in the annual Tripoli Trade Fair, and a bilateral trade agreement between Moscow and Tripoli was concluded in 1963. Libyan parliamentary delegations visited the Soviet Union in 1961 and again in 1968 after a Supreme Soviet delegation had visited Libya in 1966.

WESTERN DEPENDENCE

The state of relative tranquility enjoyed by the monarchy at the outset of independence soon changed as Libya became increasingly enmeshed in the growing politicization of the Arab world. Contemporary events, like the colonial struggles of neighboring states, the Palestine conflict, renewed Soviet interest in the Middle East, the growth of Nasserist and Baathist pan-Arabism, and anti-royalist movements throughout the region, were hardly propitious for the political development of a conservative, traditional monarchy. The United Kingdom of Libya quickly exhausted its limited anti-colonialist credits as its dependence upon income from the American and British bases fostered a policy of support for the West. Over time, the legitimizing force of nationalism, which stemmed from the achievement of independence, was increasingly challenged internally by opposition groups and externally by pan-Arab movements. In the process, issues of foreign bases and foreign aid regularly exposed the one consistent weakness of the monarchy's foreign policy, its vulnerability to decisions taken by others.

Dependent on the West, King Idris was never as pro-Western as many observers believed. While the monarchy maintained a cordial relationship with the Western powers, its approach was based, not on a widespread commitment to Western ideals, traditions, and policies, but on the monarchy's belief that the Western powers remained in the best position to guarantee Libyan security. Reflecting this position, the monarchy worked to minimize the impact of Western sociopolitical values and structures on Libya and emphasized its political nonalignment in regional and international bodies, like the Organization of African Unity and the United Nations.

Officially supporting the cause of African unity, Libyan delegations attended the 1961 Casablanca conference of self-styled African neutralists and the founding meeting of the Organization of African Unity in 1963. Libya joined its African neighbors in condemning and boycotting the white regimes in southern Africa, but its practical support for African solidarity was meager. Commercial and diplomatic ties with states south of the Sahara also were limited. Libyan support for Maghrib unity was slow to start but gained momentum in the 1960s. Viewing Maghrib unity as a potential counterweight to the wave of Arab nationalism coming from the Mashriq, Libya sent an observer to the 1958 Conference for the Unification of the Arab Maghrib, subsequently affirming its faith in Maghrib unity. The monarchy later increased its support for regional economic development; in 1967, a permanent consultative committee was established in Tripoli to draft regional plans for economic cooperation.

The appearance and the reality of the monarchy's dependence on the West rested on the financial and political assistance generated by American and British military bases in Libya. The close association of the monarchy's apparent Western orientation to its need for military base revenues was increasingly apparent once petroleum exports began to reduce its dependence on those revenues. As early as 1964, after violent protests broke out in Benghazi and Egyptian President Gamal Abdul Nasser called for assurances the bases would not be used against Arab forces in the event of a war with Israel, Libya asked the United Kingdom and the United States to reconsider their future status at those bases. The United States responded by accepting in principle a withdrawal from Wheelus Field. The British moved more aggressively, withdrawing most of their forces from Tripolitania by 1966 and completing their evacuation from Cyrenaica in March 1970.

Ironically, the exploitation of oil deposits freed Libya from one form of dependence on the West but swapped it for another. To develop fully this newly discovered natural resource, Libya needed to remain on friendly terms with the West in order to attract necessary technicians and technology under the umbrella of Western oil companies. The downstream importance of the oil companies was obvious as early as 1957 when foreign oil companies spent $43.4 million in Libya compared to total foreign aid of only $38.32 million in the 1957–58 fiscal year. In short, oil increased public interest in being freer from the West, but it did not free Libya from its long-standing Western ties. On the contrary, it bound Libya more closely to the West because the monarchy, mistrusting the Soviet Union and its allies, could only obtain the financial and technical assistance necessary to develop this natural resource from the West.

IMPACT OF OIL

Oil exploration in Libya began in 1955, and deposits in commercially viable quantities were first discovered in 1959 when American prospectors confirmed their location at Amal and Zelten, separate oilfields in Cyrenaica. The following decade witnessed dramatic increases in both production and revenues, but not in the posted price of oil, the basis of taxable income for producing countries. Like most Arab oil-producing states, Libya considered the posted price of oil to be undervalued and unjust;

nevertheless, it continued to accept a volume-oriented as opposed to a price-oriented policy. It did so because it feared a confrontation with the oil companies over posted price levels might slow the momentum of industry development.

The wisdom of this policy decision was increasingly challenged after the June 1967 War closed the Suez Canal. In response, oil companies rapidly expanded their production in Libya to maximize the transport savings derived from not having to ship Gulf oil to Europe via the Cape of Good Hope. With proven oil reserves at the time far less than those of Saudi Arabia, Libya's daily production by 1969 was comparable to that of the Saudis.

Libya succeeded in crafting a clever petroleum law in 1955, later amended, that encouraged the international oil companies to participate in the Libyan oil industry. The unique feature of this innovative approach was the number of concessions granted to the relatively hungry, and consequently more flexible and accommodating, independent oil producers. The Libyan approach, when combined with Libya's proximity to European markets, resulted in Libya granting 137 concessions to thirty-nine companies by 1968. Libyan production at this point exceeded 2.6 million barrels a day.

The Libyan government joined the Organization of Petroleum Exporting Countries (OPEC) in 1962, two years after the organization was founded to stop the petroleum companies from reducing the posted price of oil. Until the end of the decade, Libya tended to support select OPEC policies but refused to endorse any that would alter its relationship with the oil companies working in Libya. Specifically, it supported in principle increasing refining capacity in producing countries, establishing national oil companies, taking an integrated approach to oil industry operations, and coordinating the conservation, production, and exploitation of oil reserves.

Government revenues from petroleum exports increased more than fifteen-fold from $40 million in 1962 to $625 million five years later. Within eight years of its first oil shipments, Libya had become the world's fourth largest exporter of crude oil, a rate of growth previously unknown anywhere in the history of the industry. In the process, Libya moved from a stagnant to an exploding economy, from a capital-deficit state to a capital-surplus state, from an aid recipient to an aid extender. Even though it occurred from a relatively low base, economic growth of this magnitude still remained extraordinary both in real and relative terms.

In addition to enriching the government, mounting oil revenues awakened the Libyan populace, drawing increasing attention to the conservative nature of the Idris regime. Indicative of the depth and breadth of change that took place, per capita income increased from $35 in 1951 to over $1,000 in 1967. Per capita income figures can be misleading as the increase in wealth is never distributed evenly; and in the Libyan case, the majority of people were still struggling financially in 1967. That said, the numbers highlight the revolution in rising expectations that took place in Libya in the 1960s as the populace came to expect the newly discovered oil wealth to result in vastly improved personal circumstances.

Growing oil revenues, accompanied by improving economic conditions and greater social mobility, also increased demands, especially among younger Libyans, for a coherent ideology that would satisfy new, albeit vaguely understood, political and spiritual yearnings. The monarchy attempted to respond to these needs but failed to understand and accommodate them just as it failed to satisfy the growing demands of Arab nationalists in and out of Libya. In the face of the revolution in rising expectations, the monarchy's entrance into pragmatic agreements for economic and technical cooperation with its North African neighbors was no match for the romantic appeal of the pan-Arabism offered by President Nasser. By the end of the decade, increasing numbers of the Libyan population, especially the younger, more articulate segments in the urban areas of Tripolitania, had concluded the domestic and foreign policies of King Idris were parochial, if not corrupt, and must be changed.

The rapid growth of oil revenues also increased opportunities for institutions and individuals to use oil income for personal advancement and enrichment. In a highly centralized political system, influential tribal leaders, especially those in Cyrenaica, powerful families, members of the royal diwan, and Sanusi family members collectively controlled the economic bureaucracy. In so doing, they experienced opportunities for graft and corruption on a grandiose scale. The impact of their behavior was doubly ruinous because the political system created and sustained by the Libyan elite reduced the bulk of the population to the role of impotent bystanders, intensifying feelings of frustration and alienation with the system.

The reality of the socioeconomic situation contributed to the feeling of bitterness reflected in Libyan literature in the 1960s. Alienation, anxiety, and rebellion characterized the short stories of authors like Khalifa Takbali, Abdullah Algwiri, and Kamel el-Mahgor. In "Dignity", by Khalifa Takbali, a Libyan worker defies three American oil workers to protest their insulting and humiliating demands. In "The Oil and the Dates" by Abdullah Algwiri, the narrator can find no one to harvest his crops because former farm hands have all migrated to the city in search of better jobs. The story ends with a brother of the narrator deciding to sell his share of the family farm and join the flight to the city. In "Crying" by Kamel el-Maghor, a young schoolboy laments the destruction of his old neighborhood, including the family home, to make way for new construction. At the end of the decade, in the wake of the Arab defeat in the June 1967 War, Libyan author Ahmed Fagih has noted elements of malaise and pessimism often also entered the literary mix:

> But the social and cultural upheaval that came with the oil discovery had had its bitter aftermath and brought some negative phenomena, that writers could not ignore; issues such as authenticity in the face of new modernisation, the cultural assimilation, as well as a strong sense of local identity, were evoked, to help resist the invading values of the commercial and consumer society.
>
> The feeling grew that the new wealth, which should be the common property of all the people, was controlled by powers that were alien to the peoples' aspirations and ambitions. ... Libyan workers were exploited by oil companies, and the American and British bases were active in maintaining the *status quo*. All of this contributed to a feeling of bitterness that was reflected in Libyan literature of the sixties.[8]

NATIONAL IDENTITY

A very low level of national consciousness or national identity existed in Libya at the time of independence. During the Ottoman occupation, nationalist tendencies were mostly latent, and the role of the Sanusi Order in Cyrenaica remained predominantly religious. Armed resistance to Italian rule transformed the Sanusiyya into more of a political movement, but the Italo-Libyan struggle did little to foster a growing sense of national political unity.[9] In consequence, it was not surprising that a lively debate had ensued in the run-up to independence as to whether to form a united Libya or to partition the territory into two or even three entities, each under a distinct political regime.

The advent of independence unified Cyrenaica, Fezzan, and Tripolitania into the United Kingdom of Libya, but it failed to forge a deep-rooted sense of national identity as did, for example, the bitter war of independence in neighboring Algeria. Most Libyans after 1951 continued to think of themselves as Cyrenaican, Fezzanese, or Tripolitanian, not Libyan. The proclamation of statehood also coincided with the rising tide of Arab nationalism in the Middle East, together with mounting anti-colonial agitation in surrounding North African states. The monarchy correctly saw Arab nationalism as a competing ideology, inimical to its interests, and sought to contain and direct its growth and influence in the kingdom. Libyan nationalists, on the other hand, regarded the regime established under the federal union as simply another artificial structure imposed on them by foreign powers. To them, nationalism equated with political freedom.

Geographical and political differences combined to reinforce the absence of a historical sense of unity between the disparate components of the new Libyan state. Geographically, the political division of the country into three provinces mirrored its physiographical character as the three territories were separated by severe geographical barriers. The Gulf of Sirte and the great Sirte Desert effectively split Cyrenaica and Tripolitania, reinforcing the political divide between Libya's two largest provinces. Cyrenaica before independence looked east towards Egypt and beyond to the Mashriq. In turn, Tripolitania looked westward toward the three North African states comprising the Maghrib. The sparsely populated Fezzan directed its attention towards little beyond the Sahara Desert, of which it was inseparably a part, as well as the African states bordering the Sahara. Politically, the people of Cyrenaica had opposed Italian domination at considerable human and economic cost while the Tripolitanians, despite the resistance of a few, had a far higher incidence of non-resistance or active collaboration.

In the first decade of independence, the monarchy made major efforts to promote a cohesive national community to give structure and meaning to new state institutions and to enhance and capitalize on feelings of shared experience. Not surprisingly, the early results of such efforts proved inconclusive, given the existing levels of inter-provincial rivalry and enmity. Well into the decade of the 1960s, observers continued to highlight the limited level of national identity or national consciousness found in Libya. In the wake of the public outcry provoked by the June 1967 War, the monarchy intensified its efforts in this regard, stressing the existence of a Libyan identity with deep roots in pre-independence history. In response, a feeling of national consciousness began to grow under the leadership of the Idris regime but not fast enough to preserve the monarchy from the stronger, more vibrant pan-Arab ideology originating in the east.

RISE OF ARAB NATIONALISM

Before World War I, Islamism and Ottomanism served as the principal factors of Arab political solidarity. After the war, Ottomanism was irrelevant and Islamism suffered humiliation at the secularizing hands of the Turkish reformer Mustafa Kemal (Atatürk), and through the presence of European imperialists in the major cities of Arab Islam. With attention centered on obtaining political independence from European control, budding Arab nationalism and vague formulations of Arab unity were interwoven with support for Palestinian Arabs in their opposition to Jewish immigration and land purchase.

The Libyan experience in this regard was not atypical. Failing to stop the Italian invasion, many Libyan leaders went into exile in Egypt or elsewhere in the Arab world where they conducted an active, if generally ineffective, war of words against the Italian occupation. Once the allied armies had liberated Libya, nationalist expressions surfaced. In October 1944, nationalist elements led a crowd of several thousand people through the streets of Tripoli, tearing down Italian street signs and replacing them with signs in the Arabic language. In 1945, demonstrations in Tripoli became an almost daily occurrence with the Jewish community the object of repeated mob outbursts.

As events in Palestine moved toward partition in 1947 followed by the proclamation of the state of Israel in 1948, ugly demonstrations again broke out in Libya and elsewhere in the Arab world. Unable to express directly their growing anger over the situation in Palestine, Libyans and their counterparts in other Arab states often vented it locally upon Jews who in most cases had little or no connection with Zionism. The plight of the relatively small Jewish community in Libya was further aggravated by the refusal of the British Military Administration to authorize Jewish emigration until 1949 after the British government had recognized the state of Israel.[10]

A conservative, traditional monarchy, the Idris regime occasionally emphasized Libyan–Arab brotherhood and solidarity; but its policies seldom went beyond lip-service unless under extreme pressure. King Idris blocked Libyan membership in the Arab League until 1953; and his government always fell short of offering tangible support for the Arab cause in the Middle East. During the 1956 Suez Crisis when President Nasser nationalized the Suez Canal, the British government, in direct violation of the 1953 Anglo-Libyan treaty, considered using its bases in Libya to attack Egypt. When the Libyan government protested, the British reconsidered; however, the damage had been done. The mere fact the monarchy had to request the bases not be used provided ammunition to nationalist elements in Libya already frustrated with what they saw as the pro-Western policies of the monarchy.

When Libya concluded a treaty of friendship and cooperation with Tunisia in 1957, marking the practical start of the movement for greater Maghrib unity, it was hailed by the signatories as a model of bilateral collaboration. The Tunisian government of President Habib Bourguiba, like Libya, saw the pact as a potential counterweight to Egyptian influence in North Africa; however, Arab nationalist critics denounced the agreement as little more than an instrument for harmonizing the policies of the signatories with those of the West. The dispute highlighted a core issue dividing the Arab world at the time in that some Arabs viewed Maghrib unity solely within the context of North Africa while others saw it as a precursor to greater Arab and African unity.

Once oil revenues began coursing through the Libyan economy, Libyans were eager for change and sought a comprehensive ideology that would both explain and satisfy their yearning. For them, Arab nationalism supplied the answers to the political divisions bedeviling the region and also to the economic and social issues inextricably connected to them. Ironically, the expanding Libyan school system was a major source of Arab nationalist thinking. Woefully short of trained Libyan teachers, the monarchy looked to Egypt to supply both teachers and textbooks. By the end of the 1950s, hundreds of Egyptians were employed as teachers in Libya, and the curriculum they fostered constituted a form of pedagogical imperialism. Their enthusiastic activities on behalf of Egyptian President Nasser eventually compelled the Libyan Minister of Education in 1958 to contract for Lebanese teachers to offset Egyptian influence. Libyan adoption of Egyptian administrative and judicial models, widespread Egyptian cultural influence in the form of Egyptian newspapers and Radio Cairo's *Voice of the Arabs*, and large numbers of young Libyans studying in Egypt compounded the problem of Egyptian influence. In Libya, Nasser's portrait was almost as widely displayed as that of the king.[11]

The monarchy completely misread the depth and breadth of popular sentiment, totally underestimating the need of its citizenry for ideological fulfillment. Instead, it concentrated on the provision of increased material benefits. As a result, a nascent Libyan nationalism, only sometimes vital enough to satisfy their total needs, proved unable to overcome the negative impact of tribal, provincial and religious loyalties and the positive appeal of pan-Arabism.

Student demonstrations broke out in both Benghazi and Tripoli in January 1964 in support of an Arab summit in Cairo and to protest Israeli plans to divert water from the Jordan River to irrigate the Negev Desert. These demonstrations intensified after Nasser called in February 1964 for the liquidation of the foreign bases in Libya on the grounds that they were a threat to Egypt and the Arab cause and designed to support Israel. At the same time, Radio Cairo falsely alleged the bases had been used against the Egyptians in the Anglo-French invasion of the Suez Canal in 1956. Demonstrations again occurred in 1965 over the issue of retaining diplomatic relations with West Germany after it established relations with Israel. Libya withdrew its ambassador to Germany in protest, but it was one of the few Arab states not to break diplomatic relations.

The year 1967 proved pivotal for the monarchy as its weak response to the June 1967 War, in the wake of its highly criticized response to the 1956 Suez Crisis, became a catalyst for the 1969 *coup d'état* that removed it from power. With the Egyptian government blaming the sudden, overwhelming defeat of Egyptian forces on the United Kingdom and the United States, the presence of their bases in Libya made an easy target. As elsewhere in the Arab world, popular reaction in Libya to the war was widespread, prolonged, and violent, especially in Benghazi and Tripoli. The official response of the Libyan government included a public threat to close Wheelus Field, and Libya also joined Saudi Arabia and the Gulf states in briefly shutting down oil production. Despite these tentative steps, Prime Minister Hussein Maziq was later forced to resign, after he resumed oil shipments to Western Europe, in the face of widespread criticism that his government had not done enough to assist its Arab brethren in the Arab–Israeli conflict.

Faced with bitter opposition, the monarchy made some concessions to the Arab system but struggled to maintain its nonaligned orientation. At the 1967 Arab summit in Khartoum, Libya joined other Arab oil-producing states in agreeing to subsidize the losses of Egypt and Jordan in the June 1967 War; however, it rejected more stringent measures, such as shutting off oil exports to the West. Thereafter, the monarchy continued to portray itself as a general supporter of Arab causes, but it did not pursue a more aggressive role in the arena of Arab politics in general or the Palestinian issue in particular.

MONARCHY IN PERSPECTIVE

At independence, Libya had no overarching ideology to guide a diverse population; no set of common traditions to unite the tribesmen of Cyrenaica, the townsmen of Tripolitania, and the nomads of Fezzan; few trained technicians, experienced administrators, or political chieftains knowledgeable in the art of modern government; and a deficit economy wholly dependent on aid from foreign sources. As oil revenues in the 1960s reached levels unimaginable in 1951, critics of the monarchy tended to forget, in particular, the depressed state of the economy in the previous decade. In light of the prevailing socioeconomic and political situation, the choice at independence of a monarchical institution to rule the country was understandable and not a bad decision.

Given the low base from which it began, the monarchy made considerable economic and social progress after 1951 and most especially after 1960 when oil revenues gave it the wherewithal to initiate social welfare programs and to begin much-needed public works. As early as 1958, the Abdul Majid Kubar government decreed that seventy percent of oil revenues would be devoted to economic and social development in an effort to distribute the benefits of the newfound wealth throughout society. Following creation of a development council in 1960, development priorities were outlined in 1963 in a Five-Year Economic and Social Development Plan, emphasizing public works and agricultural and forestry development. Loosely constructed, the plan quickly experienced difficulties because the unexpectedly rapid growth in oil revenues meant there was much more money to spend than the planners had anticipated. The hasty addition of ambitious new projects, like the building of 100,000 new homes in only five years, corrupted the original plan which soon lost cohesion and perspective. At the same time, opportunities for nepotism, bribery, and corruption multiplied, undermining the well-intentioned, if sometimes ill-advised, attempts of the monarchy to develop a basic economic and social infrastructure for Libya.

In the end, the distinctive feature of the absolutist political system in place proved to be its isolation from society at large. The power elite in Libya consisted of King Idris, a small coterie of retainers in the court entourage, and a revolving door of ministers, constantly fluid in composition. A second notable feature was the physical remoteness and detachment of the king who preferred to reside in Cyrenaica, removed from the day-to-day pressures of government. Bemused by religious and scholarly pursuits, he left the management of public policy to his ministers, an arrangement which led to frustration, corruption, and crisis. The absolutist system also lacked viability as King Idris had no issue and the question of succession thus was somewhat clouded. Since the hereditary nature of the monarchy involved numerous cousins in the political panorama, unhealthy competition among the various family factions forced the king as early as October 1954 to decree the line of succession was restricted to the king's branch of the royal family. The heir apparent, Hassan al-Rida, a nephew of the king with a lackluster personality, was known as the man without a shadow and was not held in high regard by the king. The actions of King Idris added to the air of instability as he offered his own abdication on several occasions after 1951, enhancing his image as a detached, reluctant ruler.

Given the fragile nature of the monarchy, its survival for almost eighteen years was due largely to the fragmented nature of Libyan society. Where the Libyan elite exhibited official agreement on most policy issues, the general public more often lacked consensus. Moreover, with the masses not mobilized and political parties proscribed, Libyans lacked the organizations necessary to express dissent in any collective manner. And the threat of coercion always lurked in the background. Able for a time to control the resources of influence and power, the monarchy was unable to compete with ideology of Arab nationalism once oil revenues began to course through the Libyan economy. The rapidly transforming Libyan economy precipitated dramatic changes in the social fabric of Libya which led to demands for socioeconomic and political change that the monarchy was simply unable or unwilling to accommodate.

THE END

On 1 September 1969, a small group of Libyan army officers, calling themselves the Free Unionist Officers' Movement, executed a successful *coup d'état* against an aging monarchy and initiated a radical reorientation of the domestic and foreign policy of Libya. The movement was led by a twelve-man central committee which designated itself the Revolutionary Command Council (RCC). The composition and leadership of the RCC was at first anonymous; however, it soon issued a terse statement, announcing the promotion of Captain Mu'ammar al-Qaddafi to the rank of colonel and his appointment as commander-in-chief of the Libyan armed forces. Thereafter, the RCC remained a generally closed organization; nevertheless, it was readily apparent that Qaddafi was the chairman and *de facto* head of state. Abroad at the time seeking medical treatment in Greece and Turkey, King Idris never returned to Libya. Settling in Egypt, he lived in exile in Cairo until his death on 25 May 1983 at the age of 94.

6

ONE SEPTEMBER REVOLUTION, 1969–73

The coup had been military in conception, planning, organization, and execution, carried out without the participation or knowledge of any organized civilians or even sections among the intellectuals. Its success was more due to the sclerosis of the old system than to the vitality and broad support of its challenger.

Ruth First, *Libya: The Elusive Revolution*, 1974

The armed forces are an integral and inseparable part of this people, and when they proclaimed the principles of liberty, socialism, and unity, they produced nothing new. It is the people who believe in liberty, socialism, and unity and inspired the armed forces, their vanguard, which imposed them on the enemies of the people with the force of arms.

Mu'ammar al-Qaddafi, September 1969

Against the alarmists who saw the coup as a triumph for both Egypt and the Russians, extending Soviet influence into the western Mediterranean, [U.S. Assistant Secretary of State David D.] Newson and [U.S. Ambassador Joseph] Palmer argued that Qadhafi should be given a chance. In his despatches [*sic*] to Washington the wise, genial Bostonian, Joseph Palmer, prophesied that Qadhafi would prove to be a heaven-sent champion of American interests.

Patrick Seale and Maureen McConville,
The Hilton Assignment, 1973

The Libyan Free Unionist Officers, a group of approximately seventy army officers, most of them from the signal corps, overthrew the Libyan monarchy on 1 September 1969. Initially termed the White Revolution, because the *coup d'état* was bloodless, it later became known as the One September Revolution. Once they had seized power, the twelve-member central committee of the Free Unionist Officers constituted a Revolutionary Command Council (RCC) which exercised supreme executive and legislative authority throughout Libya. The first priorities of the RCC, like most revolutions in a traditional society, were the survival of the revolutionary government and the modernization of the country, in that order.

Mu'ammar al-Qaddafi, a captain in the army at the time he orchestrated the One September Revolution, was immediately promoted to colonel, named commander-in-chief of the Libyan armed forces and soon recognized as the head of the RCC as well as the *de facto* head of state. In contrast, the remaining eleven members of the RCC worked in the shadows for a prolonged period. Limited biographical information on them slowly emerged, but they were not named and pictured in the *Official Gazette* until 10 January 1970, more than four months after the overthrow of the monarchy.[1]

In the interim, Colonel Qaddafi was busy solidifying his control of the revolution. In theory, the RCC operated as a collegial body, discussing issues and policies until consensus was reached. In practice, Qaddafi was able to impose his will through a combination of personality and argument to the extent that all major foreign and domestic policies bore the mark of his thinking. The early policies of the revolutionary government, in particular, reflected Qaddafi's deep Islamist roots, together with his strong support for Arab nationalism. The consumption of alcohol was banned, churches and nightclubs closed, foreign-owned banks seized, and Arabic decreed the only acceptable language for use in official communications. Later on, the American and British military bases in Libya were closed, the few remaining Italian residents expelled, and the international oil companies, most of which were American, subjected to stringent operating conditions.[2]

YOUNG REVOLUTIONARIES

Qaddafi was born in the central Libyan desert some fifty miles south of Sirte near Abou-Hadi, most probably in the spring of 1943 although some accounts place his birth in 1942. Born of illiterate Bedouin parents who kept no birth records, the only certainty is that he was born during World War II at a time when competing armies battled across Libya. In the process, the Libyan people suffered a great deal; and Qaddafi, born into a crucible of conflict and change, learned early on the role colonialists played in Libyan society. A son of the desert, his childhood deeply affected his habits and personal life as an adult as well as the policies of his administration. A collection of short stories published by Qaddafi in 1998 are helpful in revealing his deeply held views. In one story, "The Village," he waxes eloquently over the benefits of life in the village and countryside vis-a-vis the city:

> City life means panting as you chase after certain desires and unnecessary, yet necessary, luxuries. When we see these social sicknesses spread throughout the city, and laws passed to combat them, we are not surprised. We do not believe that they will end, and that we will gain victory over them, for the nature of city life is thus, and these sicknesses are inevitable. The city is dizziness and nausea, madness and loss, fear of insanity, fear of confronting urban life and its urban problems.
>
> Leave this hell on earth, run quickly away. In complete happiness, go to the village and the countryside, where physical labour has meaning, necessity, usefulness, and is a pleasure besides. There, life is social, and human; families and tribes are close. There is stability and belief.[3]

Qaddafi was the only surviving son in a traditional, tribal family that included three older sisters. None of his relatives finished high school, and most of them dropped out of elementary school. With formal schooling available only in the larger population centers, his early education focused on traditional religious subjects taught by the local tribal teacher. Tribal social values, especially the religious principles learned at this time, strongly influenced him throughout his life.

Qaddafi eventually began elementary school in Sirte, where he completed six grades in four years. He then enrolled in secondary school in Sebha, a small market town in south-central Libya. His student days in this remote, relatively small, regional center proved pivotal to his later political development. For the first time in his life, he had regular access to Arab newspapers and radio broadcasts, especially the *Voice of the Arabs* news program from Cairo. In Sebha, most of his teachers, together with the school curriculum, came from Egypt, stimulating his interest in the Egyptian revolution. Active in political activities, including the distribution of subversive posters and the organization of unauthorized political demonstrations, Qaddafi and his family were asked by the authorities to leave Sebha before he graduated from high school. There are varying accounts as to exactly why he was expelled from school, but their common thread is that he was a political activist, distributing literature critical of the monarchy and organizing public protests. From this experience, Qaddafi concluded nonviolent political activities were ineffectual in changing undemocratic regimes.

During his formative years, decisive military and political events in the Middle East, including the 1948 Arab defeat by Israel in Palestine, the 1952 Egyptian revolution, the 1956 Suez crisis, and the 1958 Egypt–Syria union, had a strong impact on Qaddafi's world outlook. In the process, he became a fervent admirer of the revolutionary policies of Egyptian President Gamal Abdul Nasser. The anti-imperialist, Arab nationalist foreign policies and the egalitarian, socialist domestic reforms of the Egyptian revolution were wildly popular throughout the region, and support for them was hardly unique. What separated Qaddafi from most of his generation was his determination to bring the Egyptian revolution to conservative Libya.

Once the Free Unionist Officers had seized power, analysts were quick to point out the similarities between the One September Revolution and its Egyptian predecessor. Borrowed from the structure of the latter, the Free Unionist Officers movement and the Revolutionary Command Council were outward signs of Egyptian influence. And the goals of the One September Revolution, freedom, socialism, and unity, were the same goals Nasser had proclaimed in 1952. The dependence of the RCC on the Egyptian experience became even more noticeable when it began to issue policy statements. It declared Libya to be neutral in great power disputes and against any form of colonialism or imperialism at home or abroad. The RCC also proclaimed its intent to take a more active role in espousing Arab nationalism and supporting the Palestinian cause against Israel. The policy similarities between the Egyptian and Libyan revolutions were doubly significant because Qaddafi in 1969 was speaking almost two decades after Nasser initiated the Egyptian revolution in 1952. With many of the policies associated with the Egyptian revolution long discredited elsewhere in the Arab world, early critics dismissed the One September Revolution as anachronistic.

Qaddafi completed his secondary schooling in the coastal town of Misurata, the third largest city in Libya and a much more cosmopolitan urban environment than the tribal market center of Sebha. Lacking good recommendations, he encountered some difficulty transferring to another high school, finally gaining admission to Misurata High School. Qaddafi's time in Misurata was a defining moment in the development of his political theories. The early 1960s were a time of considerable political ferment in the Arab world with groups like the Arab Socialist Resurrection (Baath) Party, the Muslim Brotherhood, and Arab Nationalist Movement competing for support. Qaddafi refused to join any of these groups on the grounds that he rejected factionalism. He also feared membership would undermine his chances of obtaining admission to the Royal Military Academy. Focused on his own political education, he read widely, including books by the Syrian political theorist, Michael Aflak, and biographies of Sun Yat-sen, Mustafa Kemal Atatürk, and Abraham Lincoln. He also read all the books he could find on Gamal Abdul Nasser and the Egyptian revolution as well as everything available on the French revolution.

In Misurata, Qaddafi renewed contacts with childhood friends. He also recruited new adherents to his political thinking among like-minded students who shared his commitment to the principles of Islam, Arab unity, liberty, and social equality. He convened secret meetings of his fellow students in which the young revolutionaries discussed their plans to transform Libyan society. Recognizing the army was the only organization in the country capable of overthrowing the monarchy, Qaddafi in 1963 enrolled in the Royal Military Academy in Benghazi after a brief stint as a history student at the University of Libya. Several members of his Misurata circle followed him into the military and later served the revolutionary government in prominent positions.

At the time, the Libyan armed forces offered good opportunities for higher education and upward socioeconomic mobility, most especially for ambitious and talented young men, like Qaddafi, from the lower echelons of Libyan society. The military also represented an obvious potential avenue for decisive political action. With political parties banned and other political activities severely regulated by the monarchy, Qaddafi viewed military service, not as a career, but as an instrument for socioeconomic and political change. During his two years in military school, he created the Free Unionist Officers movement and selected its twelve-member central committee.

Qaddafi graduated from the Royal Military Academy in August 1965 and was commissioned a communications officer in the signal corps. In April 1966, he was sent to the United Kingdom for advanced military training. Over the next nine months, he completed an English language course at Beaconsfield, a Royal Air Corps signal instructors course at Bovington, and an infantry signal instructors course at Hythe. In the admission form to the Bovington course, in what he later described as a purposeful deception, Qaddafi declared himself to be pro-British and stated the British troops in Libya were an asset. The director of the signals course at Bovington noted in Qaddafi's profile that he had successfully overcome early language problems and demonstrated a sound knowledge of voice procedure. Adding Qaddafi's main interests were football and reading, the director described the young Libyan as an "amusing officer, always cheerful, hard working, and conscientious." Later accounts generally suggest Qaddafi experienced difficulty in adopting to the British way of life and did not enjoy this brief sojourn abroad. One of the few photographs of him dating from this time shows Qaddafi walking the streets of London around Piccadilly Circus dressed in traditional Libyan robes. Returning to Libya, he was assigned to a military post near Benghazi where he continued to organize the network of conspirators that toppled the monarchy on 1 September 1969.

Given the background of Qaddafi and his fellow revolutionaries, it should be clear the revolutionary government was not *sui generis*. The twelve members of the RCC and most of the Free Unionist Officers shared similar backgrounds, motivations, and world views; and their attitudes and convictions were reflected in the policy positions adopted by the One September Revolution. Most came from poorer families and minor tribes and attended the Libyan military academy in search of education and socioeconomic advancement. Their language was the language of Arab nationalism, guided by the precepts of the Qur'an and shari'a, the traditional code of Islamic law, and strengthened by the conviction only the RCC spoke for the Libyan people. In this sense, the One September Revolution can be characterized as a revolution of the oases and interior against the established society of dominant tribes and prominent coastal families.

GREAT POWER DENOUEMENT

The timing and composition of the One September Revolution caught the Western powers, especially the United Kingdom and the United States, by surprise. Some kind of *coup d'état*, probably led by senior military personnel with little policy change, had been widely anticipated for weeks, even months, but no one expected a bold stroke by junior army officers intent on a broad socioeconomic and political revolution. Ambassador David D. Newson,

U.S. Ambassador to Libya from 1965 to 1969, who returned to Washington to become Assistant Secretary of State for African Affairs less than two months before the *coup*, confirmed as much in later comments to the Foreign Affairs Oral History Project:

> The agency [Central Intelligence Agency] had reports of a group that was forming, called the Black Boots, probably a group that was centered around an officer by the name of Abdul Aziz Shalhi. But that group, if they had any intention of trying to seize power, was preempted by the Qadhafi group on which we had no information.

At the outset of the One September Revolution, diplomats representing the Four Powers (France, Great Britain, the Soviet Union, and the United States) were called individually to meet with members of the Revolutionary Command Council. Thereafter, representatives of the United Kingdom and the United States enjoyed much greater access to the Libyan leadership than those of France and the Soviet Union because the RCC wanted to resolve the military base issue. That said, from September to November 1969, there were notably few occasions for any diplomat to meet and talk with Qaddafi.

In the erroneous belief it was possible to maintain their economic and military interests in Libya, both the United Kingdom and the United States soon concluded it was in their best interests to extend diplomatic recognition to the revolutionary government. Consequently, the British government rejected an urgent appeal from supporters of King Idris to intervene militarily on his behalf and to restore the monarchy to power. The RCC at this point was especially solicitous toward the United States. In marked contrast, it was wary of the British government because the latter had been closely identified with the monarchy after independence.

American and British diplomatic correspondence in 1970–71 suggested growing disillusionment with the revolutionary government; however, many analyses and reports were dominated by the thought that Qaddafi remained the right man in the right place at the right time. For example, a 30 September 1971 assessment of the first two years of the One September Revolution, authored by the U.S. embassy in Libya, concluded Qaddafi was "close to being the indispensable man" in Libya, adding "a period of instability would in all likelihood ensue" should he disappear from the scene. Consistent with this view, the United States government in the early months of the revolution, on at least one occasion and probably on two or more, furnished the Libyan government with information on budding counter-*coup* attempts.[4]

At the time of the One September Revolution, the American embassy was between ambassadors as Ambassador Newson had departed in July 1969 and his replacement, Joseph Palmer, did not arrive until later in the year. David L. Mack, a junior diplomat at the time who later served as Deputy Assistant Secretary of State for Near Eastern Affairs (1990–93), spoke Arabic and served as a translator for the acting chargé d'affaires and then Ambassador Palmer. He later recounted the early meetings with Qaddafi which all took place in the Tripoli radio station. Mack was struck by Qaddafi's intelligence, his excellent command of the Arabic language, which he spoke like a Radio Cairo announcer, and his seemingly perfect recall of the content of previous conversations. It was immediately apparent to Mack that Qaddafi was the Alpha Male in the RCC; nevertheless, a debate raged for months in the U.S. embassy in Tripoli, as well as in Washington, as to who was in charge of the revolution.

In February 1964, the monarchy had announced that it would not renew the base agreements with the United Kingdom and the United States due to expire in the early 1970s; nevertheless, the base rights question remained an extremely controversial issue in Libya. Therefore, it came as no surprise when the RCC immediately began to pressure both governments for an early termination of the agreements. In a public address on 16 October 1969, Qaddafi made the revolutionary government's position quite clear.

> Today's stand towards the Mellaha [American] base which you ask should be eliminated, has become abundantly clear. Our attitude towards this and other bases is no longer equivocal. The Arab people in Libya which rose on September 1 can no longer live with

foreign bases side by side. Nor will the armed forces which rose to express the people's revolution tolerate living in their shacks while the bases of imperialism exist in Libyan territory.

The lifetime of the bases has become limited the same as that of the occupier. The fate of the bases in our land is already doomed for we accept no bases, no foreigner, no imperialist, and no intruders. This is a clear-cut attitude which is understandable to both friend and enemy. We will liberate our land from bases, the imperialist and foreign forces whatever the cost involved.[5]

In the end, negotiations with the British went relatively well as they soon accepted the principle of evacuation, departing from Al-Adem Base at the end of March 1970. Negotiations with the United States on Wheelus Field were more prolonged as Washington insisted for a time on strict compliance with the terms of the 1954 treaty which remained in force until 24 December 1970. In an effort to avoid moving the facility to Europe, the Americans even proposed the joint use of Wheelus for training exercises; however, when the Libyans rejected this initiative, the Americans on 23 December 1969 agreed to evacuate the base. When the last American plane took off from Wheelus on 11 June 1970, the U.S. embassy in Tripoli cabled Washington, "Wheels up, Wheelus." Once the British and the American forces had departed, 28 March, the day the British evacuated Al-Adem Base, and 11 June, the day the Americans evacuated Wheelus Field, became national holidays in Libya, commemorated each year with popular festivities, normally highlighted by a strong nationalistic address by Qaddafi. Similarly, 7 October 1970, the day Italian-owned assets were confiscated and the Italian community expelled from Libya, also became a national holiday in Libya.

Early on, Qaddafi had turned the base negotiations over to Major Abdel Salam Jalloud, a fellow RCC member who for a long period of time was considered Qaddafi's chief deputy. Once the base negotiations were resolved, Qaddafi moved on to other issues, including talks with the oil companies. Eager to cultivate a positive relationship with Qaddafi, the American embassy hoped at this time to discuss other questions with him, like a technology transfer agreement, but issues like these were simply not on Qaddafi's agenda. Consequently, the Americans could not get access to him. Ambassador Palmer, in the course of a three-year assignment, saw Qaddafi only three times: when he arrived, at the outset of the Wheelus talks, and when he departed. And this was two more times than most ambassadors met with Qaddafi. Standard practice was for Qaddafi to meet with an ambassador only once, upon his arrival in Libya.

At the same time, the Libyans continued to pressure the United States and other diplomatic missions in different ways. Shortly after the revolution, they nationalized the Seventh Day Adventist mission hospital in Benghazi without paying compensation, and later did the same thing with the American Church in Tripoli. Apart from squeezing U.S. and other property interests, including the American stake in the Libyan oil and gas industry, there was constant criticism of U.S. policy, particularly in the Middle East, an ominous military build-up with significant regional implications, and a claim to territorial waters out to two hundred miles. As part of this latter policy, Libya claimed control of the entire Gulf of Sirte, a policy the United States would challenge later with military force.

To be fair, U.S. policy, at times, encouraged aggressive Libyan behavior. When the Libyans sought permission to purchase C-130 cargo planes, for example, they were told they could order them, but an export license was not guaranteed. After the Libyans paid for the planes, the United States embargoed the aircraft, and they sat parked in Marietta, Georgia for more than three decades.

In 1972, the Americans, together with the British, Soviets, and others, received notes from the Libyan foreign office demanding a staff reduction to fifteen people. As a result, staff levels at the U.S. embassy dropped from eighty-five people in September 1969 to only thirteen in December 1973. To reach these levels, the U.S. embassy closed its last outpost, the consulate in Benghazi, and eliminated the entire marine security contingent, leaving embassy security in the hands of the Libyan government. The downside to this decision became apparent seven years later when the embassy was attacked and trashed by angry mobs while local police forces stood by, refusing to intervene. At the end of 1972, Ambassador Palmer retired and was not replaced, reducing U.S. diplomatic representation to the chargé d'affaires level until the embassy was shuttered in 1980.

Even as the United Kingdom and the United States were discussing with Libya the closure of their respective military bases, their ally France was negotiating the sale of sophisticated new weapons to the revolutionary government. Within six weeks of the successful One September Revolution, the French government offered to sell Libya one hundred supersonic Mirage warplanes; and in January 1970, the RCC agreed to purchase 110 instead of the original one hundred Mirages over a period of three years at a total cost of $300 million. As part of the deal, the French agreed to train pilots and technicians on a rotating basis in France. Both countries considered the agreement, the largest French armaments sale in history to that time, as a major economic and diplomatic *coup*. For the remainder of the decade, French relations with Libya were closer than those enjoyed by any other Western state, largely because French policy in the Middle East was more acceptable to the Arab side.

The Soviet Union, which had enjoyed very limited diplomatic and commercial relations with the Idris regime, also moved quickly to strengthen its position in Libya. Officially recognizing the revolutionary government on 4 September 1969, the Soviets indicated a willingness to provide any assistance required. Soviet interests and activities gradually broadened over time, but the RCC initially limited its relationship with the Soviet Union to the commercial sphere, in particular the purchase of armaments. Early Libyan policy statements described communism as a godless system alien to Islam and to Arab socialism and totally unsuitable to the Libyan milieu. The first consignment of Soviet weaponry arrived in July 1970 and was displayed at the parade commemorating the first anniversary of the One September Revolution. Thereafter, the RCC continued to purchase Soviet military equipment throughout the decade, including a $1 billion package in 1974–75 that constituted its single largest arms agreement. Given the prevailing bipolar logic of the Cold War, it was this deepening relationship between Libya and the Soviet Union, as much as anything else, that estranged Qaddafi from the United States.[6]

PRIMACY OF OIL

In the early days of the revolution, the RCC, preoccupied with consolidating power, directed conciliatory statements toward the international oil and gas industry, promising to honor existing agreements. On 18 September 1969, for example, Prime Minister Mahmud Suleiman al-Maghrabi sought to reassure the oil and gas sector, emphasizing there would be no spectacular changes in hydrocarbon policy. Two weeks later, he suggested the posted price of Libyan crude oil, the basis of taxable income for producing countries, was probably lower than it should be. On 6 October 1969, the petroleum minister took a stronger stand when he charged the posted price of crude oil had been set, unilaterally and unfairly, by the petroleum exporting companies in contravention of Libyan law, adding his ministry intended to rectify the situation. Ten days later, Qaddafi signaled a major policy change.

> It is well-known that [oil] prices are unfair and were fixed for the interest of companies more than the Government. The action we have taken is that we set up a committee to study the matter. In the light of this study, our share of oil income will be determined after technicians have made careful study of the matter so that when we claim something, we shall get it.[7]

In retrospect, it seems obvious the RCC was determined from the start to reduce oil production to conserve supplies, increase oil revenues by maximizing the price, develop upstream and downstream capabilities, and use oil revenues to diversify the economy.

The honeymoon the international oil companies had enjoyed since the discovery in 1959 of petroleum deposits in commercially viable quantities ended abruptly ten years later. In December 1969, the RCC opened talks aimed at increasing the posted price of oil.

The Libyans focused on the independent oil companies, especially Occidental Petroleum, because they were most vulnerable to a negotiating strategy based on reducing production quotas on a company-by-company basis. When the independents rejected initial demands for contract modifications, the RCC in the summer of 1970 increased the pressure by cutting overall oil production by 800,000 barrels per day. In addition, Esso was told to stop exporting liquefied natural gas; and to add to the uncertainty, Libya nationalized the local marketing of petroleum products. The production cuts implemented by the RCC coincided with a break in Tapline, the Saudi Arabian pipeline through Syria; and the two events combined to produce a global oil shortage, especially in Europe.

On 1 September 1970, exactly one year after the Free Unionist Officers seized power in Libya, Occidental Petroleum, soon followed by the other producers in Libya, agreed to an increase of $0.30 per barrel in the posted price of oil. This was the first hike in the posted price since the formation of the Organization of Petroleum Exporting Countries (OPEC) in 1960, and it was soon followed by similar price increases throughout the oil-producing world as other OPEC member-states joined Libya in taking price hikes. The hardline policy of the RCC thus ended the long-standing myth that the oil producers alone could set the posted price of crude oil.

Following the One September Agreement in Libya, the OPEC states met in Caracas in December 1970. Reflecting Libyan leadership, the major resolution adopted at the Caracas meeting called for an increase in both oil prices and income tax rates, together with the elimination of marketing allowances and the adoption of a new system to adjust specific gravity. Two months later, the Gulf states concluded a new agreement with the oil companies, known as the Teheran Agreement, incorporating many of the gains won by the Libyans, including an immediate price increase and additional price increases over five years. In return, the Gulf states rejected the principle of leapfrogging, agreeing not to negotiate separately for better terms. They also agreed not to limit production in an effort to achieve better financial terms.

The terms of the Teheran Agreement infuriated Qaddafi and the other members of the RCC who strongly criticized the level of price increases negotiated, rejected the principle of collective bargaining, and denounced the prohibition on production restrictions. In response, the RCC immediately opened new negotiations with the oil producers in Libya, ending its short-lived OPEC leadership role. The product of these talks, the Tripoli Agreement, was actually a series of separate agreements between Libya and the individual oil companies. Similar in structure to the Teheran Agreement, the Libyans succeeded in the Tripoli Agreement in extracting much better pricing, income tax, and specific gravity commitments from the oil companies. To compensate for alleged under-pricing during the monarchy, the oil companies also agreed to a supplemental payment on every barrel of oil exported for the duration of their concession. The combination of price increases and retroactive payments in the Tripoli Agreement brought Libya an estimated $1 billion in additional revenues in the first year alone.

Successful in improving the terms of its contracts with the oil companies, the RCC moved to increase its control over them. Libya nationalized the British Petroleum share of the British Petroleum–N. B. Hunt Sarir Field in December 1971, subsequently nationalizing the N. B. Hunt share in June 1973. With commercial considerations generally dictating Libyan oil and gas policy, the action against British Petroleum was unique in that it was a political gesture in retaliation for the failure of the British government, which owned more than forty-eight percent of British Petroleum, to block Iran's seizure of three islands in the Persian Gulf. On 1 September 1973, Libya announced it was nationalizing all foreign oil producers. One month later, in response to the October 1973 Arab–Israeli War, it imposed a partial oil boycott, doubling the price of oil. The OPEC boycott ended in April 1974, but the higher oil prices stuck.

In stark contrast to the oil sector, the RCC failed initially to develop a clear strategy for natural gas, despite plans for gas-based industrialization. Petroleum Regulation Eight, adopted in early

1969 to ensure oil and gas operations were based on sound conservation measures, encouraged the exploitation of natural gas. It gave the government the option to take, free of charge at the well-head, natural gas not being used for "economically justified" purposes and imposed penalties for the excessive flaring of gas; nevertheless, all gas fields, with the exception of two owned by Esso, were abandoned with their wells plugged. Esso had built a liquefied natural gas (LNG) plant at Marsa al-Brega in the 1960s; however, production at the plant was effectively limited to the associated fields for the next twenty-five years. When the RCC attempted to carry its tough negotiating position on oil prices over into the LNG arena, it enjoyed limited success due to price disputes with its major buyers, Italy and Spain.

SOCIOECONOMIC CHANGE

Socialism was an integral part of most twentieth-century revolutions, especially those in North Africa and the Middle East, and Libya was no exception. In trumpeting the revolutionary trinity of freedom, socialism, and unity, Qaddafi and his colleagues depicted socialism as the solution to the economic problems of mankind. The RCC soon made control of the oil and gas industry, together with other sectors of the economy, a prominent policy because, in addition to being a first step on the road to socialism, it helped solidify its control in Libya. Early policy statements stressed the indigenous character of Libyan socialism, describing it as an integral part of Libyan political culture as well as being a necessary corrective action. Qaddafi's approach here reflected contemporary practice in the Middle East where the origins and character of socialism have often been discussed in the context of local history and customs. In the end, Libyan socialism proved doctrinal, as opposed to pragmatic, and highly nationalistic in a region where socialism and nationalism have often been found together.

In dealing with the oil companies, the RCC successfully pursued a strategy of confrontation, based on an assumption of past exploitation by colonialists and quasi-colonial agencies, calling the bluff of the international oil cartels and the Western consuming nations. Unfortunately, it misread the political lessons to be drawn from its aggressive approach to the oil industry, much to the detriment of domestic socioeconomic policy in other areas. Delighted with the results of its confrontational approach, the RCC applied the same management style elsewhere only to find that none of the nation's other resources were amenable to such aggressive solutions. The RCC also failed to apply lessons learned in the area of oil and gas conservation to other areas. On the contrary, scarce and precious resources in areas like water and rangeland pasture were managed for much of the decade with little concern for their sustained use.[8]

Concerned with domestic opposition, the RCC delayed implementation of the more radical elements of its socialist program until the second half of the 1970s. In the first half of the decade, socioeconomic policy emphasized social welfare programs, like increased housing, and improved health care, that enjoyed widespread popular support and where the revolutionary government had clear goals. Regime support for education was comparatively less and somewhat selective. Education was not a goal in itself; instead, the revolutionary government aimed to create a new man, supportive of the new regime.[9] Working to transform existing educational institutions, the authorities were particularly cautious in the area of academic inputs because their selection and regulation had major socioeconomic implications. Determined to move in a direction different from the capitalist and communist systems, Qaddafi viewed any and all input from these systems as potentially threatening to his incipient form of mass democracy.

In conjunction with the measured introduction of socialism, the government also distributed largesse to a broad segment of the population in a conscious effort both to share the oil wealth and to build legitimacy for the regime. The increases in public sector expenditure for housing, health care, and education in 1969–73 were accompanied by government initiatives designed to profit directly workers and consumers. The minimum wage for workers was raised, workers were allowed to share in company profits, and free housing was made available to the poorest members of society. Farmers gained access to land confiscated from Sanusi or Italian farms, and they were allowed to purchase the implements and livestock necessary to work the land at an estimated ten percent of real value. Subsidies for new housing, especially in rural areas, were readily available from a banking system in which the government had taken a fifty-one percent holding in 1970.[10]

FREEDOM, NATIONALISM, AND UNITY

The foreign policy of the One September Revolution was far more aggressive and comprehensive than that of the monarchy. Even after the air bases were evacuated, the United Kingdom and the United States remained favorite targets for criticism by Qaddafi. On 11 June 1972, at ceremonies commemorating the second anniversary of the U.S. withdrawal from Wheelus Field, Qaddafi's remarks dwelled on the indignity and injustice suffered by the Arabs at Western hands in such vitriolic tones that the American and British ambassadors both walked out in the middle of the ceremonies. The Libyan leader was especially critical of the United States because of its support for the state of Israel. The Palestinian issue had a profound effect, not only on the policy of the revolutionary government toward an overall Middle East settlement, but on almost all areas of foreign policy, including relations with many African states. Early relations with the United Kingdom were complicated by many issues, in addition to its prior relationship with the Idris regime and the question of military bases, including Qaddafi's demand that the British repay funds advanced by the monarchy for a radar system that had not been delivered. This issue contributed to the Libyan decision to withdraw its reserves from British banks and later to nationalize British Petroleum assets in late 1971.

Concerned with colonial imperialism, the RCC attempted to neutralize the Mediterranean Sea by reducing the presence of

North Atlantic Treaty Organization (NATO) forces, especially those operating from Malta. Qaddafi argued the use of Maltese air and naval facilities by British forces, and indirectly by NATO, perpetuated excessive Western power and influence in the region. In 1971, Libya intervened in ongoing talks over the future status of NATO facilities, promising Malta large amounts of foreign aid in return for the reduction or elimination of NATO forces. In the end, Malta agreed to a temporary continuation of NATO base use; however, the final agreement was something of a Libyan victory in that it included a clause prohibiting the use of the bases for attacks against an Arab country.

In his 11 June 1972 Evacuation Day speech, Qaddafi also made broad statements of support for various dissident or minority groups, including Muslim insurgents in the Philippine Islands, the Irish Republican Army in Northern Ireland, and Black militant groups in the United States. In addition, he announced he was opening a center in Libya to train and equip guerrilla fighters in the struggle against Israel. Volunteers were told to apply at Libyan embassies, and Qaddafi himself opened the First Nasserite Volunteers Center on 23 July 1972. The revolutionary government later played down its support for liberation movements, but it clearly sponsored and sustained a wide variety of them throughout the 1970s. The motives behind this support were complex and varied. Early on, the Libyans used overt support for liberation movements to symbolize that the Arab revolution was passing from the defensive to the offensive. Support for some movements, like the Filipino Muslims, was also an important expression of Islamic solidarity. Finally, Libyan support for liberation movements enhanced its international status as a leader in the Third World struggle against colonialism and neocolonialism.

Qaddafi believed the key to Arab unity was the unification of the lands comprising the Arab nation into a single state. In his first press conference in February 1970, he produced a formula for a united Arab politics; and in a July 1972 speech, he described Arab unification into a single state as an absolute necessity. In the interim, he proposed a federation with Egypt, Syria, and Sudan in

November 1970 and a merger with Egypt in February 1972. In January 1974, Qaddafi proposed a merger with Tunisia, an idea he had raised initially in December 1972. A strong and vocal advocate of Arab unity, Qaddafi's many attempts to unite Libya with one or more Arab states all ended in failure. Qaddafi continued to discuss Arab unity after 1973, but it became more a long-term goal than an immediately recognizable objective.[11]

During the monarchy, evidence of nationalism and anti-Western feeling surfaced in Libya; however, it fell to Qaddafi to articulate a nationalist ideology targeted at the Arab nation. His variant of Arab nationalism was associated closely with the revolutionary concepts of freedom, socialism, and unity and thus served to unite the major policies of the One September Revolution into a coherent ideological framework. Central features of this nationalist ideology incorporated the broad concept of an Arab nation; a consciousness of backwardness owing to more than four hundred years of foreign domination; a revulsion against the degenerate, corrupt, and repressive Idris regime; and a sense of massive injustice, bordering on a persecution complex, because of the wrongs inflicted by foreigners over the centuries. In expressing a feeling the Arab people were equal to any other people in the world, Qaddafi argued they had a right to control their own destiny. In this context, the Palestinian issue became a focal point of Qaddafi's Arab nationalism because he perceived the creation of Israel as the ultimate indignity in the long history of oppression visited on the Arab nation by Western colonial imperialism.

Qaddafi saw himself as Nasser's heir and claimed that Nasser had designated him the trustee of Arab nationalism. But Qaddafi was inspired by and sought to emulate the flamboyant, idealistic Nasser of the fifties and early sixties and not the more moderate, experienced, and battle-weary Nasser of the post-1967 war. Both men were animated by similar ideological tenets, but socioeconomic and political factors affected them and their philosophies in very different ways. The revolutionary government in Libya was the first Arab revolutionary government to be wealthy. It was also the first government to combine two forces, oil and pan-Arabism, generally at odds in recent Arab history. In contrast, Nasser's base, an overpopulated, impoverished land, set real limits on his expectations and possibilities, especially later in his career. Libya's small population and immense wealth, on the other hand, encouraged Qaddafi to dream the impossible dream. The Libyan leader and his people also benefited from having escaped the traumas and wounds suffered by Nasser and the Egyptian people in the course of thirty years of war with Israel. Moreover, while Nasser's approach bore the maturity and leveling influence of a long association with Cairo, the Arab world's largest and most cynical city, Qaddafi's Arab nationalism was a pure, simple desert philosophy, strongly influenced by his Bedouin origins.

POPULAR REVOLUTION

The One September Revolution was completed without the knowledge or participation of organized civilian groups; and for a considerable time, the Revolutionary Command Council maintained the military direction of the revolution. Members of the RCC retained their military ranks, after promoting themselves one or more times, and often appeared in uniform to emphasize their military affiliation and discipline. Assuming executive and legislative functions, the RCC ruled by decree with new laws taking effect as soon as they were published in the *Official Gazette*. Eventually, a few civilians were brought into the cabinet to help operate the government; but even then, the RCC reserved supreme authority for itself. It sat at the top of the pyramid, issuing policy directives and legislation, retaining the support of the armed forces, and overseeing all actions of the government to ensure they were consistent with the objectives of the revolution.

Convinced it represented the Libyan masses, the RCC patently refused to allow civilian support to be channeled into an autonomous political party or organization. The formation of political parties was prohibited under the RCC just as it had been under the monarchy. These decisions and others highlighted a basic contradiction in the Libyan revolution, particularly in its early days. While the Free Unionist Officers, especially the twelve RCC members, felt they were close to the masses and mirrored their thoughts and wishes, they also distrusted the masses and refused to allow them to share in the direction of the revolution. The first rule of the One September Revolution was total dominance by the armed forces as confirmed by the leadership of the RCC. Qaddafi later captured the early ambivalence of the RCC in a short story, "Escape to Hell," published in 1998:

> I love the freedom of the masses, as they move freely, with no master above them. They have broken their chains, singing and rejoicing following their pain and tribulation. Yet how I fear them! I love the masses as I love my father, yet fear them in the same way. In a bedouin society, with its lack of government, who can prevent a father from punishing one of his children? It is true that they love him, but they fear him at the same time. In the same way, I both love and fear the masses, as I love and fear my father.[12]

To help solidify its control of the revolution, the RCC moved to reduce tribal and regional power and identification, increase political mobilization, and implant new local leadership supportive of revolutionary goals. As part of this strategy, every effort was made to tie traditional leadership to the former colonial powers. On 17 August 1971, for example, a special military court was convened in Tripoli to try traditional tribal leaders in the Sebha region accused of allying with foreign interests to overthrow the revolution. The RCC also tried to link traditional leaders to the negative aspects of the Idris regime. A special people's court was convened in late 1971, for example, to try members of the former regime accused of treason and corruption.

In conjunction with its efforts to discredit traditional leadership, the RCC attempted to reduce their influence by redrawing long-standing administrative and political boundaries and appointing a new type of local leadership. The creation of new administrative areas, crossing old tribal boundaries and combining different tribes into a single zone, helped reduce regional identity and accompanying socioeconomic power. The replacement of traditional leaders with youthful revolutionaries was less effective because the latter mostly lacked the attitudes and background necessary to become successful modernizers. The public quickly perceived their shortcomings, rejecting them as community leaders. The checkered performance of these appointed modernizers also reflected a wider failure of the RCC which both underestimated the power base of traditional leadership and overestimated the appeal of its revolutionary message. The reluctance of the RCC to delegate authority to civilians was another reason for the failure of the modernizers. As long as the RCC followed the Nasserite precept of hegemony to the armed forces, civilian modernizing leaders seeking to generate popular support and build viable civilian institutions faced an almost impossible task.[13]

By the spring of 1971, the RCC realized the new system of local and regional government was not mobilizing the general populace in support of revolutionary goals to the extent required to transform traditional Libyan society into a modern socialist state. Scrapping the system less than two years after its creation, Colonel Qaddafi on 11 June 1971 announced the formation of the Arab Socialist Union (ASU), an official mass mobilization party patterned after its Egyptian namesake. The ASU was firmly controlled by the RCC with Qaddafi serving as president and the remainder of the RCC as "the Supreme Leading Authority of the Arab Socialist Union." In the beginning, constituent committees at the regional level were appointed by the RCC with one of their number chairing each regional committee. Later, committees at both regional and local levels were elected; however, with ideological and policy discussions prohibited, voters mostly resorted to family and factional politics.

In retrospect, the ASU was stillborn. The rigid control maintained by the RCC stifled local initiative and suffocated local leadership. In so doing, the ASU was unable to resolve the inherent contradiction of attempting simultaneously to be sensitive to local demands and a reflection of government interests. In addition, the ASU was undercut by existing government organizations that saw it as a threat to their authority and responsibility. The complex structure of the ASU and the negative perceptions arising from the earlier performance of its Egyptian counterpart also contributed to its demise.

On 15 April 1973, Qaddafi initiated a popular revolution based on a five-point program. First, all existing laws were to be repealed and replaced by revolutionary enactments designed to produce the requisite change. Second, all opponents to the revolution were to be removed. Third, an administrative revolution would eliminate all forms of bourgeoisie and bureaucracy. Fourth, the general populace would be armed to defend the revolution. Finally, a cultural revolution would be initiated to eliminate imported ideas and to fuse the people's genuine moral and material potentialities.

To consummate this popular revolution, Qaddafi urged the Libyan people to seize power through the creation of people's committees which were to be elected throughout the country. In the early stages of the popular revolution, the absence of guidelines or procedures led to considerable uncertainty as to how and where popular committees were to be elected. In the end, direct popular election was largely restricted to organizations within zones, the lowest level of government organization, with higher levels of representation achieved through the election of zone committees to municipal and provincial committees. Direct elections were also held in public corporations and select government bureaucracies; however, concerned anarchy could develop, the RCC did not allow the popular revolution to take over the revolutionary administration.

In the context of the original goals of the One September Revolution, the initiation of the popular revolution in April 1973 had four objectives. First, it was designed to mobilize the public behind the RCC since both the appointment of modernizing leaders and the proclamation of the ASU had failed to accomplish this task. Second, it was hoped the creation of a new type of community leadership, based on a combination of knowledge, ability, and loyalty to the regime, would further erode the power base of traditional leaders. Third, it was thought the legal and administrative obstacles in the path of revolutionary change would be reduced by giving the people some power to create rules and regulations suitable for the revolutionary era. Finally, the popular revolution aimed at the destruction of the traditional bureaucracy by giving the people the authority and power to elect and dismiss public officials at all levels with the significant exception of the RCC, cabinet members, and security personnel. In the final analysis, the people's committee system provoked a relatively high level of public response and involvement within the limits the RCC allowed. The net result was an increase in levels of mobilization and participation, together with a simultaneous strengthening of the RCC's control of the revolution.

On the darker side, the initiation of the popular revolution proved a reflection of the paranoia of the Revolutionary Command Council. Too often, people's committees became an adjunct of the security services, denouncing individuals critical of the revolution. In conjunction with their creation, a wave of arrests took place, targeting Libyans associated with Marxist, Baathist, Muslim Brotherhood, or other political circles, who had not satisfactorily associated themselves with regime policies. The majority of the arrests were initiated by the secret police; however, in some cases, the newly formed people's committees denounced individuals. The activities of the people's committees also impacted negatively on regime development objectives, disrupting the management and functioning of a variety of institutions, from public sector companies to agricultural development projects. Occasionally, the activities of the people's committees also led to jurisdictional disputes with the Arab Socialist Union.

THIRD UNIVERSAL THEORY

Two months after the April 1973 announcement of the popular revolution, Qaddafi opened a campaign to give the One September Revolution a theoretical underpinning in what he called the Third Universal Theory. In search of a "Third Way," he attempted to develop an alternative to capitalism and communism, competing systems he rejected as unsuitable to Libya. Condemning both as monopolistic systems, he considered capitalism a monopoly of ownership by capitalists and companies and communism a state monopoly of ownership. In addition, he considered both the Soviet Union and the United States to be imperialist states, intent on developing spheres of influence in North Africa and the Middle East. He also denounced the atheistic nature of the Soviet regime.[14]

Qaddafi based his Third Universal Theory on nationalism and religion, the two forces he considered the paramount drivers of history and mankind. He viewed nationalism as the natural result of the world's cultural and racial diversity and thus a necessary as well as a productive force. Arab nationalism, in particular, was considered to have especially deep and glorious roots in the ancient past. With the Arab nation the product of an age-old civilization based on the heavenly and universal message of Islam, he argued it had the right and the duty to be the bearer of the Third Universal Theory to the world. Qaddafi firmly believed it would take a united Arab nation, stretching from the Atlantic to the Gulf, to unite both the Muslim community at large and the wider Third World against the pressures of global imperialism.

Qaddafi never published a coherent, comprehensive discussion of his religious views; however, his public statements focused on the centrality of Islam to religion and the Qur'an to Islam. He considered Islam to be God's final utterance to humanity, arguing there was nothing in life for which the principles could not be found in Islam. For Qaddafi, the unity of God was the essence of religion; therefore, he made no distinction between Christians, Jews, and Muslims, what he termed the followers of Jesus, Moses, and Muhammad. Because there was only one religion, Islam, all monotheists were Muslims. Qaddafi argued Islam was addressed not only to the followers of the Prophet Muhammad but that Islam meant a belief in God as embodied in all religions. He referred to this contention that anyone who believed in God and his apostles was a Muslim as the "divine concept of Islam."

Calling for an Islamic revival based on the Qur'an, he argued Muslims had moved away from God and the Qur'an and must return. In the process, he attempted to correct contemporary Islamic practices that in his mind were contrary to the faith. Condemning formal interpretation of the Qur'an as blasphemy and sin, for example, he argued the Qur'an was written in Arabic so that every Arab could read it and apply it without the help of others. Similarly, he criticized the hadith, the traditions or collected sayings of the Prophet Muhammad, on the grounds the Qur'an was the only true source of God's word. He also criticized the different schools of Islamic jurisprudence as the product of power struggles and thus removed from either Islam or the Qur'an.

While the similarities can be overstated, the fundamentalist elements of the Third Universal Theory and the doctrines of the puritanical Sanusi Order shared some important continuities. For example, the Sanusi Order, in an effort to promote Islamic unity, accepted the Qur'an and the Sunna as the basis for Muslim life, downplaying the role of the various schools of Islamic law. In a similar vein, Qaddafi in the early years of the revolution emphasized these fundamental aspects of the religion, in part because they served to legitimize the revolutionary government. As he succeeded in consolidating his control of the One September Revolution, his approach later became increasingly reformist, if not secular.[15]

In the wake of the military *coup d'état* on 1 September 1969, Qaddafi repeatedly stressed that what had taken place in Libya was not a simple *coup* but a socioeconomic and political revolution. His aim was not simply regime change, the replacement of one government with another; instead, he planned to create a new socialist society that would need no government. This early emphasis on revolution proved premature as it took Qaddafi and his colleagues an extended period of time to consolidate the new regime and to define the parameters of the One September Revolution. The articulation of the Third Universal Theory thus marks the end of the beginning, as opposed to the beginning of the end. After 1973, Qaddafi would lead Libya down a path of increasingly radical domestic and foreign policies in the second half of the 1970s.

7

REVOLUTION ON THE MOVE, 1973–86

The instrument of government is the primary political problem facing human communities.

Mu'ammar al-Qaddafi, The Green Book, 1975

The popular direct authority is the basis of the political system in the Socialist People's [Libyan] Arab Jamahiriya. The authority is for the people who alone should have the authority. The people exercise their authority through the popular congresses, the people's committees, the syndicates, the unions, the professional associations, and the General People's Congress.

Declaration of the Establishment of the People's
Authority, March 1977

Do not doubt for a moment that Libya has a military dictatorship, that the Libyan government is an aggressive trouble-maker in international affairs, and that Libya is not a country to cross authority in. It is a place where rules are arbitrarily applied, and where uncertainty intrudes into those areas of life which most Westerners and many Libyans prefer to be certain about.

John Davis, Libyan Politics, 1987

Qadhafi deserves to be treated as a pariah in the world community.

Ronald Reagan, January 1986

In the early years of the revolution, Revolutionary Command Council policy was a dynamic combination of bold strokes, like the early evacuation of Western military bases and the increase in oil prices, and more cautious, tentative steps in areas like socio-economic and political reform. In retrospect, it was not surprising that officials in the U.S. embassy and elsewhere experienced difficulty in defining the revolution. To a very real extent, the young revolutionaries, often unsure as to where they wanted to take the revolution, were still in the process of defining themselves. As they gained experience and confidence, the One September Revolution gained strength and momentum, and economic and political reform expanded in breadth and depth. As it moved to remake Libyan society, the RCC also initiated an increasingly aggressive foreign policy, openly challenging the *status quo* in Africa, the Middle East, and elsewhere in the world.

THE GREEN BOOK

Six years after he led a *coup d'état* in Libya overthrowing the ruling monarchy, Mu'ammar al-Qaddafi began to summarize the ideological tenets of the revolution in a series of three short volumes, totaling fewer than one hundred pages, known collectively as *The Green Book*. The publication of *The Green Book* marked a new phase in the evolution of Qaddafi's thought, a process with several identifiable stages, not always distinct from one another. The first stage, which began when Qaddafi was a student in Sebha and Misurata, was a period of exploration and learning. Heavily influenced in youth by the words and deeds of Egyptian President Gamal Abdul Nasser, the early days of the One September Revolution marked a second stage which was strongly Nasserist in tone and content. When the worn and tired ideology of the Egyptian revolution failed to resonate in Libya, a third stage began in April 1973 when Qaddafi initiated the popular revolution. Over the next three years, this stage combined early efforts to give the revolution a theoretical foundation, principally through articulation of the Third Universal Theory, and practical experimentation with a nascent political structure. Stage four began in the fall of 1975 with the publication of the first part of *The Green Book* and the concurrent initiation of wider reforms to the political system. Activity in this stage intensified in March 1977 with the issuance of the Declaration of the Establishment of the People's Authority.

The first part of *The Green Book* was entitled *The Solution of the Problem of Democracy – "The Authority of the People"* and developed the theoretical foundations for direct democracy, the unique political system based on congresses and committees that Qaddafi had begun to implement throughout Libya.[1] In part one, Qaddafi argued the instrument of governing was the prime political problem facing human communities. In his mind, a political campaign in which a candidate obtained fifty-one percent of the votes led "to a dictatorial governing body disguised as a false democracy" because forty-nine percent of the electorate would be ruled by an instrument of governing imposed upon them. He dismissed Western parliamentary democracy as "a misrepresentation of the people," and parliamentary governments as "a misleading solution to the problem of democracy." In turn, the political party system was "the modern dictatorial instrument of governing" because it enabled "those with one outlook and a common interest to rule the people as a whole." His thinking here led to revolutionary slogans like "representation is fraud" and "no representation in lieu of the people" being repeated *ad nauseam*.

Qaddafi's solution to the dilemmas of representative democracy was a form of direct democracy grounded in the establishment of people's conferences and people's committees throughout the country. Emphasizing democracy was the "supervision of the people by the people," he stressed there could be "no democracy without popular congresses and committees everywhere." In outlining his system of direct democracy, Qaddafi provided a relatively accurate description of the structure of government actually implemented; however, the discussion was notably brief and illustrated by a single diagram. And the simple diagram found in early editions of *The Green Book* did little to clarify Qaddafi's approach to direct democracy as it could well have been the diagram of any hierarchical organization with a plurality of different groups. The units in the diagram were not explained in any detail, either in the legend accompanying the diagram or in the text, and there also was no explanation of the lines connecting the various squares, rectangles, and triangles in the diagram. In addition, the part played by the RCC was ignored as were issues crucial to the discussion of any political system, like how money is distributed or who controls the use of violence. Later editions of *The Green Book* provided a revised, more accurate, and easier to understand circular diagram of direct democracy, but it remained the single illustration in the entire book.

Qaddafi concluded part one of *The Green Book* with the following enigmatic statement which appeared to contradict everything he had said earlier about direct democracy. "Theoretically, this is the genuine democracy. But realistically, the strong always rule, i.e. the stronger part in the society is the one that rules." The dichotomy between the theoretical and real mechanisms of power in Libya would grow dramatically in the years ahead. Despite rhetoric to the contrary, the political system remained one in which Qaddafi and a few close advisors made all important decisions on economic and political development. And the institutions and economic sectors the regime considered essential to its survival remained off-limits to direct popular management.

The second part of *The Green Book* was entitled *The Solution of the Economic Problem – "Socialism"* and was first published in 1978.[2] Rejecting in part one the political systems of East and West, Qaddafi in part two rejected their economic systems, communism and capitalism, concluding socialism was the optimum economic order. In so doing, he argued the wage earner was a slave to the master who hired him with the solution to the problem being abolition of the wage system thus emancipating humankind from its bondage. Where "power to the people" characterized his political thinking in part one, the slogan "partners, not wage earners," summed up his economic thinking in part two. With inequality of wealth unacceptable in the "new socialist society," Qaddafi in the latter half of the 1970s implemented major reforms in traditional socioeconomic practices aimed at creating a more egalitarian society. Broad in scope and content, *The Green Book* as a whole failed to address many important questions, and nowhere was this more evident than in the second part where Qaddafi's simplistic, under-developed economic thoughts brought to mind early experiments in utopian socialism.

The third part of *The Green Book*, entitled *The Social Basis of the Third Universal Theory*, explored selected social aspects of the Third Universal Theory, focusing on the family, tribe, and nation.[3] Published in 1979, it was in some ways the most interesting part and certainly the most theoretical. Basically, it was an attempt to examine the role of the individual, especially women, in Islamic society. Qaddafi pointed to the family as the basic social unit, arguing proper family life could come about only if men and women performed their natural roles. In so doing, he strongly supported the idea that men and women were equal, maintaining acts like marriage and divorce should be approached on the basis of equality. Yet, while men and women were equal, he also argued, in a condescending and patently sexist manner, they should not be doing the same things. Because of their biological differences, he suggested both sexes have a role to play, and neither could opt out of what nature intended for them. Where Qaddafi asserted radical political views in part one of *The Green Book* and proposed radical economic thoughts in part two, he projected conservative, even reactionary, social values in part three.

The first part of *The Green Book* proved the most enduring. The political system implemented in the mid-1970s experienced little meaningful change after that time. Over the ensuing three decades, Qaddafi repeatedly emphasized the Libyan form of direct democracy was superior to the representative democracy found in the United States, United Kingdom, and elsewhere. In contrast, Libya in the late 1980s began to move away from the socialist command economy outlined in part two and implemented in the second half of the 1970s. The breadth and depth of economic reform broadened considerably at the outset of the twenty-first century as Libya struggled to implement market reforms. In turn, the third part of *The Green Book* proved the most controversial with Qaddafi's insular, contradictory, and even reactionary views on a potpourri of subjects, like the tribe, women, education, minorities, the arts, and sport, an endless source of debate.

DIRECT POPULAR AUTHORITY

In August 1975, a dispute within the Revolutionary Command Council over Qaddafi's distributive economics led to a failed *coup d'état* led by two of its members, Bashir Saghir al-Hawaadi and Omar Mehishi, who favored more orderly, technocratic solutions to the country's economic problems. In the wake of the abortive revolt, only five of the original twelve RCC members remained in place. Until late 1996, these five men, Qaddafi, Abu Bakr Yuunis Jaabir, Kweildi al-Hemeidi, Mustafa al-Kharuubi, and Abdel Salaam Jalloud constituted the elite leadership of the revolution. The failed *coup* proved a watershed for Libya because it freed Qaddafi to pursue his vision of a stateless society while spending enormous sums of money on military purchases and foreign adventures. The abortive revolt also spelled the end of the Revolutionary Command Council as a political institution (even though it was not formally abolished until March 1977) and destroyed any pretense of collegial decision-making with Libya yielding inexorably to one-man rule.[4]

In the wake of the revolt, Qaddafi, in conjunction with the publication of the first part of *The Green Book*, announced in September 1975 a fourth major stage of political reform. He was dissatisfied with the level of political participation generated by the people's committee system; this new phase was designed to increase the level of popular mobilization. Specific objectives included an increase in the level of coordination between the people's committees and the Arab Socialist Union (ASU) and a reduction in the conflict and competition which often typified their relationship.

At the bottom of the direct democracy system, zones and the direct popular election of zone committees, together with the election from their membership of a district basic popular congress, were retained. At this level, the major change was the call for each basic popular congress to elect from its membership a smaller people's committee with administrative responsibilities for the congress. In turn, political authority was delegated to the district Arab Socialist Union whose membership was to be elected from the basic popular congress. The position of the Arab Socialist Union was further strengthened by a requirement that the chair of the each basic popular congress be an ASU member. At the top of the system, Qaddafi announced the creation of a new, national level representative body called the General People's Congress (GPC) with himself as the Secretary-General of the organization and the remaining members of the Revolutionary Command Council forming its General Secretariat.

The chairmen and assistant chairmen of the district people's committees and district ASUs were automatically delegates to the General People's Congress. District union leaders and their deputies were also entitled to be delegates. Scheduled to meet annually, the General People's Congress became the major arena in which the policies, plans, and programs of the Revolutionary Command Council, together with those developed at the district level by the popular congresses, were discussed and ratified. Formal ratification carried with it responsibility for implementation by the members of the Arab Socialist Union, unions, and people's committees. At its first session in early 1976, the General Secretariat surprised many observers by submitting major domestic and foreign policy items to the General People's Congress for review and authorization, including the general administrative budget for 1976 and the 1976–80 development budget.

On 2 March 1977, Qaddafi clarified the authority and structure of the new organization in the so-called Declaration of the Establishment of the People's Authority. Affirming the official name of Libya to be "The Socialist People's Libyan Arab Jamahiriya" and the Qur'an to be the law of its society, the declaration announced the "establishment of the authority of the people" in "the dawn of the era of the masses." Jamahiriya was a neologism coined by Qaddafi to describe a political system allegedly marked by popular rule but absent political parties and their representatives. With popular direct authority the basis for this new political system, the Libyan people were to exercise their authority only through approved, official organizations, like the popular congresses, people's committees, syndicates, unions, professional organizations, and General People's Congress.

The institutional changes introduced in 1975–77 strengthened mobilization and participation, within carefully defined parameters, by reducing competition between the Arab Socialist Union and the people's committees and providing the General People's Congress with limited policy review and ratification powers. Revolutionary control was tightened by restricting political activity to the organizations established and controlled by the General Secretariat of the General People's Congress. Workers were obliged to join unions where their activities could be closely monitored, and popular congresses and committees continued to be reelected whenever their activities generated excess turmoil or their recommendations were inconsistent with those of the General Secretariat.

At the same time as the Qaddafi regime promoted political reform and encouraged institutional change, it actively fostered ideological change in the form of revisionist Libyan history. The Libyan Studies Center, formally known as the Center for the Study of the Jihad of the Libyans against the Italian Occupation, was one of several research units founded by the regime around 1978 to support the creation and dissemination of a fresh interpretation of Libyan history more in line with the ideology of the One September Revolution. Serious scholarship on the prehistoric and classical periods of Libyan history was not abandoned; however, the regime encouraged study of the Ottoman Empire and the Italian occupation in particular. The Sanusi were given their due, particularly the important role of the sheiks in the resistance to the Italians, but information on the dark side of the Sanusi family also became more readily available.

In addition to biographies of important resistance figures, like Umar al-Mukhtar, and accounts of significant military battles, research was encouraged on the role played by Ottoman officers in aiding the Libyan resistance to the Italian occupiers. The new scholarship also stressed the role of the Tripoli Republic in upholding the interests of Tripolitanians after World War I. In providing a niche for professional historians, the work published by the Libyan Studies Center and similar research bodies made an important contribution to the official, revolutionary interpretation of Libyan society as a cohesive, nationalist, anti-imperialist body, loyal to its Arab-Muslim culture.

In the process, historical interpretation often changed quickly and dramatically; consequently, the close nexus between the interests of the regime and its support of historical research inevitably raised the issue of politically subservient history. In a fluid political climate, studies greeted with enthusiasm in the 1970s were often unavailable, confined to the restricted access rooms of Libyan libraries, less than a decade later. In 1984, an American-trained Libyan historian warned a Tunisian audience of the dangers of official history that wholly or largely supported ideological and political ends. By that time, the ideological framework of the Qaddafi regime was in place, and independent, professional historians in some research units found they had outlived their usefulness.

On 1 September 1978, Qaddafi called for a resurgence of the people's committee system to eliminate what he termed the bureaucracy of the public sector and the dictatorship of the private sector. In response, several hundred companies were taken over by newly elected people's committees with several elections often necessary before the composition of a given people's committee was sufficiently revolutionary and loyal to satisfy Qaddafi. On 3 February 1979, a major reshuffle of the General Popular Committee or cabinet was announced, reducing the total number of ministers from twenty-six to nineteen. In coming years, frequent cabinet reorganizations, designed to prevent any one individual from gaining enough power to challenge Qaddafi, became a hallmark of the regime.

In December 1978, Qaddafi announced he was stepping down from his post as Secretary-General of the General People's Congress to concentrate on revolutionary activities with the masses, effectively separating instruments of government from instruments of the revolution. Continuing as commander-in-chief of the armed forces, he adopted the title, Leader of the Revolution, a designation he retained after that time. His close associates on the General Secretariat, Abu Bakr Yuunis Jaabir, Kweildi al-Hemeidi, Mustafa al-Kharuubi, and Abdel Salaam Jalloud, also resigned their posts to concentrate on revolutionary activities. While some observers considered Qaddafi's move a devolution decision, no evidence surfaced to suggest a significant change in the power structure had taken place. On the contrary, by freeing themselves of the formal duties of cabinet-level positions, Qaddafi and his close associates divested themselves of responsibilities and constraints but retained the power and authority they had wielded since the outset of the One September Revolution.

When the General People's Congress on 2 March 1979 made the official announcement of the separation of instruments of government from instruments of the revolution, it also formally announced the creation of revolutionary committees, a new echelon of organization not mentioned in *The Green Book*. Already in operation for some time, revolutionary committees were a delayed reaction to the lethargy long prevalent in the congress and committee system. Qaddafi had been noting the need to reduce absenteeism since 1976, and the first revolutionary committee was formed at Tripoli's al-Fateh University as early as November 1977. By the end of 1978, a loose network of revolutionary committees was active throughout the country, infiltrating popular congresses, people's committees, and university faculties. With no defined assignment, they mostly performed ideological surveillance at this point, guiding the masses and defending the revolution but not yet assuming the security dimension that would later dominate their operations.

Following the March 1979 announcement, revolutionary committees were established at all levels of government and society,
from popular congresses to schools and universities to factories
and offices to the military. The revolutionary committee system
attracted self-proclaimed zealots intent on becoming the true
cadre of the revolution. In contrast to the people's committees,
which reported to the General People's Congress and had largely
administrative responsibilities, the revolutionary committees
reported directly to the Leader of the Revolution and were responsible for monitoring and promoting revolutionary ardor throughout Libyan society. Beginning in 1979, Qaddafi met annually with
the revolutionary committees, and a Central Coordinating Office
for Revolutionary Committees was established to coordinate their
activities in the interim.

Originally without formal authority, the revolutionary committees soon gained the power to make revolutionary arrests, hold
revolutionary courts, and inflict revolutionary justice. The psycho-
logical impact of these denunciations was later captured by Libyan
writer, Hisham Matar, in his critically acclaimed novel, *In the
Country of Men*. In the following paragraph, the protagonist of the
novel, a young Libyan boy, describes the impact on him of witness-
ing the televised execution in 1979 of the father of a friend, earlier
denounced by a neighbor, in the National Basketball Stadium:

> Apart from making me lose trust in the assumption that "good
> things happen to good people," the televised execution of Ustath
> Rashid would leave another, more lasting impression on me, one
> that has survived well into my manhood, a kind of quiet panic, as
> if at any moment the rug could be pulled from beneath my feet.
> After Ustath Rashid's death I had no illusions that I or Baba [his
> father] or Mama were immune from being burned by the madness
> that overtook the National Basketball Stadium.[5]

In contradiction to the directives in *The Green Book* and the
Declaration of the Establishment of the People's Authority, the
revolutionary committees by early 1979 were dominating
the activities of the popular congresses and effectively controlling

the agenda of the General People's Congress. Following an April 1979 decision to create revolutionary committees within the armed forces, Qaddafi called in November 1979 for their creation within the police force. In 1979, the revolutionary committees also began publication of their own weekly magazine, *al-Zahf al-Akhdar* (The Green March), and in 1980, they added *al-Jamahiriyya* which soon became the voice of the regime and the pulse of the revolution. Revolutionary committees were also established outside Libya where they were charged with implementing a strategy of revolutionary force against counterrevolutionaries, a policy that led to reprisals and assassinations and contributed to worsening relations with the West. A long anticipated takeover of the Libyan press also occurred in October 1980.[6]

RUSH TO SOCIALISM

Following a period of cautious experimentation, the Libyan approach to socialism clarified in the second half of the decade. After the second part of *The Green Book* defined man's basic needs as a house, an income, and a vehicle, rental housing and hired vehicles were denounced as forms of domination over the needs of others. In the case of home ownership, Resolution Four, issued by the General Secretariat of the General People's Congress in March 1978, established strict guidelines for home redistribution. No family had the right to own more than one home with only a few exceptions, namely widows whose only source of income was rent and families with at least one son over eighteen years of age. Committees were set up in every province to carry out the resolution, and by July 1978, the permanent secretary of the Municipalities Secretariat was able to announce substantial progress in the takeover and redistribution of houses and apartments owned by government bodies and private companies. The second phase of home redistribution, the takeover of homes owned by private individuals, took longer due to the legal and personal complications involved. Housing redistribution was very popular with people who were tenants because their new monthly mortgage payments averaged around one-third of their former rent. In addition, the government subsidized the purchase price by deliberately undervaluing the property; consequently, the cost of a new home was up to forty percent less than its actual value.

After Qaddafi in the fall of 1978 urged greater self-management of public and private enterprise, workers rushed to take over some two hundred companies. A widespread redistribution of land on the Jefara plain west of Tripoli began in 1979, continuing into 1980–81. In May 1980, Libya also declared all currency in denominations larger than one dinar to be void, giving citizens one week to exchange their cash. With the maximum exchange set at one thousand dinars, all deposits in excess of that amount were frozen. The de-monetization campaign was a straight-out socialist measure, redis-tributive in intent and effect. Novelist Hisham Matar provided a vivid description of the impact of the currency change, setting the event in *In the Country of Men* one year earlier than it actually occurred:

> In 1979, a few days after I was sent to Cairo, the entire Libyan population was given three days to deposit liquid assets into the National Bank. The national currency had been redesigned, they were told, to celebrate the revolution's tenth anniversary. People deposited pockets of coins and others suitcases of notes and some a truckful of money only to be told afterward that individual bank withdrawals would be limited to one thousand dinars annually. My parents were badly affected by this, their monthly output alone was in excess of that amount. The following year, private savings accounts, which were effectively what most accounts had become, were eliminated, and my parents watched their money vanish "like salt in water."[7]

Finally, the General People's Congress announced in early 1981 that the state would take over all import, export, and distribution functions by year end. Future imports were restricted to ten state import agencies that purchased everything from sophisticated oil and gas technology to basic foodstuffs. To replace local entrepre-neurs, the regime established state supermarkets throughout the country. About the same time, religious endowment property was also abolished, effectively undermining the limited economic power the religious leadership in Libya still possessed.

If socialism is defined as a redistribution of wealth and resources, a socialist revolution clearly occurred in Libya after 1969 and most especially in the second half of the 1970s. The management of the economy was increasingly socialist in intent and effect with wealth in housing, capital, and land significantly redistributed or in the process of redistribution. Private enterprise was virtually eliminated, largely replaced by a centrally controlled economy. In the process, the Libyan approach to socialism became more fundamental than that found in neighboring states. Whether or not Qaddafi intended in 1969 for Libyan socialism to become as radical as it had done by the early 1980s remained open to question. What was clear was that precept and theory generally preceded practice in the Libyan case. Moreover, the domestic turmoil produced by the regime's increasingly radical socioeconomic policies had an adverse impact on its own development goals, sometimes paralyzing decision-making for weeks on end.

The widespread redistribution of power and wealth also had a negative affect on the economic well-being of many Libyans, eventually resulting in growing opposition to the regime. In the first decade of the revolution, distributive largesse, funded by rapidly increasing oil revenues, tempered the impact of Qaddafi's ideological revolution, translating into substantial regime support throughout most of the 1970s. Per capita income increased from around $35 in 1951 to a little more than $2,200 in 1969 to almost $10,000 a decade later. Housing redistribution was bothersome to property owners, but fair compensation was generally forthcoming, and individual families often made arrangements to temper the impact of official decrees. In the second decade of the revolution, opposition to the socioeconomic policies of the regime increased sharply because a drop in oil revenues due to lower prices meant the revolutionary government no longer had the resources necessary to buy popular consensus. Economic austerity policies, coupled with Qaddafi's struggle with the religious establishment and his confrontational foreign policies, generated mounting dis-satisfaction in the early 1980s. The presence of a large, costly, and socially explosive foreign work force fuelled internal discontent, provoking ridicule for regime slogans like "partners, not wage earners."

Opposition outside Libya was also on the increase. The revolution created a growing number of enemies in exile, including the dispossessed monarchical elites, fellow revolutionaries who had fallen out with Qaddafi, a religious leadership whose role was severely constricted, and ordinary citizens opposed to the theory and practice of the One September Revolution. In response, a plethora of organized opposition groups began to surface outside Libya with the most prominent one being the National Front for the Salvation of Libya (NFSL), founded in 1981 by Muhammad Mugharyif.

The turn towards radical socialism after 1975, which included the creation of a parallel system of justice to circumvent ordinary courts, resulted in a sustained period of neglect for codified law, individual liberty, and basic human rights. The revolutionary courts were staffed with revolutionary committee members, not regular judges, and they were not bound by the penal code. On the contrary, the revolutionary court system routinely ignored normal legal safeguards, leading to a significant number of well-docu-mented abuses. The elimination in May 1981 of the private practice of law, along with other professional occupations, removed the last constraint on the revolutionary court system. For the next seven years, the regime paid little attention to formal legal rules, instead relying on an arbitrary and repressive system of justice that con-tributed to the growing tension in Libya.[8]

HYDROCARBON POLICY

In 1974, Libya moved to the current phase of oil and gas regulation when it converted all existing concessionary agreements to explo-ration and production sharing agreements (EPSAs). EPSA, phase one, provided for thirty-five-year agreements with five years allotted for exploration and thirty years for production. The agreements called for production to be shared in a ratio of eighty-five to fifteen percent onshore and eighty-one to nineteen percent offshore with the state taking the larger share in each case. To encourage timely exploration, they expired at the end of the five-year period if no discovery was made. The oil companies were required to spend approximately $500 million on exploration activities, regardless of their success, but their share of all crude oil found was exempt from fees, rents, royalties, taxes, or other state charges. Occidental Petroleum was the first oil company to conclude an EPSA with Libya; however, by 1978, Exxon, Mobile, Total, Elf Aquitaine, Braspero, and Agip had all signed similar agreements.

Initiated in 1980, the revised terms of EPSA, phase two, reflected Libyan concern for reserve depletion. The National Oil Company (NOC), established in March 1970, together with the international oil companies operating in Libya, were simply incapable of finding and developing sufficient new deposits to replenish the country's diminishing reserves. In an exception to standard practice, political considerations also entered into the commercial mix at this point. As Libya pursued an increasingly radical foreign policy into the early 1980s, its diplomatic relations with the West, especially the United States, deteriorated. In response, Libya decided to involve East European countries in the hydrocarbon industry. Recognizing the limited financial capacity of the East Europeans, NOC officials opposed this political decision; nevertheless, Rompetrol, the Romanian state oil company, and Geocom, the Bulgarian state oil company, were both assigned blocks in EPSA, phase two. This decision to broaden the network of potential oil producers appeared judicious at the time as Libya's deteriorating relations with the United States were causing American producers to rethink their Libyan strategy. Exxon announced its complete withdrawal from Libya in November 1981, and following months of unsuccessful talks, Mobil also announced its withdrawal in January 1983.

Otherwise, the second phase of EPSA agreements resembled the first with the important exception that the production sharing pattern in the second varied in accordance with the prospects of the acreage. For top category concessions, the split was eighty-five to fifteen percent in Libya's favor, but the state reduced its share to eighty-one to nineteen percent for medium category concessions and to seventy-five to twenty-five percent for less-promising areas. All oil companies concluding contracts under EPSA, phase two, were expected to spend around $1 billion in exploration activities in the first five years of the contract. Collectively, the terms of EPSA, phases one and two, resulted in the drilling of 694 exploratory wells, 270 of which were successful, and the discovery of some eight billion barrels of crude oil and forty-five trillion cubic feet of natural gas. The new reserves added approximately 250,000 barrels a day to Libya's production capacity.

In 1986, the United States ordered all American oil companies out of Libya and began to impose an increasingly comprehensive regime of bilateral sanctions. As relations with the United States worsened, Libya had taken steps to solidify its European connections, purchasing a majority stake in Tamoil, a European oil services company with European-based refineries and more than eight hundred retail outlets in Germany, Italy, the Netherlands, Spain, and Switzerland. A cornerstone of Libyan hydrocarbon policy from the beginning had been its determination to avoid domination by the larger international oil companies. When combined with expansion into Europe, this policy served the state well after the American oil companies were forced to withdraw as Libya was able to maintain, albeit not expand, annual oil production levels well into the following decade.

In 1988, Libya announced EPSA, phase three, which increased the return of the oil companies to give them additional incentives to undertake exploration and development. While the terms of agreement again varied according to the prospects of the acreage, the oil company share was increased with a seventy to thirty split in the state's favor for first-class category prospects and a sixty-five to thirty-five split for second-class category prospects. The cost of exploration was to be recovered from production, but the NOC did agree in phase three to share development costs equally with the oil companies. The more lenient terms of EPSA, phase three, were driven by the severe cash flow problems the Libyan government experienced in the mid-1980s, primarily because a collapse in oil prices precipitated a drastic fall in oil revenues. In 1981–86, Libya's annual oil revenues dropped from $21 billion to $5.4 billion, causing the regime to reconsider both its macroeconomic strategies and its traditional policy of distributive largesse. Necessary adjustments to U.S. sanctions and the mounting cost of large development projects, like the Misurata Iron and Steel Works and the Great Manmade River, compounded its economic woes as did heavy defense and military spending. With twenty-five foreign oil companies exploring in Libya by 1995, EPSA, phase three, clearly succeeded in attracting new exploration; unfortunately, most of it was not productive.

CONFRONTATION WITH THE WEST

Following a brief period of flirtation with the new Libyan government, Washington, for the remainder of the 1970s, pursued an ambivalent policy in which the United States enjoyed relatively normal commercial relations with Tripoli even as diplomatic relations deteriorated. In this period, Libya became one of the Soviet Union's staunchest clients in the Arab world, purchasing a Soviet-supplied arsenal far beyond what its armed forces could use effectively. At the same time, it retained close commercial ties with the West, selling the bulk of its oil to the United States and its European allies in return for substantial imports of Western technology. Libyan students continued to go abroad for higher education, mostly to the United States or Western Europe, as opposed to the Soviet Union. Moreover, Qaddafi continued to proclaim his friendship for the American people even as official relations with the United States spiraled downward.

Basic, long-standing policy differences were at the center of the deepening imbroglio between the United States, its Western allies, and Libya. The Palestinian issue was the crucial one as Libyan support for the Palestinians had a profound impact on its policy toward an overall Middle East peace settlement as well as its policies in other parts of the world. When Libya aggressively denounced the 1978 Israeli–Egyptian peace agreement and took a leadership role in Arab attempts to isolate Egypt, any remaining constituency in the United States for improved diplomatic relations evaporated. American attitudes toughened further when Libya, at the January 1980 Islamic Conference in Islamabad, sought to tone down criticism of the Soviet invasion of Afghanistan, arguing the conference should take an equally strong stand against U.S. policy in the Middle East.

Libya's image in the United States and elsewhere was damaged further by its increasingly close identification with international terrorism. From the outset, the Revolutionary Command Council enthusiastically endorsed terrorism as a useful and effective tactic, especially in the war against Israel. Following the 1972 Munich massacre, in which eleven members of the Israeli Olympic team died, Qaddafi had the bodies of the five Arab guerrillas killed in the action flown to Tripoli where they were given a martyr's burial. The Libyans continued to support the use of terrorism even after the October 1973 War strengthened the position of the Palestine Liberation Organization (PLO) and oil proved to be a more effective weapon than terrorism. In contrast, the PLO recognized terrorist movements were vulnerable when their actions alienated support, announcing in January 1975 that the hijacking of airplanes, ships, or trains would be considered a capital crime if they involved loss of life.

While the Palestine Liberation Organization recognized that terrorism could be counterproductive, Libya did not. This ongoing dispute over the use of force in general, and terrorism in particular, eventually led Qaddafi to a public feud with PLO Chairman Yasser Arafat. In a Palestine Solidarity Day address in November 1979, Qaddafi called on the PLO to step up its attacks on Israel as well as on the Suez Canal which he claimed was being used to support Israel. Later, he attacked Arafat's leadership of the PLO movement, charging the latter was imitating the "capitulationist" policies of

Egyptian President Sadat and was prepared to sell out the Palestinian people. Qaddafi's criticism of Arafat and his Fatah organization centered on its increasingly moderate attitude toward the West at a time when Libya, and possibly Iraq and Syria, remained the only truly unregenerate rejectionists in the Arab world. Thereafter, Qaddafi devoted considerable time and attention to differentiating between revolutionary violence, which he continued to advocate, and terrorism, which he allegedly opposed. The United States failed to see the difference, and Libya in 1979 became an inaugural member of the State Department's list of state sponsors of terrorism.

Libyan relations with the United States reached a new low at the end of 1979 when Libyan demonstrators sacked the U.S. embassy in Tripoli. William L. Eagleton, the chargé d'affaires at the time and later U.S. ambassador to Syria, later recalled the attack had all the earmarks of "a planned military event."[9] The embassy had been under the protection of the Ministry of Foreign Affairs since the early 1970s, when the U.S. marine contingent was withdrawn; however, no Libyan force came to its defense when the building was attacked. On the contrary, Libyan authorities later complained the embassy's use of tear gas during the attack made local citizens ill.

Diplomatic relations with the United States and its Western allies continued to deteriorate in the wake of a January 1980 attack by Libyan-sponsored guerrillas on the Tunisian town of Gafsa. Paris dispatched military aircraft and warships to the region in support of the Tunisian government, and Washington accelerated its military assistance program to Tunisia. Following new attacks on diplomatic premises in Libya, France withdrew its ambassador and the United States shuttered its embassy. By the summer of 1980, Libyan fighters were intercepting American planes over the Mediterranean Sea, and American–Libyan relations overall had reached a level of tension not seen since the American bombardment of Tripoli in 1804.

After taking office in January 1981, President Ronald Reagan systematically increased diplomatic, economic, and military pressure on Libya. Unfairly and inaccurately dismissed as a Soviet puppet, Qaddafi was labeled an international pariah to be restrained if not replaced. Within a year, the Reagan administration fundamentally altered U.S. policy toward Libya in both commercial and diplomatic terms. Citing a wide range of Libyan provocations and misconduct, the Libyan embassy in Washington was closed, Libyans were subjected to mandatory security advisory opinions, and U.S. oil companies operating in Libya were advised to begin an orderly reduction in the number of their American employees. In the process, the Reagan administration came to recognize Qaddafi, not as an inconvenience, but as an enemy.[10]

In marked contrast, the Soviet Union expanded commercial and diplomatic relations with Libya. Qaddafi was invited to Moscow for a state visit in 1977, and the Soviets made repeated offers of military and technical assistance in return for hard currency. Libya was receptive to these offers, and while the exact amount of Soviet arms purchased was never announced, it was considerable and was accompanied by several thousand Soviet advisers. Motivated in part by the opportunity to earn hard currency, the Soviets also saw Libya as a potential future source for oil when their own supplies were exhausted. In addition, Libya's constant criticism of the West supported Soviet policies in the Middle East and elsewhere in the world.

From the Libyan perspective, Qaddafi never pursued his threat in 1978 to join the Warsaw Pact; however, there were repeated rumors that Tripoli and Moscow might conclude a twenty-year treaty of friendship and cooperation similar to Soviet accords with Iraq, South Yemen, and Syria. In 1978, the Soviet Union agreed to construct in Libya a nuclear power plant and research center with a capacity of three hundred megawatts; and by 1981, the two states were discussing a further expansion of their nuclear cooperation efforts, including a power station with two four hundred-megawatt units. During a 1981 visit to Moscow, Qaddafi concluded several technical and economic cooperation agreements covering a wide variety of areas, including oil and gas, nonferrous metals, and irrigation. Libya also continued to acquire sophisticated weaponry from the Soviets to the point that its fifty-five thousand-strong armed forces were reported, in the early 1980s, to have the highest ratio of military equipment to manpower in the world.

On the other hand, the Soviets were not granted permanent use of any Libyan port or refueling facility, a Soviet objective since World War II, and the influence of Soviet advisers on the Libyan armed forces was carefully controlled. In part, Libyan policy toward the Soviet Union reflected Qaddafi's resolve to maintain some element of neutrality in the world power struggle. It also highlighted the fact that Libya's populist, Islamist, Arab nationalist views had little in common with atheistic Marxism.

The viewpoint on Libya in most Western European capitals differed from the United States in significant policy areas. Acknowledging Qaddafi's anti-Western behavior, many European analysts argued he was not as dangerous as the United States maintained. In support of this position, they cited his foreign policy failures in Chad and Uganda, together with his alienation of African and Middle Eastern leaders. Many West Europeans also felt it was a mistake to isolate Qaddafi, setting him up as the prime example of the international behavior President Reagan refused to accept. Instead, they argued in support of maintaining dialogue with Libya as a means to protect Western economic interests and to keep Libya from developing closer ties with the Soviet Union.

Undeterred, the Reagan administration continued to pressure the Qaddafi regime. In March 1982, the United States, citing active support for terrorist and subversive activities, announced an embargo on Libyan oil, together with an export-import license requirement for American goods destined for Libya with the exception of food, medicine, and medical supplies. The announcement sparked little comment at the time even though it represented the end of a policy process, the separation of commercial and political policies toward Libya, pursued by successive American administrations since 1969. Washington encouraged West European capitals to support the imposition of economic sanctions on Libya, but for a variety of reasons, they all declined.

In November 1985, the United States banned the import of all Libyan petroleum products; and in December 1985, it terminated all direct economic activities with Libya, froze Libyan assets in the United States, and called on Americans working in Libya to return home. President Reagan stepped up the rhetoric in January 1986 when he termed Qaddafi a pariah who must be isolated from the world community. In the spring of 1986, events in the Mediterranean moved inexorably toward armed conflict with the *casus belli* proving to be America's challenge to Libyan claims to sovereignty in the Gulf of Sirte. Following renewed confrontations in the Gulf of Sirte and the bombing of the La Belle discotheque in West Berlin, U.S. aircraft on the night of 14 April 1986 attacked what President Reagan termed centers of terrorist activity and training in Benghazi and Tripoli. In the first prime-time bombing in American history, targets included the military barracks at Bab al-Aziziyyah where Qaddafi resided.

ARAB DISUNITY

In February 1972, Qaddafi had proposed a merger with Egypt on or before 1 September 1973. As that date approached, he sensed the Egyptian government and the Egyptian people were having second thoughts about the union. Therefore, Qaddafi made an unscheduled, surprise visit to Cairo in late June 1973 during which time his criticism of Egyptian policy and society doomed any chance remaining for an immediate merger. Egypt and Libya did agree in August 1973 to a unified political leadership, as well as to vague provisions for merger through evolution; however, these were obviously compromise measures given Qaddafi's call for immediate and total political union.

The October 1973 War further isolated Libya from Egypt as well as from the remainder of the Arab world. The outcome of the war strengthened the domestic political position of the Sadat regime, enabling it to accelerate internal and external policy changes that threw the Libyan policy of Arab unity into total disarray. Egypt completely rearranged its regional alliances with a Teheran–Riyadh–Cairo axis replacing the former Damascus–PLO–Cairo axis. Outside the region, the United States and Western Europe supplanted the Soviet Union and Third World as Egyptian allies.

Rejected in the Mashriq, Qaddafi turned his attention to the Maghrib, where Libya and Tunisia in January 1974 announced the merger of their countries into the Islamic Arab Republic. Consistent with patterns of regional bloc formation, the idea was not a new one, but its timing seemed an act of pique in the face of Egypt's rejection. The Libyan proposal evidenced poor planning, and the merger was strongly opposed by neighboring Algeria. As a result, Tunisia had second thoughts, and the so-called Union of Djerba was effectively dead within a month. Diplomatic relations with Tunisia deteriorated in the wake of the failed talks. Following reports of Tunisian guerrillas receiving military training in Libya, one such group crossed the border in late January 1980, attacking the Tunisian town of Gafsa. The Tunisian army soon crushed the rebel force; and convinced it was supported, if not organized, by the Libyans, Tunisia withdrew its ambassador from Tripoli and closed the Libyan cultural center in Tunis.

Libya's search for North African allies in the period after the October 1973 War was not limited to Tunisia. Qaddafi also attempted to build links with Algeria and Morocco. Libya and Morocco had broken diplomatic relations in 1971–72 over alleged Libyan support for insurgents who planned to overthrow King Hassan. Libyan–Moroccan relations improved for a time after the October war but again deteriorated after 1975 when Qaddafi was critical of Morocco's role in the Western Sahara. Relations between Algeria and Libya soured in the immediate aftermath of the failed Union of Djerba but had improved by late 1975 to the point that the two states were able to conclude a mutual defense pact. Under the terms of the Hassi Messaoud Treaty, Algeria became Libya's major regional ally as well as its principal protector in North Africa.[11] Algeria later intervened on behalf of Libya when Egypt in July 1977 launched a limited air and ground attack against Libyan military installations in the Cyrenaican desert west of the Egyptian border. In turn, Libya supported Algeria in its confrontation with Morocco over the Western Sahara, supplying the Frente Popular para la Liberación de Saguia el Hamra y Rio de Oro (Polisario Front) with military and other aid.

Thereafter, Qaddafi continued to promote the idea of Arab unity through political union, for example with Syria in 1980, Chad in 1981, and again with Morocco in 1984; however, his words largely fell on deaf ears. Pan-Arabism was an exhausted, discredited idea after 1967, and after 1973 when traditional Arab rivalries reemerged in the wake of the October War, it appeared dead. Eventually, Qaddafi would abandon his dream of Arab unity, disown the Arab world, and actively promote African unity.

THIRD CIRCLE

In marked contrast to the monarchy, the revolutionary government was deeply involved in Africa in the first decade of the One September Revolution. Qaddafi never adopted formally the three-circles strategy followed by Nasser, which focused on the Arab, African, and Islamic worlds, but Africa effectively became a third circle of Libyan foreign policy. Throughout most of the 1970s, Africa was the scene of intense diplomatic and propaganda activity, eventually becoming the arena in which the regime scored some of its earliest and most stunning diplomatic victories.[12]

With its attention focused on the Middle East, the African diplomacy of the Revolutionary Command Council began tentatively with early overtures targeted at largely Muslim neighbors like Cameroun, Mauritania, and Niger. The primary objective of these initiatives was a reduction in Israeli influence in Africa. Qaddafi viewed Israel's presence in Africa as a fifth column behind the Arab front line which sapped Arab strength at the back door. Secondary goals included opposition to Western influence, the elimination of foreign bases, opposition to apartheid, support for African liberation movements, the propagation of Islam, and control over the region's resources.

To counter Israeli influence, the Revolutionary Command Council established diplomatic relations with African states, offered them economic assistance, and then urged them to break diplomatic relations with Israel. By mid-1973, Mali, Niger, the Congo, and Burundi had all severed diplomatic relations with Israel. At the same time, Libya began raising the issue at meetings of the Organization of African Unity (OAU), a body which previously had been largely neutral on the Arab–Israeli conflict. Tripoli urged member states to sever ties with Israel and to shift OAU headquarters from Ethiopia to a country more suitable for achieving freedom and unity in Africa.

In the wake of the October 1973 War, Libya skillfully exploited African concerns raised by the oil embargo and oil price increases to pressure African governments to abandon their neutrality on the Palestinian issue and rid the continent of Zionism. By the end of 1973, more than twenty additional African states had broken diplomatic relations with Israel, with many of them opening relations with Libya for the first time. By the beginning of 1974, Libya had largely achieved its foremost goal in Africa, a reduction of Israeli influence, with itself often supplanting the Israeli presence.

At the same time, Libya sought to reduce Western power and influence on the continent by eliminating Western military bases and undermining moderate African governments opposed to its policies. Libya supported African liberation movements and radical, anti-Western governments, and it repeatedly denounced the white, minority regimes in southern Africa. It also provided military assistance to liberation movements in Angola, Guinea-Bissau, and Mozambique; and in 1973, it closed Libyan air space to South African over-flights.

In many areas of Africa, Libyan foreign policy also assumed an Islamic hue in that preference was given to governments and groups expressing their opposition to the *status quo* in religious terms. Qaddafi established a Jihad Fund in 1970 to strengthen the Libyan armed forces and to support the Arab nation in its struggle against Zionist forces. At the Fourth Conference of Foreign Ministers of Islamic Countries, held in Benghazi in March 1973, African liberation through assistance to Islamic liberation movements and aid to Islamic welfare associations was touted as a central objective of the Jihad Fund. In addition, the Islamic Call Society, established in 1973 as an instrument to propagate the faith, was used for propaganda and subversion. In a little more than a decade, the society had created 132 centers in Africa. Libya also extended loans to promote Islamic culture and the Arabic language. The amount disbursed annually for purely Islamic purposes was not large, but it was often highly visible, politically oriented economic assistance.

Qaddafi's emphasis on Africa produced a series of quick diplomatic victories. Uganda, following an early 1972 meeting between Qaddafi and President Idi Amin, expelled several hundred Israeli advisers and later broke diplomatic relations with Israel. In the course of Uganda's first confrontation with Tanzania, Libya successfully intervened in September 1972 with an airlift of troops, justifying its involvement as support for the Ugandan struggle against colonialism and Zionism. Nine months later, Qaddafi saluted President Amin during the annual ceremonies marking the closure of Wheelus Field, praising him for transforming Uganda from a backward satellite of Zionism into a vanguard African state combating apartheid and Zionist colonialism.

Soon after Egypt, Libya, and Sudan had concluded a tripartite agreement in December 1969, forming an Arab Revolutionary Front, major policy differences surfaced between Libya and Sudan, and bilateral relations rapidly deteriorated. In September 1972, Sudan forced five Libyan planes transporting military hardware to Uganda through Sudanese airspace to land in Khartoum, impounding the arms and equipment. Qaddafi viewed the Uganda government of Idi Amin as an Islamist, anti-imperialist force in Africa, but the Sudanese government of Jaffar al-Numayri saw it in a different light, supporting instead deposed Ugandan president Milton Obote. When Numayri concluded the Addis Ababa agreement later in the year, ending seventeen years of civil war in the Sudan, Qaddafi refused to recognize the non-Muslim Africans of the southern Sudan. The ensuing diplomatic crises clouded Libya–Sudan relations for years to come.

Libyan foreign policy met with greater success in Chad. Following years of acrimonious relations, the governments of Chad and Libya in April 1972 resumed diplomatic ties severed in August 1971 when Chad accused Libya of aiding rebel forces. In return for Libyan friendship, the withdrawal of official support for the Front de Libération Nationale du Tchad (Frolinat), and a promise of economic aid, Chad broke diplomatic relations with Israel in November. The governments of Chad and Libya then concluded a treaty of friendship in December 1972. Around this time, Libya moved troops into the Aouzou Strip, raising the Libyan flag over the ramshackle remains of the former French fort at Aouzou, and in August 1975, it annexed the Aouzou Strip, incorporating it into the Murzuq province of Libya.[13]

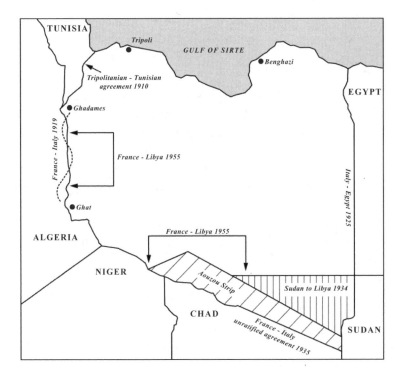

Map 7 Libya's Borders

Qaddafi's occupation of the Aouzou Strip concerned more than a simple dispute over boundaries in the sand. It involved Libyan support for the Arab, Muslim politicians of Chad, together with their non-Arab Toubou allies, against the mélange of Black African traditionalists and Christians who controlled the government in N'Djamena. Libyan occupation of the Aouzou Strip raised considerable concern in the OAU where an immutable principle, defined in article two of its constitution, was recognition of the colonial boundaries inherited from the European powers. The Aouzou Strip was little more than a desolate area of sand seas, mountain massifs, and arid plateaus; however, African leaders rightly feared the readjustment of boundaries in this relatively worthless desert could establish a precedent for frontier rectification throughout Africa and thus precipitate an untold number of disputes.

DECLINING INFLUENCE ABROAD

Libya maintained the anti-Israeli focus of its African foreign policy for the remainder of the decade while paying increased attention to the related issues of colonialism and neocolonialism. The favorite targets of the Qaddafi regime were the white minority regimes of Rhodesia and South Africa which it grouped with Israel as racist regimes. Libyan emphasis on this tie helped set the stage for the controversial UN General Assembly vote in November 1975, equating Zionism with apartheid. Twenty-eight African states voted in favor of the measure with twelve abstaining and only five opposing. Libya also continued to use the Organization of African Unity as a forum to advocate stronger policies against all forms of colonialism and imperialism. A member of the OAU Liberation Committee, Libya in February 1978 also became a member of a new military committee charged with securing sophisticated weaponry for African liberation movements.

By the end of the decade, Libyan influence in Africa was on the wane, and nowhere was this more evident than in Uganda and the

Central African Republic. Libyan troops sent to Uganda in 1978 to assist in repelling a mixed force of Ugandan exiles and Tanzanian forces suffered a crushing defeat. In the Central African Republic, self-proclaimed emperor Jean Bedel Bokassa was deposed in September 1979 while in Tripoli seeking aid from Libya. Uncritical support for notorious regimes like those of Amin and Bokassa reflected badly on Libya but was consistent with Qaddafi's approach to Africa. For the most part, personalities and policies were irrelevant to him as long as governments supported Islam and opposed imperialism, colonialism, and Zionism.

By the end of 1980, nine African states including Gabon, Gambia, Ghana, and Senegal either had expelled Libyan diplomats, closed Libyan embassies, or ended diplomatic relations with Libya. Many African governments were especially concerned with the intricate nexus of politics, religion, and foreign aid that characterized Libyan policy. Some African states resented Tripoli's use of Islam as an instrument of foreign policy while others, with large Muslim communities or a geographic split between Muslims and Christians (or animists), complained Libya's emphasis on religion often exacerbated sensitive national cleavages. Ongoing Libyan recruitment into the Islamic Legion was another source of widespread concern. Finally, African states complained, with good reason, the discrepancy between Libyan aid commitments and disbursements continued to widen.

Events in Chad highlighted Libya's growing isolation on the continent. The two neighbors in June 1980 concluded a treaty of friendship that formalized Libyan support for Chadian independence and territorial integrity but also provided legal justification for a December 1980 Libyan intervention on behalf of the Gouvernement d'Union Nationale Transitoire (GUNT). A stillborn merger agreement with Chad, proclaimed in Tripoli on 6 January 1981, was greeted with dismay throughout Africa. Five days later, the chairman of the Organization of African Unity called for the withdrawal of Libyan troops; and later in the month, the organization condemned the projected union and openly denounced Libya for the first time. In a more tactful approach, the Organization of

African Unity later passed a resolution thanking Libya for establishing peace in Chad but calling for a pan-African peacekeeping force to replace Libyan units there.

As the decade progressed, a number of states located in sub-Saharan Africa expressed concern Libya would use control of Chad to increase its influence in the Sahel, the western stretch of the Sahara Desert bordering on the Atlantic Ocean, and West Africa as well as to harass Sudan. Around the time of the Chad–Libya merger, the governments of Ghana, Mauritania, Niger, and Nigeria joined Gambia and Senegal in citing evidence of Libyan interference in their internal affairs. Qaddafi's nebulous plans to create an Islamic Republic of the Sahel, together with concern over how the Islamic Legion might fit into those plans, intensified such fears. To many observers, Qaddafi's vision of an Islamic Republic appeared to be little more than a thinly veiled pledge to destabilize Libya's neighbors.

In an effort to cut both military and political losses, as well as to buttress his candidacy for the OAU chairmanship, Qaddafi in November 1981 abruptly withdrew his armed forces from Chad. This move reduced whatever leverage Libya retained over events in Chad but greatly improved its diplomatic position in much of the rest of Africa. Ghana restored relations with Libya in January 1982 after Tripoli supported the successful *coup* of Jerry Rawlings and provided oil on favorable terms to the new government. Relations with Tanzania also improved after it backed Libya in its dispute with OAU members over seating the Polisario Front. Elsewhere, Nigeria expelled Libyan diplomats in February 1981 after Tripoli announced it was converting its embassy in Lagos into a People's Bureau, and diplomatic relations with Zaire were terminated abruptly after it resumed diplomatic contacts with Israel.

The key multilateral issue for much of 1982–83 remained the abortive Libyan effort to convene the nineteenth OAU summit in Tripoli under Qaddafi's chairmanship. Strong opposition came from moderate African leaders unwilling to attend a high-level meeting which appeared to vindicate Libyan policy in Africa. Many of these states acted from conviction while others were pressured by European governments, the United States, or both. The war in the Western Sahara, together with the bitterly divisive question of whether or not to seat the Polisario Front, also fuelled opposition to a Qaddafi-hosted summit. Following two unsuccessful attempts to convene the summit in Tripoli, an OAU panel recommended moving it to Addis Ababa where it opened in June 1983 under the chairmanship of the Ethiopian head of state. Qaddafi made a cameo appearance at the meeting but quickly departed after being denied the chairmanship and seeing the Polisario Front effectively barred. Qaddafi was the first African leader to be denied the chairmanship of the Organization of African Unity, a dramatic illustration of how limited and counterproductive his influence had become.

In Sudan, the failure of Qaddafi's Sudanese allies to overthrow Numayri in 1976 was followed by an abortive *coup* attempt in early 1983 led by Sudanese expatriates supported by Libya. The ill-conceived scheme was soon discovered, and Sudanese forces quickly rounded up Libyan agents in Khartoum while Egypt mobilized its reserves in support of Numayri. The United States dispatched AWACS aircraft to the region in support of its allies; and when asked what threat Libya posed for Sudan, Secretary of State George Shultz defiantly responded, "at least for the moment, Khadaffi is back in his box where he belongs."[14] Although the crisis quickly subsided, the aggressive American response embarrassed both Egypt and Sudan and underlined the difficulty of sanctioning Libyan policies without incurring the wrath of African and Arab states.

CONFINED TO THE LIBYAN PLAYHOUSE

In the first long decade of the One September Revolution, from 1969 to the early 1980s, Libyan society experienced a radical redistribution of wealth and resources in which private enterprise was largely eliminated, replaced by a centrally controlled economy. The separation of the instruments of revolution from the instruments of government in the latter half of the 1970s guaranteed this socioeconomic and political revolution would continue as long as the regime remained in power and so desired.

In turn, revolutionary foreign policy deeply affected, where it did not reconstitute, Libyan relations with most countries of the world. Where the foreign policy of the monarchy had been largely regional in scope and impact, the Revolutionary Command Council addressed the wider Arab world and beyond. The Arab–Israeli conflict in general and the Palestinian issue in particular remained Qaddafi's central concern. No compromise was possible with the so-called Zionist enemy, and Arab unity remained the ideal path to Arab victory. In addition to the Palestinians, Qaddafi also provided economic and political support to a number of African states and to a wide range of revolutionary movements around the world.

The radical oil policies of the 1970s initially provided the financial means to address this wider audience; however, when Libyan oil revenues plummeted in the early 1980s, sharply reduced finances severely restricted foreign policy initiatives. In the process, the small population and limited geopolitical and military strength of Libya proved totally disproportionate to the ambitions of Qaddafi. Consequently, the Libyan government repeatedly set foreign policy objectives its national resources proved insufficient to achieve. Much to his dismay, Qaddafi also found his socioeconomic and political message, encapsulated in *The Green Book*, had little appeal outside Libya. Desperately searching for a wider stage, Qaddafi found himself largely confined to the Libyan playhouse.

8

CONSOLIDATION AND REFORM, 1986–98

History should show that if there was any mold, I have contributed toward its destruction. If there has been any shackle binding the Libyan people, I have participated in its demolition until the Libyan people have become free.

Mu'ammar al-Qaddafi, November 1987

[The UN Security Council] condemns the destruction of Pan American flight 103 and *Union de transports aérens* flight 772 and the resultant loss of hundreds of lives [and] strongly deplores the fact that the Libyan Government has not yet responded effectively to the above requests to cooperate fully in establishing responsibility for the terrorist acts referred to above against Pan American flight103 and *Union de transports aérens* flight 772.

UN Security Council Resolution 731, January 1992

Mu'ammar al-Qaddafi is one of the revolutionary icons of our times.

Nelson Mandela, June 1999

The nose cone of the 747 [Pan American flight 103] lying on its side in a Scottish field is an immediately recognizable icon of terrorism.

Allan Gerson and Jerry Adler, *The Price of Terror*, 2001

In the extended decade between the April 1986 American attack on Libya and the April 1999 Libyan decision to remand the suspects in the bombing of Pan American flight 103, the Libyan people suffered a long night of trials and tribulations. The United States progressively tightened its bilateral sanctions package after 1986, and the United Nations in 1992 imposed mandatory international sanctions. As isolation and privation increased, opposition to the Qaddafi regime mounted inside and outside the country. Many observers thought the regime could not possibly survive the ensuing turmoil, and articles forecasting Qaddafi's imminent demise became a staple in the Western press.

REVOLUTION WITHIN THE REVOLUTION

The socialist process in Libya continued into the second half of the 1980s when Qaddafi adopted a more moderate tone and signaled an interest in returning to a more open system in a package of reforms sometimes referred to as green *perestroika*. After delegates to the General People's Congress in February 1987 criticized regime economic policies, Libyan involvement in Chad, and the zeal of the revolutionary committees, Qaddafi in March announced a number of economic and political reforms, describing the liberalization measures as a "Revolution within the Revolution." In May 1987, he called for reform in both the agricultural and the industrial sectors, including a reversal of import substitution policies and the adoption of modern management practices. Qaddafi later called for a new role for the private sector as well as increased liberalization. He also promoted a form of self-management, encouraging the creation of cooperatives in which partners could contribute either capital or labor. In response, some 140 companies had been turned over to self-management committees by August 1988.[1]

In March 1988, Qaddafi created the Ministry for Mass Mobilization and Revolutionary Leadership to narrow the role of the revolutionary committees to their original charter, indoctrination of the masses through persuasion, not violence. The power of the revolutionary courts was curtailed two months later. Qaddafi also intervened personally in March 1988 to destroy a border post on the Tunisian border, declaring all Libyans were free to travel.

Armed with a relatively generous cash allowance, approximately one million Libyans visited Tunisia before the end of the year. In September 1988, Qaddafi called for an end to government control over trade, abolishing the state import and export monopoly. After injunctions against retail trade were lifted, markets and *souks* in urban areas began to reopen. The petroleum sector and heavy industry were exempt from the new privatization measures, but Qaddafi did call for greater efficiency in state enterprises.

With the actual results of Qaddafi's socioeconomic and political experiments often in striking contrast to the intent of the regime, a complex web of economic and political factors prompted this sudden moderation in the socialist policies of the regime. The state-run supermarket system, plagued with endemic shortages, was faltering under the weight of corruption and a disorganized distribution system; and the unofficially tolerated black market, where almost anything was available at a price, provided little relief to the average Libyan. The expulsion in 1985 of large numbers of expatriate workers, a political decision with severe economic consequences, brought the agricultural and service sectors to a virtual standstill. Finally, as oil prices fell in the first half of the 1980s, oil revenues plummeted, constraining the regime's ability to support the extravagant socialist policies at the heart of its distributive economic system.

The impact of these economic issues was intensified by Libya's growing political isolation. After closing its embassy in Tripoli in 1980, Washington in 1982 suspended travel to Libya, prohibited Libyan oil imports, and expanded controls on goods destined for export to Libya. Already stung by failed African adventures and diplomatic setbacks throughout the Arab world, Libya's confrontation with the United States culminated in the American bombing of Benghazi and Tripoli in April 1986. Following the attack, Washington imposed economic sanctions, froze all Libyan assets, and ordered American oil companies operating in Libya to cease operations. At the time, American firms were central players in the Libyan oil industry, and this latter decision threatened the overall health of the entire Libyan economy.

Expert at reading public opinion, Qaddafi realized internal discontent was approaching an explosive level and responded with corrective measures, moderating many of the socialist policies advocated since the outset of the 1969 revolution. His ability to execute a policy *volte-face* at a vulnerable time was facilitated by the April 1986 bombing raid. Designed by the United States to destabilize the regime, the attack had the opposite effect, strengthening Qaddafi's hold on power. On the one hand, the bombing attack was met with almost total apathy throughout the country with the size and intensity of demonstrations outside Libya protesting the raid much greater than those inside Libya. On the other hand, the attack invigorated a radical minority led by members of the revolutionary committees who became much more aggressive in their efforts to silence voices of dissent, so aggressive that Qaddafi one year later was describing the committees as overzealous and power-hungry.

The relative impunity with which the raids were executed also discredited and demoralized the armed forces, the institution the United States had counted on to force change in Libya. This encouraged Qaddafi to proceed with plans to abolish the formal military hierarchy and replace it with a vaguely defined "people's militia," an idea he had first surfaced in 1977–78. Finally, the American crusade against Libya embarrassed exiled opposition groups, undermining their popularity and weakening their already limited capabilities. Torn by internal rivalry and dissent, these often small groups were concerned they would be dismissed as nothing more than pawns of American foreign policy. Qaddafi seized on the moment to consolidate his domestic political position even as he continued to oppose the international *status quo*.

To make matters worse, the impact of the bombing attack was totally misread by the Reagan administration which held it up as a great victory against international terrorism when something less was the case. According to a little-known U.S. Department of Defense document which did not become public until February 2000, the Qaddafi regime responded almost immediately to the raid, and the Libyan campaign of retaliation lasted some four years.

Libyan reprisals included the execution of two kidnapped Britons and one American in Beirut, an attack on a U.S. embassy employee in Sudan, and a Libyan missile attack in the direction of a U.S. installation on the Italian island of Lampedusa. In September 1987, Abu Nidal, working for Libya, hijacked Pan American flight 73, causing the death of several Americans; and in April 1988, the Japanese Red Army, under contract to Nidal, bombed the United Service Organizations (USO) facility in Naples, Italy, killing an American soldier. Libyan officials were later tied to the December 1988 bombing of Pan American flight 103 over Scotland and the September 1989 bombing of UTA flight 772 over Niger. During this period, Libyan officials also attempted to recruit a Chicago street gang to attack American airliners with shoulder-fired weapons, a move interdicted by U.S. authorities. These activities, and probably others, contradicted the popular myth propagated by the Reagan administration that the raid ended Libyan support for international terrorism.[2]

GREAT GREEN CHARTER ON HUMAN RIGHTS IN THE ERA OF THE MASSES

Qaddafi's human rights initiatives culminated in the Great Green Charter on Human Rights in the Era of the Masses, adopted by the General People's Congress on 12 June 1988. Intended to open the way for increased economic and political liberalization, the twenty-seven articles comprising the document addressed a variety of personal goals, rights, and guarantees. Based on earlier statements by Qaddafi, the charter guaranteed Libyans freedom of movement, the right to work, and respect for personal liberty. It restricted the scope of the death penalty, stating its total abolition was a regime goal. It outlawed degrading punishment and the ill-treatment of prisoners and proclaimed the right of everyone to a fair trial. It also called for an end to the arms race at a time when Libya boasted one of the highest per capita arms ratios in the world. And it called for the suppression of biological, chemical, and nuclear weapons shortly after Libya had begun its own chemical weapons program, a program it continued for the next twenty years.[3]

The Great Green Charter was issued at a time when Qaddafi was openly questioning the roles and responsibilities of the revolutionary committees and the security services. Highly critical of the failings of the rule of law and acknowledging abuses had taken place, he became overnight the foremost Libyan advocate of legality, freedom, and human rights. While supporters embraced the charter, critics noted it lacked a variety of provisions necessary to give Libyans the civil and political rights traditionally assumed under domestic and international law. Article 11 described private property as "sacred and protected" but noted it could be attacked in the "public interest" without defining what the public interest might entail. Article 25 called on each member of the Jamahiriya to defend his or her country to the death. Article 26 committed all Libyans to the "bases" of the charter, and in so doing, introduced gray areas as to what could be considered treasonous by the government. In turn, Article 27 endorsed *The Green Book* as the guide for the emancipation of the world, in effect sanctioning Qaddafi and the regime.

In the spring of 1989, Libya began to implement many of the provisions in the Great Green Charter. The General People's Congress in March 1989 enacted a law on the consolidation of liberty that retained a ban on religious and political activities. It also passed a law calling for an independent judiciary and later extended this call to include strengthening the people's courts and expanding legal accountability. In May 1989, Libya became a party to the UN Convention against Torture and Other Cruel, Inhuman, or Degrading Treatment or Punishment as well as to the Optional Protocol to the International Covenant on Civil and Political Rights. The process of restoring the rule of law continued into 1990; however, human rights groups noted there was little improvement in the protection of basic rights and freedoms. On the contrary, the position of religious and political dissidents appeared unchanged in the post-Charter era.

In the final analysis, the Great Green Charter on Human Rights in the Era of the Masses could be described most accurately as an attempt to codify many of the principles advocated in theory, if not in practice, by Qaddafi. The essence of the Charter had been foreshadowed in *The Green Book* although a few of its provisions represented a retreat from earlier pronouncements. In any case, elementary human rights continued to be denied the citizens of Libya after 1988. There remained no room for a free press on the false assumption the Libyan people were free to express themselves at the people's congresses. There was no right to strike because Libyans theoretically were the owners of the factories where they worked. There was no place for organized opposition because Libyans theoretically were free to express their opposition within the congress system.

In conjunction with the newfound emphasis on human rights, Libya announced in 1989 the creation of the Qaddafi Prize for Human Rights to recognize annually a Third World figure, organization, or movement in the forefront of "liberation struggles." Founded in Switzerland under a $10 million trust, the first winner of the $250,000 award was jailed South African activist Nelson Mandela. Subsequent winners included Native Americans in the United States and the children of the Palestinian uprising against Israeli occupation. In 1996, Libya awarded the prize to Louis Farrakhan, leader of the Nation of Islam, a Chicago-based organization founded in 1930. Following a prolonged controversy in which the U.S. Treasury Department rejected his request for an exemption from U.S. sanctions barring most economic ties with Libya, Farrakhan traveled to Libya to accept the award but was forced to decline the $250,000 honorarium. The United States also refused to allow the Nation of Islam to accept a $1 billion donation from Libya.

At the August 1988 annual conference of revolutionary committees, Qaddafi sharply criticized the committees, accusing them of political assassinations. He charged that "some people" had infiltrated the revolutionary committees and were physically liquidating elements they believed had deviated from the committees.

"Terrorism, if it arises," he added, "must be terrorism of the masses and not individual or committee terrorism." Qaddafi's remarks, which came less than two months after the proclamation of the Great Green Charter on Human Rights had guaranteed freedom of expression and denounced violence, were intended to shore up popular support.

Less than one month later in a speech marking the nineteenth anniversary of the One September Revolution, Qaddafi announced plans to abolish the country's regular army and police, replacing them with a new popular guard. Arguing traditional armies had proved ineffective in the struggle for freedom, he urged the General People's Congress to transfer existing military units to a Jamahiriya (state of the masses) guard. Qaddafi's announcement appeared to be an extension of earlier proposals to create a people's army parallel to the regular armed forces; however, the extent of the proposed change was unclear. His remarks indicated there would still be military officers with some authority over civilian militias, and some military service would still be required. In announcing the period of mandatory military service would be reduced from two years to one year, he stressed no one would be exempt from such service.

In 1991–92, Qaddafi proposed the division of Libya into approximately fifteen hundred self-governing communes, each of which would be a miniature of the larger state with its own executive and legislative powers and its own budget. Each commune was to create its own thirteen-man cabinet, two members of which would form part of a larger national cabinet, whose exact functions were not detailed. It also remained unclear how this new cabinet, composed of three thousand members would operate. With each commune responsible for its own defense, some observers interpreted Qaddafi's proposal as simply another attempt to fragment the armed forces, reducing the possibility of a future military *coup d'état.*

On 1 September 1994, Libya announced the establishment of cleansing or purification committees made up mostly of army officers or students. Their stated aim was to identify and eliminate counterrevolutionaries as well as to prevent the members of the people's committees from accumulating too much wealth and power. All Libyan citizens were required to give a cleansing committee a periodical accounting of their material wealth and their means of acquiring it. The cleansing committee movement was reinvigorated in the spring of 1996 in an effort to root out speculation and corruption. In a country where at least seventy percent of the economy was controlled by the state, committees were soon busy harassing local merchants and closing down private businesses. In theory, private business was encouraged in Libya, but no one was free to set their own prices. Every shopkeeper was required to post an official government list that limited profits on each sale to ten percent. In practice, some merchants, like traders elsewhere, tried to earn more than the official ten percent. The revitalized cleansing committee effort lasted until mid-1997 and resulted in dozens of arrests, hundreds of fines, and many shops closed until they had revised their prices. In early October 1998, Qaddafi again called for shopkeepers to reduce their prices to officially dictated limits, or he would once more unleash the dreaded purification committees.

WEAPONS OF MASS DESTRUCTION

In a front-page article in *The New York Times*, dated 24 December 1987, the United States charged Libya was building a factory near Rabta that American officials strongly suspected could be used to produce chemical weapons. In conjunction with these charges, the article repeated reports Libya had employed poison gas in its war with Chad and also suggested bilateral trade between Libya and Iran included chemical arms. The article marked the beginning of a prolonged and serious international crisis grounded in the Reagan administration's belief that Libya was developing weapons of mass destruction in the guise of a chemical weapons production facility. Opposed to the proliferation of chemical weapons, Washington was determined to block this new Libyan initiative.[4]

Responding immediately, Libya denied the Rabta facility was intended for the manufacture of weapons of mass destruction. At the same time, Libyan officials condemned the economic embargo implemented in January 1986, in particular what they inaccurately described as a ban on the sale of medicines and medical supplies to Libya. Section (b) of Executive Order 12543, issued by President Reagan on 7 January 1986, specifically excluded "donations of articles intended to relieve human suffering, such as food, clothing, medicine and medical supplies intended strictly for medical purposes" from the U.S. embargo. The Libyan charge was a deliberate distortion of U.S. policy that set the stage for the subsequent Libyan position that the U.S. embargo gave it no choice but to construct the facility at Rabta for the manufacture of pharmaceuticals.

Less than a year later, the United States in September 1988 announced Libya appeared to be nearing full-scale production of chemical weapons. The following month, the director of the Central Intelligence Agency (CIA) charged Libya was building the largest chemical weapons facility in the world; and by the end of year, American and Israeli officials were claiming Libya was creating a "staggering" manufacturing complex at Rabta to manufacture chemical weapons. President Reagan increased the pressure on Libya in late December 1988 when he stated the United States was considering military action against the alleged chemical weapons facility, a statement the Libyans took seriously given the April 1986 bombing raid. As if to make the point, U.S. aircraft in early January 1989 downed two Libyan warplanes off the northeast coast of Libya after the Libyans approached "in a hostile manner." Accusing the United States of a premeditated act, Libyan officials claimed their two planes were unarmed.

Libya responded to the accusations of the United States in a wide variety of different forums, including bilateral diplomatic contacts, international organizations, and numerous press releases. It claimed the technical complex under construction at Rabta was nothing more than a facility designed to produce medicines for the alleviation of sickness and disease. In so doing, it argued its interest in the chemical industry was a legitimate activity and challenged the United States, instead of persisting in its false allegations against Libya, to destroy its own weapons of mass destruction. Noting it had endorsed the 1925 Protocol for the Prohibition of the Use in War of Asphyxiating, Poisonous or Other Gases, and of Bacteriological Methods of Warfare and the 1972 Convention on the Prohibition of the Development, Production, and Stockpiling of Bacteriological (Biological) and Toxin Weapons and on their Destruction, Libya also charged the United States was assisting Israel to acquire chemical and nuclear weapons.

As the United States continued its public accusations against Libya, it exerted quiet diplomatic pressure on the governments of international corporations thought to be involved in the construction of the Rabta complex. Considerable evidence had begun to surface that German firms, in particular, were involved in the project; nevertheless, the West German government denied repeatedly the existence of prosecutable offenses. Official German attitudes changed dramatically in early 1989 following publication of a report acknowledging the involvement of several German firms, especially Imhausen-Chemie, in the construction of the Rabta facility. In response, Bonn tightened export regulations and increased penalties for violations, steps welcomed in Washington.

Fresh reports of activity at Rabta surfaced in early 1990. Again utilizing *The New York Times*, the United States released information suggesting Libya had begun production of small quantities of mustard gas and was striving to reach full-scale production capacity. The reports also suggested small quantities of the nerve gas Sarin were being manufactured. Consistent with the position of the Reagan administration, the George H. W. Bush administration called on the global community to support vigorous efforts to stop the operation. In addition, it warned of a "secondary danger" that the products of Rabta could find their way into the hands of international terrorists and refused to rule out a military attack on the Rabta facility.

In March 1990, the United States revealed it had learned from Italian diplomats that the Rabta complex appeared to be on fire. The official Libyan press soon confirmed this report, charging the United States, Israel, and Germany with collective responsibility for the act. Other Libyans blamed the fire on terrorists, and at least one opposition group claimed responsibility for the fire. Although subsequent reports suggested the entire incident was a hoax, the alleged fire at Rabta defused temporarily the chemical weapons issue; however, the United States by late 1991 was again charging Libya was producing poison gas at Rabta as well as building a second factory in nearby Tarhuna for the manufacture of chemical weapons.

In February 1993, American intelligence sources described the facility at Tarhuna as a subterranean chemical weapons plant, disguised as part of a water project, but capable of producing and storing poison gas. Given the ongoing debate, it later proved significant that Libya had refused to sign the freshly minted Convention on the Prohibition of the Development, Production, Stockpiling and Use of Chemical Weapons and on Their Destruction when the UN Secretary-General opened it for signature on 13 January 1993. In February 1996, the United States renewed charges that Libya was engaged in the proliferation of weapons of mass destruction in the form of chemical weapons. American intelligence sources described the factory under construction at Tarhuna, scheduled for completion in 1997, as the world's largest chemical weapons plant. In response, Libya again denied it was involved in the manufacture of chemical weapons, describing the Tarhuna facility as part of an irrigation system.

In the end, the full extent of Libya's involvement in the production of chemical weapons was not known until early 2004 after it had unilaterally renounced weapons of mass destruction and related delivery systems. According to the Organization for the Prohibition of Chemical Weapons, the body which oversaw the destruction of the Libyan stockpile of chemical weapons, Libya had succeeded in manufacturing a large quantity of mustard gas and possessed precursor chemicals for the production of nerve gas. In addition, it had over three thousand empty bomb casings designed to carry chemical weapons; however, it lacked the long-range missile or other delivery systems required to deliver chemical weapons beyond its own borders.

LOCKERBIE

On 21 December 1988, Pan American flight 103 exploded over Lockerbie, Scotland killing 259 passengers, together with eleven people on the ground. Nine months later, UTA flight 772 exploded over Niger killing 179 passengers. The United States and the United Kingdom issued indictments on 14 November 1991 against two Libyans for the bombing of Pan Am flight 103; and on 27 November 1991, France, the United Kingdom, and the United States issued a tripartite declaration demanding Libya hand over the suspects. When Libya failed to comply, the UN Security Council in March 1992 passed Resolution 748, imposing limited sanctions on Libya. In November 1993, the Security Council passed Resolution 883 which toughened the sanctions in place by freezing Libya's overseas assets, banning some sales of oil equipment, and tightening an earlier decision to end commercial air links.[5]

For the next few years, Libyan foreign policy was dominated by issues related to the sanctions in place. Washington repeatedly pressed for a global boycott of Libyan oil, a move opposed by its European allies as well as by many African and Arab states. Libya later benefited from the windfall in oil prices resulting from the Gulf crisis, and Qaddafi's marginal involvement in the Gulf also gave him a free hand to crack down on Islamist fundamentalists at home. In April 1995, the United Nations relaxed its ban on flights from Libya and allowed EgyptAir to take Libyan Muslims to Saudi Arabia on the annual *haj*. Six months later, Libya requested the UN Security Council's permission to repatriate more than one million African workers, a move it said was prompted by the poor state of the Libyan economy. While the mandatory sanctions imposed by the United Nations undoubtedly had a severe impact on the Libyan economy, most observers agreed the Libyan action was also driven by social unrest in Libya and a desire to use foreign workers as a bargaining chip to press the United Nations to ease the embargo. In any case, the Secretary-General of the Organization of African Unity called in February 1997 for an end to the sanctions on the grounds that African states felt Libya had taken several positive steps towards a resolution of the Lockerbie issue.

By the end of 1997, the UN sanctions were beginning to crack with African leaders taking the lead in opposing them. South African President Nelson Mandela visited Libya in October 1997 to thank Qaddafi for his support during the years of South African struggle against apartheid. Although Mandela completed the last leg of his journey by car to avoid violating the UN sanctions, he called during his visit for a lifting of the sanctions and said the Lockerbie case should be handled by an international tribunal, a view shared by the Organization of African Unity and the Arab League. The presidents of Gambia, Liberia, Tanzania, and Uganda, among others, also visited Tripoli in this time frame. Mandela later defended publicly his ties with Libya during President Bill Clinton's visit to South Africa in March 1998.

In August 1998, Libya accepted an Anglo-American proposal to try the two Libyan suspects in the Lockerbie bombing case at The Hague in the Netherlands under Scottish law. Two months later, the UN General Assembly adopted a Libyan-sponsored resolution aimed at the United States that called for the immediate repeal of laws that unilaterally imposed sanctions on companies and nationals of other countries. The vote was eighty in favor and only two (Israel and the United States) against with sixty-seven delegations abstaining, an unusually large number in a vote of this kind. In the interim, African delegations, including officials from Chad, Gambia, Nigeria, and Sudan, continued to visit Tripoli in violation of the UN ban. In the wake of intense diplomacy by Egypt, Saudi Arabia, South Africa, and UN Secretary General Kofi Annan, Libya eventually handed over the two Lockerbie suspects on 5 April 1999. Once Libya had remanded them, the United Nations suspended its sanctions against Libya, allowing air travel and the sale of industrial equipment to resume. After a lengthy review, the United States took the opposite course, announcing at year end it was continuing the bilateral sanctions on the grounds that the crisis with Libya had not yet been resolved.

The complex rationale behind Qaddafi's decision to hand over the Lockerbie suspects after resisting this action for seven years included several related considerations. First, he had the domestic political situation under control by 1998 but was faced with a rapidly deteriorating economic situation. Consequently, he no longer feared the domestic political repercussions of remanding the two suspects, on the one hand, and desperately needed to open the economy and attract foreign capital, on the other. A less tangible motive was Qaddafi's love of the international limelight and his weariness with a prolonged period of political isolation. Strategically, Qaddafi was motivated by a desire to rebuild alliances in Africa and elsewhere to prevent Libya from being isolated in any potential future conflict with the United States. Finally, the opportunity to renew and enhance ideological and strategic ties with key African states clearly positioned Libya to pursue longer-term objectives in the region.

EUROPEAN RELATIONS

European policy toward Libya after 1986 shared some similarities with that of the United States, especially the common concern for Libyan support for terrorism. At the same time, Europe remained concerned with the commercial impact of the sanctions approach advocated by successive American governments. Given their substantial commercial ties with Libya, European governments generally preferred a more cautious approach in which diplomacy played a lead role.

At the outset of the One September Revolution, France enjoyed excellent relations with Libya and soon became a major arms supplier to the revolutionary government. Bilateral relations later deteriorated with Qaddafi increasingly critical of French willingness to sell arms to all sides in the Middle East conflict. As Libyan relations with Egypt soured, Qaddafi was especially critical of the sale of French weaponry to the Cairo government. From the French perspective, Libya's increasingly aggressive policies in the Sahel and sub-Saharan Africa, a traditional sphere of French influence, became a fundamental source of disagreement.

Once Libya pulled back from its decade-long adventures in Chad, relations with France improved for a time. In a controversial move, the French government credited Qaddafi with assisting in the April 1990 release of three European hostages taken prisoner more than two years earlier by a Libyan-backed terrorist group, the Fatah Revolutionary Council, also known as the Abu Nidal group. Orchestrated by Qaddafi, ostensibly as a humanitarian gesture, their freedom coincided with the delivery to Libya of three Mirage fighters impounded by France since 1986. A senior Palestine Liberation Organization official later suggested the real intent of the Libyan decision to assist in securing the release of the hostages was to resume contacts with the United States by demonstrating Libya controlled radical elements like the Nidal organization.

France later supported the multilateral sanctions imposed by the United Nations on Libya and continued its investigation into the destruction of UTA flight 772. In early May 1997, French investigators asked a Paris court to try Qaddafi's brother-in-law and five other Libyan operatives *in absentia* on charges of bombing the airliner. French officials believed Libya ordered the strike in retaliation for the French deployment of troops to resist the Libyan invasion of Chad in the second half of the 1980s. Evidence in support of the French charges included confidential documents, dating back to one year before the bombing, instructing Libyan agents to plan a strike against French interests. In addition, a Congolese witness testified that Libyan operatives had paid a friend to check onto UTA flight 772 with a Samsonite suitcase containing a bomb. The bomb carrier was supposed to get off at an intermediate stop but was not allowed to do so and died with the rest of the passengers when the plane exploded over Niger.

Libyan relations with Germany, like those with France, suffered from long-standing legal proceedings. When the United States bombed Libya in 1986, Secretary of State George Shultz claimed radio intercepts related to the bombing of the La Belle discothèque in West Berlin, an attack that killed three people and injured 229 others, were the "smoking gun" that proved Libyan complicity in terrorism. While the claims of Shultz proved overstated, a trial opened in Germany eleven years later in an effort to bring to justice those responsible for the attack. As the La Belle proceedings played out, Libya appeared content with a German relationship based on mutual commercial interest and best characterized as normalcy at a low level.

In April 1984, political demonstrations in front of the Libyan embassy in London led to the death of Yvonne Fletcher, a London police officer. British authorities believed the shots that killed her had been fired from inside the embassy. In response, Great Britain ordered the closure of the Libyan embassy and broke diplomatic relations with Libya. In March 1985, British and Libyan representatives opened talks in Rome in an effort to improve relations; however, little progress was possible after Qaddafi repeated threats to retaliate against any European state harboring Libyan dissidents. In the wake of the April 1986 American attack on Libyan targets from British bases, Great Britain banned Libyan Arab Airways flights after evidence in a London trial implicated the national carrier in terrorist activities in Britain. In retaliation, Libya closed its airspace to British aircraft, a move with little practical effect since British carriers had not flown to Libya since the summer of 1986.

Over the next decade, bilateral relations between Great Britain and Libya were strained. In mid-1995, the British defense secretary expressed concern that Libya possessed, or was developing, a ballistic missile capacity to target British facilities on Cyprus and Gibraltar. Without specifying Libya, he added that an increasingly large area of Europe, over the next five to ten years, would be vulnerable to missile attacks from adjacent states. Six months later, the British government expelled the head of the Libyan interest section in the Saudi Arabian embassy on grounds of espionage and intimidation of Libyan opponents to the Qaddafi regime. The Foreign Office insisted the expulsion was unconnected with the death the previous month of a prominent Libyan dissident found stabbed to death in his London grocery store; however, the Libyan diplomat expelled also headed the official Libyan news agency, JANA, the organization charged with monitoring Libyan dissidents.

Following the confiscation of Italian-owned property and the expulsion of some twenty thousand Italian residents, bilateral relations between Libya and Italy improved after 1975 when a tentative agreement was reached on compensation for the property confiscated in 1970. By October 1978, Qaddafi was able to remark that modern Italy was not the imperialist power of the past; and over the next decade, Italy became Libya's primary commercial partner as well as Europe's strongest advocate for an ongoing dialogue with Libya. By the end of the 1980s, Italians dominated the expatriate business community in Libya with an estimated fifty-seven Italian firms in operation there. While commercial relations were notably strong, they did not prevent Qaddafi in October 1989 from demanding Italian compensation for the thousands of Libyans killed, injured, or deported during the 1911–43 Italian occupation of Libya, a claim he would repeat in coming years.

In April 1992, Italy joined its European neighbors in honoring the UN Security Council sanctions imposed on Libya. Rome was less enthusiastic about subsequent U.S. attempts to expand the sanctions in place to include a complete oil embargo. Italian companies insisted on honoring the oil and gas exploration and production contracts concluded with Libya. An early champion of Libyan rehabilitation, the Italian foreign minister flew to Libya to meet with Qaddafi one day after the two Lockerbie suspects were flown to the Netherlands for trial. Italian companies also rushed to expand commercial ties with ENI, the oil and gas group, landing a $5.5 billion natural gas project in July 1999. Italian Prime Minister Massimo D'Alema later flew to Libya in December 1999 for a two-day visit, the first by a Western leader in eight years. His visit reinforced bilateral economic ties that had slowed but never stopped during the embargo years.

In October 1985, Qaddafi made his third and final visit to the Soviet Union. Libyan objectives for the trip included a nuclear reactor convertible to military uses, additional military supplies, increased Soviet purchases of Libyan oil, and the conclusion of a friendship and cooperation treaty. The official Soviet news agency described the discussions as taking place in an atmosphere of friendship and mutual understanding; however, Qaddafi left Moscow with considerably less than the total package. The Soviets agreed to help construct a nuclear reactor, but not one convertible to military uses. Referring the request for additional arms to a commission, they pressed for payment of an estimated $7 billion due for earlier purchases. A deal was concluded to purchase additional Libyan oil for Yugoslavia, but it was not the doubling in the daily Soviet purchase desired by Libya. Finally, an agreement covering economic, scientific, technical, and trade cooperation through 2000 was signed; however, there was no mention in the final communiqué of the friendship and cooperation treaty agreed to in principle two years earlier. Five months later, Qaddafi ruled out any possibility of Soviet bases in Libya, and the Soviets shelved plans for a friendship treaty.

The April 1986 American attack on Libya strained already tense bilateral relations. The Soviets denounced the raid but limited practical support to Libya to a promise to help rebuild its defensive capability. When Qaddafi again threatened to join the Warsaw Pact, he received absolutely no support from Moscow. In the aftermath of the raid, a senior Libyan delegation traveled to Moscow where it found the Soviets were reluctant to extend additional arms credits, rejected a proposed mutual defense treaty, and stressed the growing confusion worldwide in differentiating between Libyan support for revolution and terrorism.

In the second half of the 1980s, the Soviets further distanced themselves from the Qaddafi regime and the multiple agreements in place were often subordinated to simple arms-for-cash deals. In the process, the Libyan–Soviet relationship was strongly influenced by the economic and political reforms initiated by President Mikhail Gorbachev, reforms that eventually precipitated the collapse of the Soviet Union. When reform opponents staged an abortive *coup* in 1991, Libya was among the first states to recognize the Communist hard-liners in their failed attempt to halt Gorbachev's reforms. Qaddafi's hasty decision to recognize the *coup* leaders contributed to a cooling in the bilateral relationship in the aftermath of the implosion of the Soviet Union.

With the collapse of the Soviet Union, Russia stopped import-ing Libyan oil; however, Libya still owed Russia approximately $4 billion, mostly for earlier arms sales. Throughout the 1990s, the Qaddafi regime delayed payment because its outstanding debt helped shield Libya from tighter UN sanctions. A cash-strapped Russia, fearing Libya would be unable to pay its debts, threatened in 1994 to veto a Security Council resolution restricting the export of Libyan oil. Russian opposition to the proposed resolution resulted in a watered-down version that prohibited the export of oil-related equipment to Libya but included no restriction on the sale of oil and gas.

STATUS QUO IN AFRICA

Israeli influence in Africa remained a high priority for Libyan for-eign policy in the second half of the 1980s. In August 1986, Cameroun became the fourth African country, following Zaire, Liberia, and the Ivory Coast, to resume diplomatic ties with Israel; and the Israelis also operated interest sections in Gabon, Ghana, Kenya, and Togo. As part of its broader campaign to undermine the Qaddafi regime, the United States actively supported Israeli efforts to restore diplomatic links with African states. In contrast, the French government was distinctly unhelpful in this regard in part because it was concerned a wider Israeli role in Africa would promote American as opposed to French interests in the region.

To strengthen its African ties, Libya relied heavily on the famil-iar tools of trade and economic aid. Libyan assistance assumed a variety of forms including economic and technical agreements with Nigeria, the establishment of joint venture companies in Benin and Upper Volta, a $1 million check to Mali, and conces-sionary oil sales in Burkina Faso and Ghana. Considerable public-ity often accompanied Libyan aid commitments; nevertheless, it remained difficult to correlate aid commitments with aid disburse-ments with the latter continuing to fall short of the former. This was especially true in the second half of the 1980s when a sharp drop in oil revenues had an adverse effect on Libya's capacity to extend foreign aid.

Elsewhere, Libya continued to rely on non-diplomatic as well as diplomatic means to regain its earlier influence in Africa. A number of sub-Saharan governments, including Burkina Faso, the Central African Republic, Ghana, and Uganda, received significant shipments of arms and military equipment in 1983–87. Over the same period, recruitment into the Islamic Legion continued unabated with Burkina Faso, Djibouti, Ethiopia, Ghana, Mali, Nigeria, and Sudan targeted as prime contributors. By early 1987, the Legion included several thousand Africans with some twenty-five hundred from Sudan alone. In the process, speculation increased as to whether the objectives of the Islamic Legion had broadened to include the establishment of an international revolutionary force.

In Sudan, the Transitional Military Council (TMC), which replaced the Numayri government in 1985, pursued improved relations with Ethiopia, Libya, and the Soviet Union. In May 1985, Qaddafi arrived in Khartoum for an unscheduled visit in which he called for unity, criticized multiparty democracy, and suggested Egyptian President Husni Mubarak would suffer the same fate as former Sudanese President Jaffar al-Numayri. Even as the Sudanese government deepened its relationship with Libya, it resisted Libyan demands for political union and rejected Qaddafi's open hostility toward Egypt. The Khartoum–Tripoli axis complicated relations with neighboring states, and Sudan also found itself increasingly entangled in the mounting crisis between Libya and the United States. The State Department reduced its embassy staff in Khartoum in late 1985 and warned Americans not to travel there because Libyan subversives were operating from the Libyan embassy. After rejecting the American charge, the TMC quietly deported several Libyan envoys. When U.S. warplanes bombed Benghazi and Tripoli in April 1986, Sudanese politicians and citizens alike denounced the raid as an unwarranted attack on the sovereignty of a fellow Arab state.[6]

Soon after Sadiq al-Mahdi became prime minister in May 1986, Qaddafi made another uninvited visit to Khartoum in which he renewed calls for political union and for subversion against Egypt and the United States. Although the visit embarrassed the Sadiq government and alarmed Sudan's neighbors, Khartoum relied increasingly over the next three years on military assistance from Libya. Sadiq was overthrown in a military *coup d'état* in June 1989 and replaced by an Islamist-oriented military government that took a tough stance toward civil strife. The political crackdown alienated Sudan's traditional supporters, including Libya. Calling for the release of Sadiq, Qaddafi strongly criticized the Islamists for mixing politics and religion and for alienating the non-Muslim communities of the Sudan; nonetheless, Libya continued to provide weapons and oil supplies. In March 1990, Khartoum and Tripoli concluded a Charter of Integration that provided for the coordination of military and security forces together with joint efforts to disseminate Arabic culture and language; and in May 1991, Sudan adopted a people's committee-type political system.

While Qaddafi criticized the politicization of Islam in Sudan, he embraced the Arabization of non-Arab peoples in the country. His policy here was consistent with his thoughts in part three of *The Green Book*, published a decade earlier:

> It is, therefore, of great importance for human society to maintain the cohesiveness of the family, the tribe, the nation and the world in order to benefit from the advantages, privileges, values and ideals yielded by the solidarity, cohesiveness, unity, intimacy and love of the family, tribe, nation and humanity.[7]

Libya also increased its military presence in Darfur in western Sudan, a battleground for Chadian forces and dissidents at the expense of local villagers. Darfur provided a vital sanctuary in Qaddafi's prolonged, eventually unsuccessful, attempt to influence events in Chad. Concerned the fighting in Chad continued unabated, the Organization of African Unity in February 1987 issued an appeal to Chad and Libya, together with interested parties, to seek a peaceful resolution to the conflict. African leaders meeting in Cairo a few weeks later condemned foreign intervention in Chad. Chadian forces eventually inflicted a devastating defeat on Libyan forces at Wadi Doum in March 1987, an event that marked a turning point in the war as it made the Libyan position untenable. Libyan forces soon retreated north to the Aouzou Strip.

Chad and Libya resumed diplomatic relations on 3 October 1988; and they later agreed to submit their border dispute over the Aouzou Strip to the International Court of Justice (ICJ) at The Hague. After the court ruled in favor of Chad's claim in February 1994, Chad and Libya signed a joint communiqué in which Libya returned the Aouzou Strip to Chad. With the collapse of Libyan foreign policy in Chad, Qaddafi's interest in Sudan also waned. In the early 1990s, Libyan–Sudanese relations were strained by Sudanese support for militant Islamist reformers, and Libya played a greatly reduced role in Sudanese politics in the second half of the decade.

At the same time, Libya continued to be implicated in destabilization attempts across Africa. Kenya in April 1987, Benin in August 1988, Burundi in May 1989, and Ethiopia in March 1990 expelled one or more Libyans accused of activities incompatible with their diplomatic status. In Ethiopia, two Libyan diplomats were also implicated in a plot to blow up the Hilton hotel in Addis Ababa. Elsewhere, Libya held talks with Burkina Faso, Ghana, and Uganda in November 1988 to strengthen political ties and concluded trade agreements the following year with Burkina Faso, Mali, Rwanda, Uganda, Zanzibar, and Zimbabwe. Reports continued to surface in the early 1990s of Libyan involvement in the internal affairs of neighboring states, like Mali, Nigeria, and Rwanda, and bilateral relations with many of them remained tense.

The next few years were difficult ones for the Qaddafi regime as well as for most Sahelian and sub-Saharan states. Many countries in Africa, especially the Francophone states, endured an extended period of international decline driven by poor economic performance, destructive corruption, and political stagnation. In turn, Libya entered a period of international isolation in which global sanctions, combined with lower oil prices, crippled the economy and invigorated opposition to the Qaddafi regime.

TURN TO THE MAGHRIB

As the Libyan government wooed, threatened, and cajoled a wide variety of African states, it moved to improve relations with its North African neighbors. In the Treaty of Oujda, concluded in August 1984, Libya and Morocco agreed to a form of federation in which each state retained its sovereignty. The union promised economic benefits to both parties; however, its long-term prospects were never good as the political outlooks of the signatories too often were diametrically opposed. Therefore, it came as no surprise when Morocco declared the agreement null and void in August 1986.

In search of a major ally in the region, Libya turned to Algeria where unity talks were held as early as November 1986; and in a June 1987 address to the People's National Assembly in Algiers, Qaddafi called for unity between Algeria and Libya. A new Tunisian government, following the 1987 deposition of Qaddafi's arch-rival, Habib Bourguiba, led to a restoration of diplomatic relations in February 1988. The Libyan–Tunisian rapprochement led to a number of economic and political agreements, including the removal of all obstacles to the movement of people between the two states and a tripartite agreement with Algeria on a gas pipeline. In May 1988, Algeria and Morocco agreed to resume diplomatic relations. While the reconciliation did not involve Libya directly, it invigorated talk of a Grand Maghrib that had begun earlier in the year. In mid-December 1988, Libya and Tunisia agreed to several practical steps toward integration, including free cross-border trade, joint offshore exploration for oil and gas, and linking electrical grids. The two neighbors also created an Executive Committee to ensure decisions on cooperation, integration, and unity moved forward.

On 17 February 1989, Libya joined Algeria, Mauritania, Morocco, and Tunisia in a new body, the Arab Maghrib Union (AMU), intended to improve regional economic cooperation. For the first time since the mid-1960s, a North African unity agreement included all the Maghrib states and thus was not vulnerable to being undermined by a rival alliance. In a communiqué announcing its creation, the new organization was described as a "fundamental phase on the path of Arab Unity" that supported the Palestinian people and was prepared to consolidate ties with other African states to promote economic development. Prompted by upcoming changes within the European Community, the member states viewed the newly created Arab Maghrib Union as essential to their survival after the European Community in 1992 had removed all tariff and customs duties on goods moving between their countries. The European Union (EU) posed a direct threat to Maghrib export markets, especially agricultural products, textiles, and light industrial goods. In addition, labor migration from the Maghrib to Europe had slowed, and European tourism in North Africa was on the decline.

With Qaddafi often appearing deliberately controversial, Libyan enthusiasm for Maghribi integration in general and AMU activities in particular was a recurrent subject of discussion among fellow member states. At one point, he proposed Chad, Niger, Mali, and Sudan should join the organization; and at another, he argued AMU resources should be mobilized to continue the struggle against Israel. Early AMU sessions highlighted some of the problems that would continually plague the new organization. Qaddafi twice postponed the opening of the second summit, claiming prior engagements; and before it eventually opened, he declared publicly that he would refuse to assume the six-month rotating chairmanship, like he had refused to be president of Libya. His position here surprised many observers who recalled that he had precipitated a crisis in the Organization of African Unity in 1982–83 when he aggressively sought to assume the chairmanship of that organization.

Over time, the AMU states reached a number of economic and political agreements; nevertheless, the governments of Algeria, Mauritania, Morocco, and Tunisia found it difficult to maintain regular links with Libya. The borders between Algeria, Libya, and Tunisia were closed on more than one occasion in the mid-1990s after Libya's neighbors expressed concern with its apparent support for radical factions within their countries. The AMU states also opposed occasional attempts by Libya to involve Egypt in North African affairs. Finally, the UN sanctions imposed on Libya after 15 April 1992 highlighted its regional and international isolation, thwarting serious attempts at economic or political integration.

RULE OF INTERNATIONAL LAW

In contrast to Qaddafi's recurrent manipulation of domestic law, he turned to international law on three occasions in the first twenty-five years of the revolution to resolve disputes with neighboring states. In 1978, Libya and Tunisia brought a dispute involving delimitation of the continental shelf before the International Court of Justice (ICJ). Libya contended the continental shelf was a prolongation to the north of the continental landmass and that a boundary due north from its border post at Ras Ajdir would reflect this prolongation. Tunisia argued the natural prolongation of the continent in the area was much further east and that the continental shelf at issue was effectively a submerged portion of Tunisia. The court in 1982 rejected both proposals, treated the boundary area as two separate sectors, and proposed a delimitation line in two segments which both Libya and Tunisia accepted.

In May 1976, Libya and Malta asked the International Court of Justice to rule on the delimitation of the continental shelf between their respective states. Under the terms of a special agreement, the court was asked to decide the applicable principles of law and how those principles should be applied to the dispute; however, the task of actually drawing a boundary line was to be negotiated by the disputing parties. In June 1985, the court delivered a judgment limited by the terms of the special agreement and by the competing claims of Italy, not a formal party to the dispute. Rejecting Libya's main argument in favor of that of Malta, the court found that customary international law governed the case and that any delimitation should reflect equitable principles. Accordingly, it initiated the process of delimitation, adjusted a possible boundary out of equitable considerations, and left Libya and Malta to complete the task.

After Libya and Chad concluded a peace agreement in August 1989, the settlement called for the parties to resolve ownership of the disputed territory through negotiation. When that proved impossible, they submitted the issue to the International Court of Justice in August 1990. Libya argued there was no existing boundary with Chad and asked the court to determine one. Chad took the position that a recognized frontier with Libya had existed for decades, and simply asked the court to determine the course of the frontier. The court delivered its judgment in February 1994, ruling the boundary between Libya and Chad was defined by the Treaty of Friendship and Good Neighborliness concluded by France and the United Kingdom of Libya in August 1955. The treaty referred to a line that had featured commonly in atlases and maps published after 1919 as the Chad–Libya boundary. Since the court rejected Libyan claims south of that line, Chad clearly emerged the winner in this case.

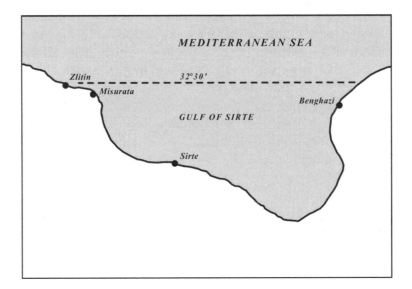

Map 8 Gulf of Sirte Closing Line

In contrast to these successful applications of international law, Libya found itself without legal grounds when it came to its alleged sovereignty in the Gulf of Sirte, also known as the Gulf of Sidra, the large gulf in the Mediterranean Sea off the central coast of Libya. On 9 October 1973, Libya declared its sovereignty over the waters of the gulf, sending the United Nations a *note verbale* to that effect. Describing the gulf waters as internal waters, the note argued the gulf was surrounded by Libyan territory on three sides, was located within its territorial waters, constituted an integral part of Libya, and was under its complete sovereignty. It concluded defiantly that public and private ships would no longer be allowed to enter gulf waters without prior Libyan approval.[8]

With the Gulf of Sirte enclosing almost three percent of the Mediterranean Sea, a number of states, including the United States, immediately challenged the Libyan claim. Most of these protests were based on the argument that the Libyan action converted international waters into internal waters in an unlawful abuse of the high seas. After 1974, the United States regularly challenged Libyan claims in the gulf through formal protests and direct action. In 1977–80, the United States conducted no fewer than ten exercises in the vicinity of the gulf; and in August 1981, American aircraft shot down two Libyan aircraft some sixty miles off the Libyan coast. A second incident occurred in March 1986 during the fourth major U.S. naval exercise off the Libyan coast in only three months. When fired upon by surface-to-air missiles from an anti-aircraft battery near Sirte, American aircraft responded, attacking the missile battery and sinking four Libyan patrol craft in the process. Both in 1981 and 1986, the United States justified its actions as necessary to maintain freedom of navigation in international waters.

The United States was not alone in challenging Libyan claims in the Gulf of Sirte. France, Great Britain, Greece, Italy, Malta, Turkey, and the Soviet Union, among other states, protested the declared enclosure of the gulf. Italy had protested the Libyan action from the start and repeated its strong reservations in its intervention before proceedings at the International Court of Justice involving the Libya–Malta continental shelf case. Malta was also quick to reject the Libyan argument that the gulf fell within Libyan sovereignty, reiterating its reservations twelve years later during the March 1986 UN Security Council debate occasioned by the fighting in the region. The Arab League, which condemned the American resort to force in 1981 and 1986, also refused to support the Libyan claim, accepting the right of the United States to challenge it peacefully.

MOUNTING OPPOSITION

Opposition to the Qaddafi regime, much of it led by Islamist groups like the Muslim Brotherhood and the Islamic Liberation Party, grew in the second half of the 1980s. In May 1984, an attempted attack on Qaddafi's residence by a group with ties to the National Front for the Salvation of Libya was foiled; and in the spring of 1985, two new attempts to assassinate him were reported. In September 1986, twenty-six men were arrested, accused of belonging to the Islamic Jihad Organization, a group Libyan authorities had discovered only months earlier; and in October 1986, seven alleged members of Hizbullah, the Party of God Group, confessed on television to the murder of a revolutionary committee member who had attempted to stop their private trading activities. In February 1987, nine alleged members of two Islamist groups, Hizbullah and the Islamic Jihad Organization, were executed in public, accused of two assassinations, the attempted assassination of Soviet military personnel in Libya, and acts of sabotage and treason. Six of the accused were civilians and were hanged in public in Benghazi. The remaining three were soldiers and were executed by firing-squad in their barracks. In March 1989, Qaddafi attacked Islamist extremism, arguing radical religious movements were an attack on Arab nationalism, Arab unity, socialism, and progress.

Unrest spread throughout much of Libya in early 1989 after security forces raided a Benghazi mosque, closing its teaching section for public criticism of Qaddafi's religious views. Several mosques in Tripoli were also raided. Protests in Benghazi, Tripoli, and elsewhere decried deteriorating economic conditions and the limited job opportunities for recent graduates as well as the attacks on religious leaders and institutions. Forced conscription into the army, combined with the deadly defeat suffered at the hands of Chadian forces in early 1987, combat in which several thousand Libyans died, was another source of discontent. Opposition activity outside Libya was also on the increase. In January 1987, for example, a number of exiled opposition groups, including the National Front for the Salvation of Libya, Libyan National Struggle Movement, Libyan National Democratic Front, and Libyan National Organization, met in Cairo where they formed a joint working group to oppose the Qaddafi regime.

Qaddafi responded to the mounting opposition with a mixture of carrot and stick with the emphasis on the stick. In March 1988, he freed hundreds of political prisoners, including former colleagues who had run afoul of the regime. Qaddafi was shown on Libyan television bulldozing the walls of Furnaj Prison where many detainees were held, falsely stating there were no more political prisoners in Libyan jails. Qaddafi claimed to be tormented by the very idea of people behind bars, realizing the futility of imprisonment as a punishment. A few days later, he went to an emigration office and allegedly destroyed lists of Libyans forbidden to leave the country, generally for political reasons. Qaddafi's human rights initiatives in this period culminated in the adoption in June 1988 of the Great Green Charter on Human Rights.

In March 1990, when delegates to the General People's Congress rejected government efforts to reduce public expenditures, calling instead for lower taxes, cheaper housing loans, and increased spending on state-owned industries, Qaddafi responded by attacking corruption in government. Later in the session, the congress elevated Qaddafi to the status of supreme leader, a position which gave him authority to overturn any policy decision with which he disagreed. After the congress adjourned, Qaddafi took fresh steps to reassert his control over the General People's Congress, replacing key members of the General People's Committee in a move widely interpreted as a victory for hard-liners.

By the early 1990s, opposition to the regime had become better organized and more outspoken. There were also occasional signs of an alliance emerging between militant Islamists and disaffected members of the Libyan armed forces, a potentially serious threat to the regime. In October 1993, a major army rebellion, with links to the National Front for the Salvation of Libya, took place in Misurata, and army units also may have staged revolts in other military installations. With local troops thought insufficiently loyal to quell the rebellion, the regime deployed the air force to bomb the rebels into submission. In September 1995, Islamist militants again battled security forces in Benghazi. Subsequent *coup* attempts in 1996–97 also suggested an alignment between Islamists and the military.

At the same time, popular opposition to Qaddafi became more widespread and increasingly volatile. In an unprecedented display of public criticism, football hooliganism in July 1996 turned into political demonstration when a crowd at a Tripoli football match began to chant anti-Qaddafi slogans. The riot was sparked by the fact that one of the teams on the field was financed by one of Qaddafi's sons, a connection not lost on the referees who made some highly controversial calls in favor of young Qaddafi's team. When fans began to protest, invading the pitch and attacking the referees, security officials opened fire on the crowd, killing as many as fifty people.

New arrivals on the opposition landscape included the Libyan Martyrs Movement, founded in 1993, and a more mysterious group, the Libyan Islamic Fighting Group, which first surfaced in 1995 although some sources claimed it was established as early as 1991. Both organizations successfully recruited Libyan veterans who had fought against Soviet forces in Afghanistan and returned home to bleak economic prospects. Ironically, the United States in 2003 designated the Libyan Islamic Fighting Group a foreign terrorist organization on the grounds that it opposed the United States as well as Libya. The regime also faced opposition from various tribal factions, principally in Cyrenaica, as well as ideological movements, mostly operating outside the country. Exiled Libyan opposition groups grew in number but continued to lack cohesion and integration.

After three decades in power, considerable opposition to the Qaddafi regime clearly existed; however, it was badly fragmented and had to deal with substantial regime support, especially among younger, less well-to-do elements of Libyan society. Qaddafi's charismatic leadership and the regime's distributive economic policies, generally successful in providing its citizens with necessary goods and services, combined to generate a relatively high level of regime support. Moreover, the Libyan leader continued to balance skillfully the three institutions, the armed forces, the congress-committee system, and the revolutionary committees, that formed the core of his support. The careful juxtaposition of these separate but related institutions, intertwined as they were with tribal alliances, allowed Qaddafi to dominate the overall political system.

9

LIBYA RESURGENT

The whole world is moving towards the [political] system governing Libya. The entire world is now talking about the third way, the
third theory, popular socialism, people's security and people's
leadership. They are all saying that people should take part in the
leadership and that there is no escape from making people participate in the leadership. All heavy weights, from [Bill] Clinton to
[Tony] Blair, the pillars of capitalism, have recognized this fact.

Mu'ammar al-Qaddafi, June 2001

End the Barcelona Process. When that happens, you can say that
Europe andAfrica are two distinct entities separated by a sea. Yes,
when that process is annulled, I will be convinced that we are two
separate entities not one. However, when you talk of the Euro-
Mediterranean cooperation, you have included me in Europe.
You make me in Libya a part of Europe.

Mu'ammar al-Qaddafi, November 2006

If Africa succeeds in unity, this will be beneficial to the Africans
and to the world similar to the unification of Europe now ... I want
the major players and the world to help in Africa's unity and to
contribute towards the establishment of the United States of
Africa because this means stability, peace and security. It is also
beneficial for the world economy and world peace.

Mu'ammar al-Qaddafi, May 2007

In August 1998, almost a full decade after the bombing of Pan Am flight 103 over Lockerbie, Scotland, Libya accepted a joint American-British proposal to try the two Libyan suspects in the case, Abdel Basset Ali Mohmed al-Megrahi and Al-Amin Khalifa Fhimah, at The Hague in the Netherlands. Once the suspects were remanded into United Nations custody in April 1999, the UN Security Council suspended the multilateral sanctions regime in place since 1992. The United States pursued a different course, easing but not suspending the bilateral sanctions gradually put in place beginning in the late 1970s. In July 1999, the UN Security Council reaffirmed its position that the multilateral sanctions regime would be lifted permanently only after Libya complied with all outstanding Security Council demands.[1] Over the next few years, Libya underwent a remarkable transformation. Once an international outcast, it successfully reestablished commercial and diplomatic relations with most of the world's nations, including the United States. Domestically, it continued its slow evolution from a highly socialist state to a Western-style, free market system in which its citizens were increasingly expected to fend for themselves. Only the domestic political arena avoided meaningful change.

OUT OF AFRICA

In response to the suspension of multilateral sanctions, Qaddafi launched a series of fresh initiatives in Africa, designed to end Libya's economic and political isolation. As a growing number of African heads of state traveled to Libya to pay their respects, he unveiled a series of peace efforts to resolve disputes in the Congo, the Horn of Africa, Sierra Leone, and Sudan. In April 1999, Qaddafi brokered a cease-fire agreement between Congolese President Laurent Kabila and Ugandan President Yoweri Museveni, and he later hosted a five-nation summit on the Congo. In the interim, he dispatched a controversial peacekeeping force to Uganda; and in June 1999, he was welcomed in South Africa as the last official guest of the Mandela administration. In the Horn of Africa, Eritrea and

Ethiopia reportedly accepted a Libyan peace plan to end their border conflict; however, a final solution to the dispute proved as elusive here as in the Congo. Qaddafi also dispatched an envoy to the Sierra Leone peace talks in Togo and met with government and opposition leaders in Sudan in an effort to end the civil war. Although these diplomatic initiatives yielded few practical results, the Libyan leader sought to leverage the sympathy and support he had received from African governments when the UN sanctions were in place to play a wider regional role in the post-sanctions era.

Qaddafi had been interested in Africa since the outset of the One September Revolution, and these initiatives were a complex mix of old and new that marked a major shift in Libyan foreign policy from the Arab world to the African continent. According to senior Libyan diplomats, this shift was rooted in part in the reluctance of Arab leaders to support Libya in its conflict with the United States and the United Kingdom over the Lockerbie issue. There was still an anti-Israeli element in the overall policy, but Israel was no longer the central concern of Libyan policy in the region. Moreover, the related issues of colonialism and neocolonialism had become passé and were seldom mentioned except in a rhetorical context. And the former emphasis on Islam was also much diminished. In what became a motif of the new diplomacy, Qaddafi repeatedly proclaimed that the future was for big spaces, and Libya was part of the African space.

At the July 1999 Organization of African Unity (OAU) summit in Algiers, Qaddafi was feted as a long-lost brother by fellow African heads of state. In response, he resurrected his vision for African unity, calling for the creation of a Pan African Congress to boost political unity, together with an Integration Bank to accelerate implementation of a treaty for the Economic Community of Africa. He also invited African leaders to attend an extraordinary OAU summit in Libya, timed to coincide with the thirtieth anniversary of his One September Revolution, to discuss a restructuring of the OAU charter to strengthen relations among member states. In turn, the OAU summit in Algiers called for the immediate and complete lifting of all sanctions against Libya.

Before the extraordinary summit opened in Libya, most African diplomats took a cautious approach, stressing their leaders had agreed to attend largely out of respect for a veteran revolutionary whose steadfast support of liberation movements had helped end colonialism on the continent. On the other hand, few expected concrete actions to emerge from the meeting. In advance of the summit, Qaddafi called for the creation of a United States of Africa, pressing the idea in a meeting of OAU foreign ministers held prior to the summit. African heads of state later refused to endorse his call for a United States of Africa; however, they issued a declaration at the end of the summit calling for a stronger Organization of African Unity, together with the creation of a Pan-African parliament, African Monetary Union, and African Court of Justice. Qaddafi later reiterated his call for African unity at the Africa–European Union summit in Cairo in April 2000.

Ironically, even as Qaddafi pushed his vision of a United States of Africa, Libya itself was the scene in September 2000 of violent xenophobic attacks by the indigenous population against African migrant workers. The riots engulfed African nationals, indiscriminately injuring and killing people from numerous states, including Burkina Faso, Chad, Ghana, Niger, and Nigeria. Generated by economic competition and social strain, the events also made a statement about levels of identity in Libya which continued to reflect Arabism, family, Islam, state, and tribe.[2] As Qaddafi busied himself chasing a leadership role in Africa, Libyans at home faced serious unemployment problems and grew increasingly concerned with the large number of foreigners in the country, most of them African immigrants. Reflecting an ideological commitment to Africa, as well as the charter requirements of the Community of Sahel-Saharan States (COMESSA), more widely known as the Communauté des Etats Sahélo-Sahariens (CEN-SAD), Libya had relaxed its visa restrictions on Sahelian and sub-Saharan Africans. While the riots tarnished Libya's reputation in Africa, the flow of migrants continued, and Libya continued to pursue its African destiny.

As Libya pushed its diplomatic agenda in multilateral forums and its peace efforts in the Congo, Sudan, and the Horn of Africa, it expanded its bilateral relations with African states. Libya concluded cooperation agreements in a variety of areas from education to science to culture with Niger in 1997, Eritrea in 1998, and Senegal and South Africa in 1999. In addition, Libya extended bilateral financial aid to several African states in 1999–2000, including Ethiopia, the Ivory Coast, Mali, Tanzania, Uganda, and Zimbabwe. At the same time, Qaddafi continued to intervene in Africa's internal crises, deploying Libyan forces in May 2001 to prop up the Central African Republic after a failed *coup* attempt by dissident soldiers. In August 2001, he agreed to supply most of Zimbabwe's fuel requirements through Libyan-owned Tamoil. The 2001 agreement with Zimbabwe was a loan, where earlier aid had been a gift, and Libya later reneged on the deal when it realized the hostile international reaction the loan provoked and Zimbabwe's inability to repay. Libya also announced joint venture investment projects in Chad, Ethiopia, Mali, and Tanzania. The agreement with Chad, which established a joint company to promote oil extraction, was viewed by some observers as a throwback to Libya's old policy of seeking control over African resources.

In July 2002, the African Union (AU), a regional organization modeled after the European Union (EU), replaced the thirty-five-year-old Organization of African Unity. Accorded a prominent speaking role at the opening ceremonies, Qaddafi rejected all conditions on foreign aid, openly contradicting the call of AU chairman and South African president Thabo Mbeki for donor nations to steer aid and investment to countries demonstrating good governance. On the other hand, he later bowed to Mbeki's promotion of the New Partnership for Africa's Development (NEPAD), a scheme to promote democracy and good government in Africa in exchange for increased aid and investment from the developed world. President Mbeki also discounted Qaddafi's idea of a standing, continental army. Instead, the African Union endorsed the concept of a standby force consisting of civilian and military contingents based in countries of origin.

In July 2004, Libya agreed to allow the World Food Program to truck food through Libya to the troubled Darfur region of Sudan as well as to Sudanese refugee camps in Chad. At the same time, the Libyan foreign minister rejected any foreign presence in Darfur, apart from the framework of the African Union, on the grounds that deployment of a Western peacekeeping force would cause an "explosive" situation. The African Union deployed an observer mission to Darfur in mid-2004, and in September 2004 the Pan-African parliament met for the first time. Qaddafi later criticized UN Secretary General Kofi Annan's call in February 2005 for the European Union and North Atlantic Treaty Organization to help end the humanitarian crisis in Darfur. In a statement consistent with his long-held belief in Africa for the Africans, he argued the African Union should increase its involvement to meet the peace-keeping challenge in Darfur. Thereafter, Libya hosted a series of inconclusive mini-summits in an effort to find an African solution to the Darfur crisis as well as to ease tensions between Chad and Sudan.

Celebrating the third anniversary of the African Union's formation, Qaddafi in July 2005 hosted the fifth ordinary session of the AU assembly. In a long welcoming address, he repeated the call for greater African unity, citing specific needs like a common defense system and a single monetary zone. Amid global calls to combat poverty in Africa, Qaddafi also counseled African nations to stop begging, arguing calls to the Group of Eight (G-8) nations to forgive existing debts would not make a future for Africa. AU leaders later asked their membership to present a united front in their dealings with the developed world, exhorting the richer nations of the world to make good on promises to help Africa climb out of poverty. With banners at the summit proclaiming "The United States of Africa is the hope," Qaddafi also called for creation of a single African passport to facilitate movement on the continent. Two years later, he called for the African Union to be turned into an embryonic federal government.

Earlier, Qaddafi had taken the lead in February 1998 in establishing the Community of Sahel-Saharan States. This initiative recalled Libyan attempts in the 1970s to forge a federation of Saharan states, an objective opposed at the time by its North

African neighbors.³ With headquarters in Tripoli, CEN-SAD linked poor African states with oil-rich Libya. Burkina-Faso, Chad, Libya, Mali, Niger, and Sudan were founding members with the Central African Republic and Eritrea joining in 1999. By mid-2007, the organization's membership had expanded to twenty-five states, representing more than half the continent's population. With an objective to promote comprehensive economic union based on integrated national development plans, the Banque Sahelo-Saharienne pour l'Investissement el le Commerce (Sahel-Saharan Bank for Investment and Trade) was established in 1999 to fund external trade and development projects. CEN-SAD gained observer status at the UN General Assembly in 2001 and concluded association and cooperation agreements with a variety of UN agencies and institutions.

Expanding its regional ties, Libya in June 2005 joined the Common Market for Eastern and Southern Africa (COMESA), a regional economic community established in 1994 to promote regional integration through trade development. The organization had twenty-one members stretching from Egypt to Namibia. Both the African Union and the New Partnership for Africa's Development had recognized COMESA as a vehicle for African development, especially the development of the continent's infrastructure.

Elsewhere, Libyan policies raised the possibility of a new pan-Saharan political alliance. In August 2004, Mauritania accused Libya of supporting a failed *coup* to oust President Maaouiya Ould Taya; and in February 2005, it arranged the return of Nigerian soldiers held hostage by Tuareg rebels, including amnesty for the Tuareg involved in their capture. In April 2005, Qaddafi addressed a delegation of Tuareg at Oubari in the Fezzan, stating Libya considered itself the protector of the Tuareg and describing them as "lions and eagles of the desert." He went on to say that Libya had been the ancestral home of the Tuareg before they dispersed into what is now Algeria, Burkina Faso, Mali, Niger, and Nigeria; therefore, they should consider Libya their "base and support" as it would not allow anyone to attack them. Cloaked in ambiguity,

Qaddafi's remarks were taken by some to justify Qaddafi's tendency to meddle in Saharan-Sahelian affairs. At another level, they also appeared a warning to Algeria and the United States to curb their imperial designs in the region. Two years later, Qaddafi denounced U.S. plans to deploy an American command force, known as Africom, on the continent.

Another example of Qaddafi's influence on the region was his announced plan to expand the Libyan armed forces by creating "employment" for some three thousand Tuareg, Tubu, and other Saharan peoples. Ostensibly, the plan was designed to impress American officials by offering attractive employment to Saharan tribesmen to encourage them to forego working as guides and drivers for trans-Saharan traffickers. That said, the potential creation of a new mercenary force controlled by Libya in an already volatile area was naturally concerning to governments in and out of the region.[4]

In late July 2006, Somalia accused Libya of providing weapons for Islamist militants who had seized control of much of the country, a charge Libya emphatically denied. In January 2007, Libya announced plans to invest $23 billion in agricultural, oil, and tourism projects in Benin. Less than a week later, Qaddafi announced at a CEN-SAD summit in Sirte that Libya would provide financial support to AU peacekeepers deployed to Somalia. And in early February 2007, the Central African Republic signed a Libyan-brokered peace accord with two rebel groups. In April 2007, Libya dispatched military observers to the volatile border between Chad and Sudan as an alternative to a UN peacekeeping force; unfortunately, they were unable to prevent additional armed clashes. Nevertheless, Libya continued to host regional summits aimed at reconciling differences between neighbors Chad and Sudan and mediating the conflict in Somalia.

When it came to Africa, Qaddafi in the post-sanctions era clearly looked to the past as he moved forward to the future. Where Libyan diplomacy earlier had focused on anti-Israeli, anti-imperial, and anti-colonial objectives, largely in support of broader pan-Arab goals, the new approach was wider in scope, less ideological in tone, and more pragmatic. A mix of old and new, when compared to past policies of deceit, division, and discord, Libya's new initiatives in Africa offered the promise, if not yet the reality, to make a positive contribution to political unity and economic development in the region.

LOOKING EAST AND WEST

Qaddafi's renewed interest in Africa came at the expense of his long-standing focus on the Middle East, especially Israel and the Palestinian question. At the opening session of the OAU summit in Lusaka in July 2001, for example, Qaddafi concentrated on African issues, ignoring the Palestinian question in general and the *intifada* in particular. Elsewhere, the Libyan leader occasionally referenced the Palestinian issue; however, his comments typically combined ideology with indifference as he distanced himself from an issue that had dominated Libyan foreign policy for much of the last three decades. Early in 2004, Qaddafi suggested Libyan Jews, many of whom had fled in 1948 with the remainder forced out in 1967, were entitled to compensation for their confiscated property as long as they had not occupied a Palestinian home after 1948. A delegation of Libyan Jews visited Libya in mid-October 2004 in a trip they described as an important opening; however, the group failed to meet with Qaddafi. Thereafter, competing Jewish groups complicated negotiations with the Libyans on the issue of Jewish property claims, and little progress was made. At the same time, Qaddafi continued to promote a mixed state, Israltine, as the solution to the Israeli–Palestinian conflict.

At the fifth ordinary session of the AU assembly in May 2005, Qaddafi mocked the very concept of a Middle East:

> Colonialism divided Asia into the Middle East, Far East and Near East, which have nothing to do with Africa. From now on, I hope no one will try to link North Africa to the Middle East, because this [is] a colonialist racist tag. Please excuse my language, but we normally refer to the Middle East as the "Dirty East."[5]

Consistent with this attitude, Qaddafi repeatedly threatened to pull out of the Arab League although he never made good on his threat. On the contrary, he continued to attend Arab summits, using them as a platform to cajole and berate his fellow members. Over time, different issues and policies contributed to Qaddafi's frustration with the Arab world, but the central one remained its failure to develop a coherent pan-Arab movement. In refusing to attend an Arab summit in Saudi Arabia in March 2007, for example, Qaddafi characterized the Arab world as "not serious" and described joint Arab action as "dysfunctional." On the eve of Saddam Hussein's hanging, Qaddafi described the former Iraqi leader as a prisoner of war, and upon Saddam's death, Libya declared three days of mourning and cancelled public celebrations around the Eid religious holiday. Later, the revolutionary committees announced they would raise a statue to Saddam alongside that of Umar al-Mukhtar, the national hero who led the Libyan resistance against the Italian occupation. Qaddafi's relations with his Arab neighbors looked set to continue strained; however, as he moved to position himself on a wider political stage, there was little risk he would alienate himself completely from them.

In North Africa, Qaddafi moved to revitalize the moribund Arab Maghrib Union (AMU), founded by Algeria, Libya, Mauritania, Morocco, and Tunisia in 1989 to promote regional peace and prosperity. With the Lockerbie issue moving toward resolution, violence in Algeria diminishing, and a resolution of the Sahara question in the offering, the stage seemed set to reinvigorate an organization hamstrung by regional disputes after 1994. In May 1999, representatives of the five AMU member states agreed to hold the first AMU summit in five years. At the same time, the Libyan representative expressed interest in increasing the scope of the Arab Maghrib Union, possibly integrating the newly formed CEN-SAD grouping.

In mid-2000, Qaddafi joined Tunisian President Zine El Abidine Ben Ali in a renewed call for the North African summit, which had failed to meet in 1999, to be held as soon as possible. Unfortunately, a variety of issues, including the conflict in the

Western Sahara and the domestic political situation in Algeria, combined to block meaningful progress. The AMU foreign ministers did meet in Algiers in January 2002, but they once more failed to agree on a venue for the pending AMU summit. Informed observers agreed progress on the issue was unlikely until Algeria and Morocco resolved the Sahara dispute. The AMU summit was again postponed in May 2005 when Morocco rejected an Algerian proposal to include the Sahara issue on the agenda. Over the next few years, political disagreements hindered efforts to improve integration on economic and political goals, and only limited progress was made. For example, the AMU member states in March 2007 announced plans to liberalize regional air transport in 2008.

As it worked to expand traditional relations in the Maghrib, Libya also looked to establish new ties in the Far East, especially with the People's Republic of China. The Chinese foreign minister, Tang Jiaxuan, paid an official visit to Libya in January 2001, concluding agreements on cultural and information cooperation; and the Chinese president, Jiang Zemin, visited Libya in April 2002. In the course of the first visit to Libya by a Chinese head of state, the two governments concluded an agreement opening Libya's hydrocarbon sector to Chinese firms as well as a $40 million deal for a Chinese company to extend Libya's rail network. At the same time, Tripoli resisted Beijing's pressure to end Libyan relations with Taiwan. On the contrary, Tawian's CPC Corporation concluded an exploration and production sharing agreement with Libya in April 2007. A high-level North Korean delegation also visited Libya in mid-2002, signing agreements on scientific and technical cooperation as well as investment promotion. At the time, observers dismissed as speculative rumors that the visit also included talks related to missile sales, but the issue took on new meaning after Libya's end-2003 decision to renounce unconventional weapons, a decision North Korea denounced.

In July 2006, President Gloria Macapagal Arroyo visited Qaddafi in the first ever visit by a Philippine head of state. Acknowledging Libya's long-term role in forging an end to hostilities in the Muslim-dominated southern Philippines, she invited Libyan businessmen to invest in the Philippines while also pressing for an improvement in the contract conditions and general welfare of Filipinos working in Libya. After concluding an agreement to train Libyan nurses, President Arroyo identified construction, furniture, health services, and tourism as four areas of future cooperation.

Elsewhere, Libyan foreign policy included new initiatives in Central America and the Caribbean, an area of the world Libya had largely ignored for almost two decades. In 1977, Qaddafi had recognized Cuban efforts to fight imperialism and invited Fidel Castro to visit Libya. Following Castro's visit, the two states established diplomatic relations, initiating an era of close collaboration. Qaddafi also established close bilateral relations with the Sandinista government in Nicaragua and the New Jewel Movement in Granada during the 1979–83 reign of Maurice Bishop. In addition, he invited leftist leaders and associated revolutionaries from Antigua and Barbuda, Barbados, Dominica, the Dominican Republic, St. Vincent and the Grenadines, and St. Lucia to come to Libya for seminars and paramilitary training.[6]

Although Libya failed in the 1980s to become a major diplomatic force in Central America and the Caribbean, it renewed its efforts in 2001, promising three Caribbean states access to a $2 billion development fund, offering to buy bananas at above market prices, and providing an immediate grant of $21.5 million. The Libyan initiative was the product of a visit to Libya by the prime ministers of Dominica, Grenada, and St. Vincent and the Grenadines. Originally, the prime ministers of Antigua and St. Kitts and Nevis also committed to the visit, but they later withdrew, suggesting preparations for the trip were inadequate. The visit to Libya by senior Caribbean officials and the aid offered by Libya worried both U.S. officials and other Caribbean leaders who expressed concern about Libyan foreign policy objectives in Latin America. Qaddafi raised fresh concerns in Washington in June 2007 when he loaned Nicaraguan President Daniel Ortega, a Cold War-era enemy of the United States and an ally of Venezuela President Hugo Chávez, *bête noir* of the George W. Bush administration, a jet airplane to travel to Iran.

EUROPEAN RELATIONS

In conjunction with its overtures to Africa, Asia, and the Caribbean, the Qaddafi regime moved to expand its already extensive relations with the major European states. Throughout the 1990s, the European Union (EU) had attracted some eighty-five percent of Libyan exports and generated seventy-five percent of Libyan imports. Germany, Italy, and Spain alone absorbed eighty percent of Libya's exports. Libyan imports were dominated by Germany and Italy, but the United Kingdom was also a significant exporter to Libya. Encouraged by Libyan initiatives, the European Union in 1999 reassessed Libyan participation in the Euro-Mediterranean Partnership, commonly known as the Barcelona process, a regional body inaugurated by the 1995 Barcelona Declaration; and in April 1999, Libya was a first-time observer at the Euro-Mediterranean Conference.

Qaddafi's visit to EU headquarters in Brussels in late April 2004 marked his official rehabilitation as a credible world leader, pardoned if not forgiven for past excesses. In October 2004, the EU lifted its remaining sanctions against Libya, including the arms embargo implemented in 1986, in part because Italy hoped to supply Libya with surveillance equipment to help stem the flow of illegal migration from Africa. In addition to the provision of surveillance gear, the EU sought cooperation with Libya in training programs, asylum application management, and social awareness initiatives.

In June 2005, EU officials announced they would work with Libya to stop the flow of illegal migrants transiting Libya on their way to Europe, once again expressing the hope that Libya might engage fully in the Euro-Mediterranean Partnership. One month later, the European Commission released one million euros to support Libya in its fight against HIV/AIDS. Earlier, the European Union had rejected a guilty verdict in a case involving five Bulgarian nurses and a Palestinian doctor charged with deliberately infecting more than four hundred children with the HIV virus and urged Libya to release the detainees. Libya eventually freed the six imprisoned health care workers in July 2007; however, resolution of the immigration question remained an outstanding issue.

Libya declared its intention to join the Euro-Mediterranean Partnership as early as 2004; however, the years passed and no formal application was submitted. The Qaddafi regime was reluctant to become too active in the regional process, in part because of its self-described role as an independent intermediary between Africa and Europe. Libya also took the position that it could not participate in an initiative whose objective was to create "a zone of peace, stability, and security in the Mediterranean" when one of its members, Israel, occupied the territory of another, Palestine. Israel was an active participant in the Barcelona process, and while the *acquis* did not expressly declare that all member states must recognize the sovereignty of each other, the acceptance of fellow members' right to exist was implicit in the document. Upon accession, Libya would have to sit on the same committees and working groups as the Israelis and be prepared to enter into dialogue and share information. Additionally, Libyan participation in the so-called 5+5 Group, consisting of five Maghribi states, Algeria, Libya, Mauritania, Morocco, and Tunisia, and five European states, France, Italy, Malta, Portugal, and Spain, served to increase its participation in political dialogue as a possible precursor to wider integration in the future. Finally, Libya already enjoyed most of the advantages of a free trade regime with Europe because its energy exports were not subjected to tariffs. Recognizing it could achieve most of what it needed from Europe without committing itself to the Barcelona process, Libya along with Syria remained the missing link in the European Union's project to create a Euro-Mediterranean Free Trade Area (MEFTA) by 2010.[7]

Libyan ties with Italy have long been the closest of any European state. With extensive trade and investment at stake, Italy was an early champion of Libyan rehabilitation. The Italian foreign minister met with Qaddafi just one day after the two Lockerbie suspects landed in the Netherlands, and the Italian prime minister completed a two-day visit to Libya at that year end. Thereafter, Italian diplomatic and commercial relations with Libya were a blend of old and new. On the one hand, Libya had long provided some twenty-five percent of Italy's total energy imports; and with the activation of the Green Stream pipeline in October 2004, its share increased to thirty percent. The end to multilateral sanctions also invigorated bilateral economic ties that slowed but never stopped during the embargo era. On the other hand, Libya continued to press Italy for restitution for damages from the colonial period as part of a wider Libyan policy of encouraging all African states to press for damages from their former colonial rulers. In particular, the Qaddafi regime pressed Italy to build a coastal road from Tunisia to Egypt in a token reparation for its colonial past. Italy agreed to fund the feasibility study for the project but not construction of the road.

In 2005, Libya revived the "Day of Revenge" celebration, commemorating October 7, the day on which Italy invaded Libya in 1911 and the same day in 1970 that Libya expelled some twenty thousand Italian residents after confiscating their property. In March 2006, after rioters attacked the Italian consulate in Benghazi, Qaddafi warned the Italian government that he could not rule out future attacks on Italian property and citizens if Italy continued to refuse to pay compensation for the murder of thousands of Libyans during colonial rule. As the tension ebbed and flowed, an Italian court in April 2007 ruled that an ancient statue of Venus taken from Cyrene to Rome at the outset of the Italian rule was not part of Italy's cultural heritage and should be returned to Libya.

In late February 2006, Italian judges closed the book on the Moussa Sadr case which involved the disappearance in 1978 of the Shiite cleric Imam Moussa Sadr, concluding there was no proof of Libyan involvement in the matter. Founder of the Amal movement, Sadr vanished in the course of a visit to Libya. Shiite leaders long contended he was incarcerated or killed in Libya, a charge Libya denied, contending he most likely fell victim to an inter-Shiite power struggle after he left the country. Earlier in the year, an Italian official determined that Sadr had entered Italian territory after departing Libya, a claim Italy had denied for decades, but his whereabouts after his arrival in Italy remained a mystery. The Sadr family and the Amal movement condemned the decision of the Italian court, charging it was simply another attempt to placate the Qaddafi regime.

The tide of illegal immigrants flooding southern Europe, especially Italy, from Libya also remained a subject of ongoing discussion. Beginning in 2004, Italy financed the repatriation of immigrants from Libya to their countries of origin, along with the construction of detention camps for illegal immigrants, offered police training, and supplied material for border control. The construction of camps on Libyan soil for asylum seekers proved a controversial policy with many Europeans concerned with human rights issues, and in December 2004, Qaddafi declared in a moment of frustration that Libya was not in a position to be the "coastguard of Europe." In July 2005, the Italian and Libyan navies completed their largest joint naval exercise in the Mediterranean since their resumption in 2002; nevertheless, Libya adamantly refused to accept total responsibility for Europe's immigration problems. Concerned a migration policy increasingly influenced by Europe would antagonize its African partners, Libya pressed for a policy in which the European Union shared the burden and helped to alleviate the socioeconomic problems in Africa responsible for the flow of migrants.[8]

The British government also moved quickly to reestablish commercial and diplomatic relations with Libya. Once Libya surrendered the two Lockerbie suspects, Great Britain agreed to restore full diplomatic relations as soon as Libya assumed full responsibility for the 1984 murder of the London police officer, Yvonne Fletcher. Once Libya had satisfied this demand, diplomatic relations were restored in July 1999, and the new British ambassador to Libya took up his post at the end of the year. British officials later opened a commercial fair in Tripoli in May 2000, the largest of its kind since the suspension of sanctions. Great Britain also served as the key intermediary in the tripartite negotiations leading to Libya's renunciation of unconventional weapons and related delivery systems in December 2003, and Prime Minister Tony Blair visited Libya in March 2004, the first such visit since Prime

Minister Winston Churchill came to Libya during World War II. As the two leaders exchanged promises to fight terrorism, it was announced in London that Britain and Libya were sharing sensitive intelligence information on al-Qaida and affiliated terrorist groups in North Africa. Outgoing Prime Minister Blair later returned to Libya in May 2007 as part of a farewell tour of Africa.

In France, a Paris court in March 1999 condemned *in absentia* six Libyans to life imprisonment for the attack on UTA flight 772; however, the court failed to raise the question of Qaddafi's personal responsibility. Hamstrung by legal proceedings, French commercial interests struggled to exploit the global rehabilitation of Libya. The normalization of Franco-Libyan relations proceeded slowly after 2001, receiving a boost in early 2004 when Libya agreed to increase the compensation to the families of the victims of the UTA attack. Libya had agreed in 1999 to pay $33 million, but the families demanded more after Libya agreed to a higher payout in the Lockerbie case. Unlike Pan Am flight 103, Libya refused to accept responsibility for the UTA attack; however, as a humanitarian gesture, it agreed in January 2004 to pay $170 million in compensation to the families of the 170 UTA victims. The payment was made through the Qaddafi International Foundation for Charitable Associations, headed by Saif al-Islam al-Qaddafi, Qaddafi's eldest son by his second wife and his heir apparent.

President Jacques Chirac visited Libya in November 2004; and two months later, the French defense minister signed a letter of intent covering military cooperation with Libya. In May 2005, France and Libya agreed to cooperate in the reactivation of the Tajura research reactor for the production of radioisotopes for medical and industrial use, and in March 2006, the two states signed an accord for the peaceful use of nuclear energy. In July 2007, one day after the six imprisoned health care workers were freed, President Nicolas Sarkozy met with Qaddafi and agreed to build a nuclear reactor to power water desalination plants to meet projected water shortages in coming years.

Libyan relations with Germany also suffered from ongoing legal proceedings. In this instance, the proceedings involved the 1986 bomb attack on the La Belle discothèque in West Berlin. After a four-year trial, a German court in mid-November 2001 found four people guilty of planting the bomb that killed three people and injured 229 others. The judge said the court was convinced the Libyan government was to a large extent responsible for the attack, but he also stated the personal responsibility of Libyan leader Qaddafi had not been proven. Libya denied responsibility for the attack but agreed in mid-August 2004 to pay $35 million in compensation to the more than 160 non-American victims of the attack. Once again, the payment was made through the Qaddafi International Foundation for Charitable Associations. Lawyers sought separate compensation for two American soldiers killed and the 169 Americans wounded in the attack. At the time, Germany was Libya's second largest trading partner behind Italy, and German commercial interests later increased with the end of the La Belle affair.

Chancellor Gerhard Schroeder traveled to Libya in October 2004 where he met with Qaddafi and visited a site operated by Wintershall, the oil arm of chemicals giant BASF. Active in Libya since 1958, Wintershall accounted at the time for some ten percent of Libyan oil production, making it the country's third largest oil producer. In the course of the visit, Qaddafi complained that Libyans were still being injured by landmines planted by German forces during World War II. When he demanded compensation, the German leader suggested it was in the best interests of both countries to put the past behind them. In early May 2005, Chancellor Schroeder renewed an invitation for Qaddafi to visit Germany, and in November 2006, the German foreign minister described Libya's return to the international scene as a positive example for other states in the region.

WAR ON TERROR

Once Libya had remanded the two suspects in the Lockerbie bombing, the United States reevaluated its policy toward Libya.

Ambassador Ronald E. Neumann, Deputy Assistant Secretary for Near East and South Asian Affairs and later ambassador to Afghanistan, signaled the change in a November 1999 address in which he acknowledged the "positive steps" taken by the Qaddafi regime. Symptomatic of the change, the White House in February 2000 decided not to challenge Libyan participation in a UN mission to the Democratic Republic of the Congo, the first Libyan participation in an international peacekeeping operation in a decade. Concurrent with its evolving public diplomacy, the Clinton administration opened secret talks with Libya in mid-1999 aimed at ensuring Libyan compliance with all relevant UN resolutions. These bilateral negotiations were later suspended in the run-up to the 2000 U.S. presidential elections out of concern they might become public and cause a scandal.

In the immediate aftermath of the 9/11 terrorist attacks on the United States, Qaddafi became an enthusiastic recruit to the war on terror, condemning the attacks and expressing sympathy for the victims. In the following months, American and British officials conducted lengthy information sharing sessions with their Libyan counterparts. In commenting on these talks in January 2003, Saif al-Islam al-Qaddafi emphasized that his country was "doing our part" to support the United States in the war on terrorism, "exchanging intelligence about the al-Qaeda network." Libyan leader Qaddafi made the same points in a March 2004 *Newsweek* interview.

Libyan cooperation with the United States in the war on terror was motivated in large part by the fact that many of the Islamist organizations targeted by the White House also threatened the Qaddafi regime. At the first session of the secret talks opened by the Clinton administration in May 1999, the Libyans recognized a common threat from Islamist fundamentalism and agreed to cooperate actively with the United States in fighting al-Qaida. Long a target of Islamist radicals, the Qaddafi regime in the wake of 9/11 freely shared intelligence on alleged allies of Osama bin Laden, like the Libyan Islamic Fighting Group. In turn, the Bush administration in 2003 added the Libyan Islamic Fighting Group to its list of foreign terrorist organizations on the grounds that the group also posed a threat to the United States. Finally, Libya launched a website in January 2002, offering a $1 million reward for information on people, mostly regime opponents tied to Islamist movements, wanted by Libya.

In August 2003, Libya accepted responsibility for the actions of its officials in the 1988 bombing of Pan Am flight 103 and agreed to pay $2.7 billion in compensation to the 270 families of the victims of the attack. Following a delay occasioned by French efforts to increase the payout to the families of the victims of the UTA flight 772 bombing, the UN Security Council lifted its multilateral sanctions on 12 September 2003. While the United States welcomed the move, it announced American sanctions would remain in place until Libya fully addressed a number of concerns underlying those measures. The concerns articulated by U.S. officials included Libya's alleged poor human rights record, lack of democratic institutions, destructive role in African regional conflicts, and pursuit of weapons of mass destruction. Of the concerns cited by the Bush administration, only the pursuit of unconventional weapons, so-called weapons of mass destruction, had figured in the original U.S. rationale for imposing sanctions on Libya.

In March 2003, a Libyan representative approached the British government, initiating talks with the United Kingdom and the United States aimed at dismantling Libya's unconventional weapons programs. The three-party talks that took place in London over the next nine months, like the Lockerbie negotiations, were structured around an explicit *quid pro quo*. In return for a verifiable dismantling of Libyan weapons programs, the United States was prepared to lift its bilateral sanctions. The London talks were conducted in the utmost secrecy; however, indications of progress surfaced in the fall of 2003. In a late October 2003 interview, Saif al-Islam al-Qaddafi spoke persuasively of Libya's desire to rejoin the international community, suggesting it would soon be making an important announcement in this regard. Eventually, on 19 December 2003, the Libyan foreign minister announced that Libya had decided of its own "free will" to be completely free of internationally banned weapons.[9]

In response to its renunciation of unconventional weapons, the United States took steps to lift its bilateral sanctions regime, expanding commercial and diplomatic ties with Libya. Washington lifted the travel ban on 26 February 2004 and announced an easing of economic sanctions two months later. In April 2004, the United States announced it was lifting its veto on Libyan membership in the World Trade Organization (WTO), and in July, the organization gave Libya a green light to begin membership negotiations. On 20 September 2004, President Bush ended the national emergency with Libya, effectively lifting the remaining sanctions. Finally, the White House in mid-November 2004 asked congress to lift the U.S. ban on Export-Import Bank loans to Libya, arguing action was necessary to facilitate U.S. investment. In conjunction with these moves, Libya in late January 2005 awarded eleven of fifteen new exploration and production sharing agreements to American oil companies. In February 2005, the United States lifted travel restrictions on Libyan diplomats, allowing them to move freely about the country. As relations expanded, Washington in the summer of 2005 announced a plan to establish military relations with Tripoli, and later in the year, Qaddafi invited President Bush to visit Libya.

At the same time, Libya remained on the State Department's list of state sponsors of terrorism, pending resolution of charges that Qaddafi financed a 2004 plot to assassinate Saudi ruler Crown Prince Abdullah bin Abdulaziz al-Saud, a potentially volatile situation that Saudi Arabia calmed in August 2005 by pardoning the alleged plotters. Frustrated by the perception of a lack of good faith and action on the U.S. side, Libya in 2005 withdrew the outstanding $540 million from the escrow account in Switzerland established to compensate the families of the victims of the Lockerbie bombing. Under the terms of the August 2003 agreement, the Libyans had agreed to pay the families $4 million each when the UN sanctions against Libya were lifted, another $4 million each when the United States lifted its bilateral sanctions, and the final $2 million each when Libya was removed from the terrorism list. The Lockerbie agreement also stipulated a deadline for

Libya's removal from the list, after which time the final payment would be forfeited.

In an effort to maintain good relations with the United States and to avoid antagonizing the families of the Lockerbie victims, Libya extended the deadline for the final payment several times; however, when it again expired in February 2005, Libya refused another extension in an effort to push U.S. officials to comply with the terms of the deal. With the time schedule for the third payment long past and the bulk of the compensation paid, the Lockerbie case appeared to be secondary to other developments in bilateral relations, and the initial U.S. reaction to the Libyan withdrawal was surprisingly muted. For a time, the focus shifted to trade, investment, and security cooperation; however, congressional allies of the families of the Lockerbie victims later blocked meaningful progress in the bilateral relationship until the families received full restitution. In June 2007, the House Appropriation Committee passed an amendment blocking funds for a new embassy in Tripoli until the Bush administration certified Libya was complying with its agreement to compensate the families. In July 2007, following the administration's appointment of Gene Cretz as the next American ambassador to Libya, four U.S. senators announced they would delay Senate confirmation of the appointment until Libya made the third and final payment owed the families.

ECONOMIC REFORM

Throughout the 1990s, oil production flagged for a number of reasons, including the imposition of economic sanctions, falling demand, and aging oil fields. With the level of domestic dissatisfaction tied closely to economic issues, the Qaddafi regime recognized the need to revitalize the ailing economy; however, it was reluctant to initiate broad reforms as long as the country was subject to economic sanctions. As the decade ended, the economy responded positively to the suspension of sanctions, increased demand for petroleum products, and stronger global oil prices. Oil-based revenues increased sharply, contributing some fifty percent of gross domestic product (GDP), ninety-seven percent of exports, and seventy-five percent of government revenues in 1999–2003.

Dependent on the hydrocarbon sector, the economy also remained largely state controlled. In July 2006, the World Bank described Libya as one of the least diversified oil-producing economies in the world with its hydrocarbon sector representing about seventy-two percent of GDP, ninety-three percent of government revenues, and ninety-five percent of export earnings. The hydrocarbon sector accounted for less than three percent of employment, with an estimated seventy-five percent of employed Libyans continuing to work in the public sector, and private investment remained low at approximately two percent of GDP. Libya also faced a serious unemployment problem, compounded by a high rate of population growth and a low rate of job creation.[10]

In September 2001, Qaddafi had launched a strong attack against corruption and the inefficient use of oil resources; and over the next two years, the regime promoted economic liberalization, focused on diversification, privatization, and structural modernization. In so doing, government officials skillfully employed terms, like "transparency" and "partnership," largely foreign to them in the past. Dissatisfied with the slow rate of progress, Qaddafi, in a June 2003 speech to the General People's Congress, initiated a major shift in economic policy when he declared the country's public sector a failure, called for the wholesale privatization of the oil industry, together with other sectors of the economy, and pledged to bring Libya into the World Trade Organization. In October 2003, newly appointed Prime Minister Shokri Ghanem, a vocal proponent of privatization, announced a list of 361 public sector firms targeted for privatization or liquidation in 2004. His administration also unified the multi-tiered exchange rate in a much-needed currency devaluation that increased the competitiveness of Libyan companies and attracted foreign investment. Efforts at privatization accelerated in 2004 after Libya renounced unconventional weapons and the means to deliver them and the United States began to ease the bilateral sanctions long in place.

Foreign direct investment in Libya totaled some $4 billion in 2004, up six-fold from the previous year.

Addressing a December 2004 strategy conference in Dubai, Prime Minister Ghanem outlined a development strategy centered on economic diversification. Emphasizing the gradual nature of proposed reforms, he stressed an increased role for the private sector did not mean the role of the public sector would end abruptly. On the contrary, he saw the public and private sectors complementing each other for an extended period of time. This proved a difficult balancing act as public reaction to regime decisions to cut subsidies and lift import tariffs soon demonstrated. Public criticism of liberalization policies escalated after the government in May 2005 imposed a thirty percent hike on fuel prices and doubled the price of electricity for consumers of more than five hundred

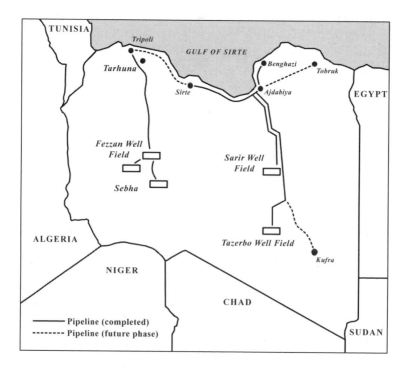

Map 9 Great Manmade River Project

kilowatts a month. A related decision in July 2005 to lift custom duties on more than 3,500 imported commodities raised concerns about job security in factories ill-equipped to face competition. With the speed and scope of the reform process uncertain, Saif al-Islam al-Qaddafi, a strong supporter of economic reform, took a symbolic step in early 2006, changing the name of his organization from the Qaddafi International Foundation for Charitable Associations to the Qaddafi Development Foundation.

Even as Libya reiterated its commitment to a course of economic liberalization, work continued on the Great Manmade River (GMR), a grandiose scheme conceived by Qaddafi to transport underground water via pipeline hundreds of miles from its origins in the southern desert to agricultural projects along the coast. Begun in 1983, construction was originally envisioned to be a five-year project; however, work continued well into the twenty-first century. With up to thirty years estimated to complete the GMR project, its expected cost, including related infrastructure, mushroomed to $25 billion. The project's intended use evolved over time as fresh water demand for domestic consumption and industrial applications increased more quickly than originally forecast. Given its size and complexity, the scheme naturally was not without its critics. Detractors argued it was too costly and encouraged agricultural development that would necessitate permanent subsidies. Subsequent studies suggested it was cost-effective for municipal uses, especially when compared to alternative costs for desalination, albeit not for agricultural applications. When other critics charged the project could damage the entire North African aquifer system, supporters countered the water supplied by the Great Manmade River would supply Libya's water needs for 800 years.

A major cabinet reshuffle in March 2006 replaced the reform-minded Ghanem with his more malleable deputy, Ali Baghdadi al-Mahmudi. As part of the reshuffle, the energy ministry was eliminated, and Ghanem was named chairman of the National Oil Company (NOC). The cabinet shake-up was widely viewed as a victory for conservative hardliners, and the much-trumpeted privatization program, which in the non-hydrocarbon sectors had gained little traction under Ghanem, slowed to a crawl. Prime Minister Mahmudi refrained from attacking the policies of his predecessor, but he did little in support of the economic reforms touted by Ghanem. As a result, the reform process outside the hydrocarbon sector continued to be implemented in an ad hoc, opaque manner with its pace and effectiveness compromised by human capacity constraints.

In the wake of the cabinet reorganization, a series of statements by Qaddafi added to the confusion as to the speed and direction of reform policy. After Libya's planning minister in June 2006 encouraged international companies to look beyond the oil sector and think of investing in construction, health, or tourism, the Libyan leader in a July speech said he wanted to curb the role of foreigners in the economy to ensure Libya's wealth remained at home. One month later, he scolded the nation for its over-reliance on oil and gas revenues, foreigners, and imports, telling Libyans to manufacture the things they needed. In a speech marking the thirty-seventh anniversary of the One September Revolution, Qaddafi subsequently encouraged unemployed Libyans to emigrate to Africa, warning them they must move quickly before the best-paid jobs were taken by Chinese and Indians. The regime later arrested several Libyan businessmen on grounds that they were monopolizing the commercial environment and violating the principles of "people's socialism," a new term employed by Libyan officials to emphasize economic liberalization must be consistent with the principles of *The Green Book*. Difficult to interpret, Qaddafi's contradictory remarks, together with the actions of isolated Libyan officials, did little to reassure potential investors.

HYDROCARBONS, THE EXCEPTION

In contrast to the uncoordinated, piecemeal approach to reform which characterized other sectors of the economy, the reform process in the hydrocarbon sector was more efficient from the

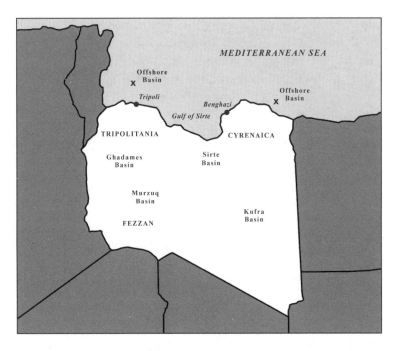

Map 10 Oil and Gas Deposits

start. Libyan crude oil production had peaked at 3.7 million barrels a day (b/d) in 1970, dropping to less than 1.0 million b/d in the mid-1980s. With proven reserves estimated to be 39.1 billion barrels, the largest in Africa, a central objective of Libya's new economic policy was to return to a level of 3.0 million b/d no later than 2015. This was to be accomplished in two stages with the first stage an increase to 2.0 million b/d by 2010. Oil production in 2005 exceeded 1.6 million b/d and approached 1.8 million b/d in 2006 so 2.0 million b/d by 2010 was readily achievable. The target of up to 3.0 million b/d no later than 2015 was more problematic. Moreover, the target year for reaching 3.0 million b/d varied from 2010 to 2012 to 2015, depending on which Libyan official was speaking, with no earlier than 2015 the most realistic date.[11]

The Ghanem administration also assigned a high priority to the expansion of natural gas production, a relatively new objective for

Libya. Proven natural gas reserves were estimated to be 51.3 billion cubic feet, the third largest in Africa, and unexplored reserves could double that figure. Wider exploitation of this resource, most especially increased domestic use, promised to free up oil for export as well as to increase natural gas exports. The Western Libya Gas Project (WLGP), designed to move natural gas from the off-shore Bahr Essalam field in the Mediterranean and the onshore Wafa field near the Algerian border to a coastal processing plant at Melitah, became the showpiece for Libya's renewed interest in exploiting natural gas reserves. In full operation, WLGP was expected to provide some thirty percent of Italy's energy needs. Central to the project, the Green Stream pipeline, a 322 mile pipeline connecting Libya and Sicily, came on line in October 2004, and trial production from the Bahr Essalam field began in August 2005. Achievement of a related objective, attracting $30 billion in foreign investment by 2010, was essential if Libya was to achieve its longer-term goals in oil and gas production.

The principal vehicle used by Libya to stimulate foreign investment in the hydrocarbon industry was a new round of Exploration and Production Sharing Agreements (EPSAs), offering enhanced incentives for oil and gas exploration in an open, competitive bidding environment. The first round of EPSA, phase four, marked a significant shift in the way Libya did business, validating the claims of Prime Minister Ghanem that the National Oil Company was committed to a more open business environment with streamlined approval procedures. For the first time, the primary factor in choosing bid winners was the percentage of oil and gas production the oil companies were willing to share with the state, with the higher the share, the better their chances. A secondary factor was the bonus the companies paid the state when the contracts were signed. Subsequent bid rounds refined, but mostly mirrored, the process adopted in round one. The new process, which incorporated public opening of bids with automatic awards based on pre-set criteria, was a welcome change from the earlier system in which the NOC negotiated in parallel with competing bidders, a process that lacked transparency and often resulted in delays in concluding agreements.

After 1974, EPSAs were the preferred Libyan approach to the hydrocarbon industry; however, Libya also developed a bilateral model to spur infrastructure development. Royal Dutch/Shell announced in May 2005 an agreement with Libya covering an upgrade of the existing liquefied natural gas plant at Marsa al-Brega, together with the exploration and development of five blocks in the Sirte Basin. After winning acreage in nine of fifteen exploration areas in round one of EPSA, phase four, Occidental Petroleum negotiated in July 2005 a resumption of operations in its historical contract areas. In December 2006, Italian authorities announced that ENI was set to renew its long-term energy partnership with Libya in a deal that included construction of a liquefied natural gas plant; and in May 2007, BP announced a seven-year development agreement that covered seventeen exploration wells, together with related investment in gas processing, transport, and liquefaction. One month earlier, Dow Chemical had announced a joint venture agreement with the NOC to upgrade the existing petrochemical complex at Ras Lanuf.

The National Oil Company also encouraged production sharing agreements, known in the industry as Development Production Sharing Agreements (DPSA), in which foreign companies revived and expanded output at fields that were losing production after decades of use. Finally, it considered offering service contracts to companies to develop untapped fields previously thought too small to be economically viable. In both scenarios, the development of known reserves was attractive to oil companies because it eliminated the risks associated with drilling in new areas.

From the very beginning, a cornerstone of Libyan hydrocarbon policy has been its determination to avoid domination by one or more large international oil companies. This policy served the state well, especially in the mid-1980s when the American oil companies were forced to withdraw. In the first three phases of EPSA, round four, more than two dozen companies from over a dozen countries were successful in the bidding. The wide variety of companies awarded acreage, when tied to the various other agreements Libya was negotiating with oil and gas producers, aptly demonstrated that diversification remained a core state goal.

SOCIAL CONDITIONS

In the mid-1990s, Qaddafi suppressed dissent within the military and tribal groups; thereafter, internal opposition came largely from Islamist fundamentalist groups. Dismissing Islamist radicals as "mad dogs," Qaddafi checked their influence in a three-part policy which entailed undermining the religious authority of the *ulema,* refuting Islamist ideas, and harshly repressing Islamist opposition. To enhance his political legitimacy and establish his undisputed authority, Qaddafi called for a stricter application of Islamic law. The General People's Congress responded in February 1994, extending the application of Islamic law and granting new powers to religious leaders, including the right to issue religious decrees.

At the same time, the regime sought to refute Islamist authority through an anti-Islamist campaign. Steering a middle path between hard-line religious opponents and the general population, which was largely opposed to militant Islam, Qaddafi directed the security forces to deal severely with radical Islamists. As part of this policy, the General People's Congress in 1997 passed a series of measures authorizing collective punishment for tribes or individuals harboring Islamists. In April 2000, Libya executed three of eight Islamist militants extradited from Jordan. Benghazi was a center of opposition activity in the 1990s; and anti-regime activities, including the assassination of two senior security officers, were again reported in mid-August 2000. After that time, the Qaddafi regime appeared to have largely contained, but not eliminated, the radical Islamist threat.[12]

Outside Libya, a plethora of opposition groups continued to operate, but they were unable to coalesce into an effective, united front. Six of these groups, the Libyan Movement for Change and Reform, Libyan Constitutional Grouping, Libyan Islamic Group,

Libyan National Organization, Libyan National Democratic Rally, and National Front for the Salvation of Libya, met in August 2000 to discuss joint strategy. The vagueness of the joint statement issued at the end of the meeting suggested ideological differences and factional disputes continued to bedevil attempts to work together. Prior to the meeting, the Qaddafi regime made an attempt to entice exiles to return home and called on the General People's Congress to establish a committee to resolve the cases of exiled opponents willing to return to Libya. In May 2003, only weeks after the United States-led occupation of Iraq, five opposition groups, the Libyan National Alliance, the Republican Assembly for Democracy and Social Justice, the Libyan Tmazight Congress, the National Front for the Salvation of Libya, and the Libyan Movement for Change and Reform, signed a Declaration of Agreement on the Principles, Fundamentals, and Objectives of the Libyan Struggle. In the document, they affirmed their commitment to the struggle against the Qaddafi regime, stressing that struggle was the responsibility of the Libyan people and the Libyan people alone.

A renewed attempt to coalesce opposition groups took place on 25–26 June 2005 when the National Libyan Opposition Conference held its inaugural meeting in London. Emphasizing a return to constitutional legitimacy, the conference brought together seven generally moderate, mainstream opposition groups, but it was not for everyone. Among others, the Muslim Brotherhood Movement, which rejected the narrow agenda insisted upon by the organizers, did not attend. The Declaration for National Consensus issued at the end of the conference called for a return to constitutional legitimacy, the creation of a transitional government, and the prosecution of all members of the Qaddafi regime who had committed crimes against humanity. In calling for Qaddafi to resign, the conference rejected armed action, saying the United Nations was responsible for restoring Libya's constitution. In a statement before the conference opened, the organizers distanced themselves from the United States, stressing political change in Libya should be undertaken without foreign interference. They also criticized the United States for normalizing ties and practicing a double standard when it came to human rights in Libya.

Over the years, a variety of organizations, including Amnesty International, Human Rights Watch, and the U.S. Department of State, have catalogued the human rights violations of the Qaddafi regime. The legacy they detailed included arbitrary arrest, detention without trial, torture, disappearance, unfair trials, and the death penalty. Criticism of Libya's dismal human rights record intensified in January 2003 when the Libyan ambassador to the United Nations was elected to a one-year term as chairman of the UN Human Rights Commission. In April 2004, Amnesty International, following its first visit to Libya in fifteen years, issued a scathing report, calling on the regime to address the grave human rights concerns detailed in its report.

Human Rights Watch in May 2005 concluded Libya had taken important first steps to improve its human rights record but indicated serious problems remained, including the use of violence against detainees, restrictions on freedom of expression and association, and the incarceration of political prisoners. In a report entitled *Libya, Words to Deeds: The Urgent Need for Human Rights Reform*, Human Rights Watch in January 2006 summarized the human rights situation in Libya:

> Civil and political rights in Libya are severely curtailed. Individuals are not free to express views critical of the government, the unique Jamahiriya political system, or the country's leader, Mu'ammar al-Qadhafi. Those who do express criticism or try to organize opposition political groups face arbitrary detention and long prison terms after unfair trials. Despite improvements, torture remains a serious concern. A pervasive security apparatus monitors the population to a high degree.[13]

In February 2006, violent demonstrations broke out in Benghazi. Sparked by the row over the publication of Danish cartoons of the Prophet Muhammad, they also reflected the ongoing frustration and simmering discontent long present in Libya's second largest city. Rioters trashed the Italian consulate in demonstrations that left up to eleven people dead, the highest single death toll in a series of protests throughout the Muslim world against publication of the caricatures by European media outlets. The riots began after a minister in the Italian government declared his intent to print t-shirts bearing the cartoons; however, the protestors soon were also shouting anti-regime slogans.

In March 2006, the General People's Committee created a human rights office, and one day later, Libya pardoned 132 political prisoners, including all eighty-four members of the banned Muslim Brotherhood. While these were hopeful signs of reform, the Department of State, in its annual report on human rights practices, issued in March 2007, described Libya as an authoritarian regime with a poor human rights record in which Qaddafi and his inner circle monopolized power. Reporters without Borders in its 2007 report stressed that no independent media outlet existed in Libya. Three out of four daily newspapers, *Al-Jamahiriya*, *Al-Shams*, and *Al-Fajr al-Jadid*, were funded by an arm of the information ministry, and the fourth, *Al-Zahf al-Akhdar*, was controlled by the revolutionary committees. Only satellite television stations, which lured people away from the state-run stations, lightened the grim picture.

POLITICAL DEVELOPMENTS

Having earlier divided Libya into fifteen hundred communes, each with its own budget and executive and legislative powers, Qaddafi in March 2000 abolished a number of central government executive functions, devolving responsibility to the twenty-six municipal councils making up the General People's Congress. While a number of government ministries were eliminated, central control was retained in areas like defense and security, economy and finance, energy, foreign affairs, infrastructure, social security, and trade. With the elimination of the Energy Ministry, responsibility for hydrocarbons policy passed to the National Oil Company. In

October 2000, the public security minister was replaced, the Information Ministry liquidated, and the finance minister removed. The duties of the Finance Ministry were divided in March 2001 between the newly created Economy and Foreign Trade Ministry and the former Finance Ministry, and other ministerial changes occurred later in the year. Qaddafi again reshuffled ministerial positions in January and March 2003, appointing Shokri Ghanem head of the General People's Committee and later replacing him with his deputy in March 2006.

Long characteristic of the Qaddafi regime, frequent ministerial changes were a favored way to prevent potential political competitors from building a power base and seldom heralded a substantive shift in the domestic political environment. On the contrary, they served to underscore the relative stability of the power balance in Libya and the dominant power position of Qaddafi. Over the years, the highest body in the political system, the General People's Committee or cabinet, consisted mostly of a small group of individuals who were reshuffled every few years. According to one estimate, Libya between 1969 and 1999 had only 112 cabinet ministers, a remarkably small number when one considers that some of them stayed only a year or two. Most of these ministers were technocrats, similar in age to Qaddafi, who were content to take various positions arbitrarily offered over the years. The system enabled Qaddafi to remain aloof from petty politics while his subordinates were unable to gain too much political power nor to feel too comfortable in their positions. Most importantly, it ensured that the power position of any one individual in Libya at any given moment was almost totally dependent on the whim of Qaddafi himself.[14]

After Fidel Castro stepped down in 2007, Qaddafi became the longest-serving head of state in the world. In spite of occasional signs of public discontent over issues like official corruption and the uneven distribution of resources, the vast majority of Libyans remained either generally supportive of Qaddafi, politically apathetic, or skeptical of the intentions of any government faction, reformist and old guard alike. Popular dissent remained a regime concern but less so than in previous years as Qaddafi employed his enhanced international status to co-opt the opposition. As a result, there was little opportunity for an effective anti-Qaddafi opposition to arise within the country. With a plethora of organizations and institutions comprising the formal political system, supplemented by an informal network of power brokers, Qaddafi maintained a sense of orchestrated chaos in which he was seen as the calming voice of wisdom.

Facing no obvious rival and not old for a head of state, Qaddafi over four decades has demonstrated the political skills necessary to continue in power. No clear rules exist for succession to his role as Libyan leader and head of state; and while Saif al-Islam al-Qaddafi is often mentioned as a possible successor, he has denied repeatedly interest in the job. Nevertheless, progressive elements see Saif and his reformist colleagues as the best hope to reconstruct a nation worn down by corruption, mismanagement, and isolation. In any case, Qaddafi's unique role as charismatic leader of the revolution will almost certainly disappear with his passing. As for the institutions created by Qaddafi, which offer elements of participation and representation as well as fulfilling important distributive and security functions, they could well prove valuable to Qaddafi's eventual successor and may be retained for some time without major overhaul.

QADDAFI'S LIBYA

After 1998, Qaddafi introduced major changes to the direction, tone, and content of Libyan foreign policy. Moving to end Libya's commercial and diplomatic isolation, he focused initially on the African continent, largely ignoring the Palestinian question and often chiding his former allies in the Middle East. He also expanded existing ties with the European Union and key European states and developed new relationships in Asia and elsewhere. However, the critical Libyan initiative, following resolution of the Lockerbie question and the lifting of UN sanctions, was the decision to renounce unconventional weapons and related delivery systems.

In so doing, Qaddafi paved the way for full commercial and diplomatic relations with the United States, a foreign policy objective dating back to the 1970s and the final step in Libya's international rehabilitation.

The Libyan economy has relied heavily on the hydrocarbons sector since the discovery of petroleum deposits in commercial quantities in 1959, and it will continue to do so in the foreseeable future. In 2007, oil reserves were estimated to be over thirty-nine billion barrels and natural gas reserves to be more than fifty-one billion cubic feet, and with numerous EPSAs and related bilateral agreements negotiated after 2003, confirmed reserve levels are expected to grow as much as three-fold in coming years. After three decades of socialist experimentation, it is thus not surprising that Libya has remained the classic example of a rentier economy, a state relying upon externally generated monies or rents for income instead of extracting income from domestic production.

Tentative attempts at economic reform in the late 1980s and early 1990s were frustrated by this rentier state pattern which remained deeply rooted in distributive mechanisms originated by the monarchy and extended by Qaddafi to attract regime support. Similar attitudes again constrained efforts at the outset of the twenty-first century to move from a socialist state to a free market economy. The latest reform process is geared toward strengthening global economic ties and attracting new foreign investment, particularly in the hydrocarbons sector. Progress in other economic sectors has been hindered by policy inconsistency, structural problems, and bureaucratic bottlenecks, with entrenched interests constraining the pace of policy implementation. As a result, economic reform remains a two-speed, two-track process with the regime prioritizing development of the hydrocarbons sector over other areas of the economy.

Whatever the speed and scope of economic reform, it is not expected to be accompanied by political liberalization. As the Qaddafi regime approaches four decades in power, well over half the Libyan population has known no other political leader or system in its lifetime. Moreover, a significant percentage of the population, in an innately conservative society, has a vested interest in the *status quo* with many Libyans accepting an implicit trade-off between limited social and political freedom and a relatively high standard of living. In lieu of political reforms that might compromise his hold on power, Qaddafi is more likely to introduce changes designed to consolidate his preeminent position in the political system he created. In the process, he can be expected to continue to reshuffle the country's leadership to balance competing power structures and to prevent any individual from developing a personal power base. As for the future, with no formal mechanism in place to ensure a smooth transition of power, the post-Qaddafi era, whenever it occurs, can be expected to be a time of considerable tension and uncertainty with numerous socioeconomic and political groups vying for power.

FURTHER READING

In the case of Libya, the problem of language can be a real one for the Anglophone, especially in regards to earlier periods of Libyan history. When I first visited Libya over three decades ago, only a handful of books were available in English, and most of those concerned technical areas or specialized periods. The situation has improved in recent years; however, there remains a paucity of English language materials on selected subjects. Therefore, while the emphasis of this essay is on English language offerings, I will mention French and Italian sources when English ones are limited.

The most extensive available bibliography of Libyan source materials is Ronald Bruce St John, *Historical Dictionary of Libya*, fourth edition (Lanham, MD: Scarecrow Press, 2006). Also recommended are Richard I. Lawless, ed., *Libya* (Oxford: Clio Press, 1987) and Mohamed A. Alawar, ed., *A Concise Bibliography of Northern Chad and Fezzan in Southern Libya* (Wisbech, Cambridgeshire: Arab Crescent Press, 1983).

For an introduction to the early history of North Africa, see Jamil M. Abun-Nasr, *A History of the Maghrib in the Islamic Period*, second edition (Cambridge: Cambridge University Press, 1987); Alasdair Drysdale and Gerald H. Blake, *The Middle East and North Africa: A Political Geography* (Oxford: Oxford University Press, 1985); Abdallah Laroui, *The History of the Maghrib: An Interpretive Essay* (Princeton: Princeton University Press, 1977); and Michel Le Gall and Kenneth Perkins, ed., *The Maghrib in Question: Essays in History and Historiography* (Austin: University of Texas Press, 1997).

For the ancient period, the following sources are recommended: Olwen Brogan, "First and Second Century Settlement in the Tripolitanian

Pre-Desert," in *Libya in History*, ed. Fawzi F. Gadallah (Benghazi: University of Libya, 1968), pp. 121–130; C. Daniels, *The Garamantes of Southern Libya* (Stoughton, WI: Oleander Press, 1970); David N. Edwards, J. W. J. Hawthorne, John N. Dore, and David J. Mattingly, "The Garamantes of Fezzan Revisited: Publishing the C. M. Daniels Archives," *Libyan Studies*, 16 (1999), pp. 109–128; D. E. L. Haynes, *Antiquities of Tripolitania* (Tripoli: Antiquities Department of Tripolitania, 1955); Mario Liverani, "The Garamantes: A Fresh Approach," *Libyan Studies*, 31 (2000), pp. 17–28; and David J. Mattingly, "Mapping Ancient Libya," *Libyan Studies*, 25 (1994), pp. 1–5.

A wider range of English language literature is available on the classical period (ca. 1000 BCE–CE 500), which includes the Phoenicians, Greeks, Romans, and Byzantines. For an introduction to the Phoenicians, see Maria Eugenia Aubet, *The Phoenicians and the West: Politics, Colonies and Trade* (Cambridge: Cambridge University Press, 1993) and Anthony Strong, *The Phoenicians in History and Legend* (Bloomington, IN: AuthorHouse, 2002). For the Greeks, Romans, and Byzantines, the general reader is well advised to begin with Antonino DiVita, Ginette DiVita-Evrard, and Lidiano Bacchielli, *Libya: The Lost Cities of the Roman Empire* (Cologne: Könemann, 1999); Paul Lachlan MacKendrick, *The North African Stones Speak* (Chapel Hill: University of North Carolina Press, 2000; and Sue Ravin, *Rome in Africa*, third edition (London: Routledge, 1993). Other recommended sources include J. Liebare, "Some Aspects of Social Change in North Africa in Punic and Roman Times," *Museum Africum*, 2 (1973), pp. 24–40; Kenneth D. Matthews, Jr., *Cities in the Sand: Leptis Magna and Sabratha in Roman Africa* (Philadelphia: University of Pennsylvania Press, 1957); and B. H. Warmington, *The North African Provinces from Diocletian to the Vandal Conquest* (Cambridge: Cambridge University Press, 1954). For those familiar with the French language, Marcel Benabou, *La résistance africaine à la romanisation* (Paris: François Maspero, 1976); Jean-Marie Blas de Roblès, *Libye: grecque, romaine et byzantine* (Aix-en-Provence: Édisud, 1999); Christian Courtois, *Les Vandales et L'Afrique* (Aalen: Scientia, 1964); and Gilbert Charles-Picard, *La civilisation de L'Afrique romaine* (Paris: Librairie Plon, 1959) are useful.

The best description in English of the Islamic conquest of North Africa is Dhanun Taha, *The Muslim Conquest and Settlement of North Africa and Spain* (London: Routledge, 1989). Also see C. Edmund Bosworth, "Libya in Islamic History," *Journal of Libyan Studies*, 1, no. 2 (Winter 2000), pp. 6–16 and Abbas Hamdani, "Some

Aspects of the History of Libya during the Fatimid Period," in *Libya in History*, ed. Fawzi F. Gadallah (Benghazi: University of Libya, 1968), pp. 321–346. The principal work in English on the Almohads is Roger Le Tourneau, *The Almohad Movement in North Africa in the Twelfth and Thirteenth Centuries* (Princeton: Princeton University Press, 1969). Although there is no comparable book on the Almoravids, a French source, Vincent Lagardère, *Les Almoravides, le djihâd andalou (1106–1143)* (Paris: L'Harmattan, 1999) discusses the Almoravid presence in Spain. On the Berber dynasties, see Michael Brett and Elizabeth Fentress, *The Berbers, Peoples of Africa* (Oxford: Blackwell, 1997); Michael Brett, "Ifriqiya as a Market for Saharan Trade from the Tenth to the Twelfth Century AD," *Journal of African History*, 10 (1969), pp. 347–364; and Ronald A. Messier, "Re-thinking the Almoravids, Rethinking Ibn Khaldun," *Journal of North African Studies*, 6, no. 1 (2001), pp. 59–80. For Islam in modern times, the reader should begin with Barrie Wharton, "'Between Arab Brothers and Islamist Foes': The Evolution of the Contemporary Islamist Movement in Libya," *Journal of Libyan Studies*, 4, no. 1 (Summer 2003), pp. 33–48; John P. Entelis, ed., *Islam, Democracy, and the State in North Africa* (Bloomington: Indiana University Press, 1997); George Joffé, "Qadhafi's Islam in Historical Perspective," in *Qadhafi's Libya, 1969–1994*, ed. Dirk Vandewalle (New York: St. Martin's Press, 1995), pp. 139–154; John Ruedy, ed., *Islamism and Secularism in North Africa* (New York: St. Martin's Press, 1996).

On the period of Ottoman occupation (1551–1911), Donald Quataert, *The Ottoman Empire, 1700–1922* (Cambridge: Cambridge University Press, 2000) and Justin McCarthy, *The Ottoman Turks: An Introductory History to 1923* (London: Longman, 1997) collectively offer the general reader a good introduction to Ottoman culture, society, and rule. For the more ambitious, see Stanford J. Shaw and Ezel Kural Shaw, *History of the Ottoman Empire and Modern Turkey*, 2 vols (Cambridge: Cambridge University Press, 1976); Lord Kinross, *The Ottoman Centuries: The Rise and Fall of the Ottoman Empire* (New York: Morrow Quill, 1979); and Roderic H. Davison, *Reform in the Ottoman Empire, 1856–1876* (Princeton, NJ: Princeton University Press, 1963).

The most comprehensive treatment of the Karamanli dynasty (1711–1835) is Kola Folayan, *Tripoli during the Reign of Yusuf Pasha Qaramanli* (Ile-Ife, Nigeria: University of Ife Press, 1979). Articles of interest include Rifaat Abou-El-Haj, "An Agenda for Research in History: The History of Libya between the Sixteenth and Nineteenth Centuries,"

International Journal of Middle East Studies, 15, no. 2 (August 1983), pp. 305–319; Kola Folayan, "Tripoli and the War with the U.S.A., 1801–5," *Journal of African History*, 13, no. 2 (1972), pp. 261–270; L. J. Hume, "Preparations for Civil War in Tripoli in the 1820s: Ali Karamanli, Hassuna D'Ghies, and Jeremy Bentham," *Journal of African History*, 21, no. 3 (1980), pp. 311–322; and C. R. Pennell, "Work on the Early Ottoman Period and Qaramanlis," *Libyan Studies*, 20 (1989), pp. 215–219. Fawzi F. Gadallah, ed., *Libya in History* (Benghazi: University of Libya, 1968) also contains relevant articles.

Traditional studies of corsairing during the Karamanli dynasty include Seton Dearden, *A Nest of Corsairs: The Fighting Karamanlis of Tripoli* (London: John Murray, 1976); James A. Field, *America and the Mediterranean World, 1776–1882* (Princeton: Princeton University Press, 1969); Godfrey Fisher, *Barbary Legend: War, Trade and Piracy in North Africa, 1415–1830* (Oxford: Oxford University Press, 1957); Ray W. Irwin, *The Diplomatic Relations of the United States with the Barbary Powers, 1776–1816* (Chapel Hill: University of North Carolina Press, 1931); and Louis B. Wright and Julia H. Macleod, *The First Americans in North Africa: William Eaton's Struggle for a Vigorous Policy against the Barbary Pirates, 1799–1805* (Princeton: Princeton University Press, 1945).

A welcome addition to the literature on corsairing, Richard B. Parker, *Uncle Sam in Barbary: A Diplomatic History* (Gainesville: University of Florida Press, 2004) relates historical events to contemporary issues in a well-researched and meticulously written book. Other recent studies of the period include Robert J. Allison, *The Crescent Obscured: The United States and the Muslim World, 1776–1815* (New York: Oxford University Press, 1995); Franklin Lambert, *The Barbary Wars: American Independence in the Atlantic World* (New York: Hill & Wang, 2005); Joseph Wheelan, *Jefferson's War: America's First War on Terror, 1801–1805* (New York: Carroll & Graf, 2003); and Richard Zacks, *The Pirate Coast: Thomas Jefferson, the First Marines, and the Secret Mission of 1805* (New York: Hyperion, 2005). For Italian-speaking students, two recent books by Italian scholars are helpful: Salvatore Bono, *Lumi e Corsari: Europa e Maghreb nel Settecentro* (Perugia: Morlacchi Editore, 2005) and Paolo Soave, *La Rivoluzione Americana nel Mediterraneo: Prove di Politica di Potenza e Declino delle Regenze Barbaresche (1795–1816)* (Milan: Dott. A. Giuffre, 2004).

For the history of the Second Ottoman Occupation (1835–1911), the reader should begin with Anthony Joseph Cachia, *Libya under the Second Ottoman Occupation, 1835–1911* (Tripoli: Government Press, 1945). Also recommended are Lisa Anderson, *The State and Social Transformation in Tunisia and Libya, 1830–1980* (Princeton: Princeton University Press, 1986); Ernest N. Bennett, *With the Turks in Tripoli* (London: Methuen, 1912); E. G. H. Joffé, "Trade & Migration between Malta & the Barbary States during the Second Ottoman Occupation of Libya (1835–1911)," in *Planning and Development in Modern Libya*, ed. by M. M. Buru, S. M. Ghanem, and K. S. McLachlan (Wisbech, Cambridgeshire: Middle East & North African Studies Press, 1982), pp. 1–32; and C. R. Pennell, "Political Loyalty and the Central Government in Precolonial Libya," in *Social and Economic Development of Libya*, ed. E. G. H. Joffé and K. S. McLachlan (Wisbech, Cambridgeshire: Middle East & North African Studies Press, 1982), pp. 1–18. Useful articles include Lisa Anderson, "Nineteenth-Century Reform in Ottoman Libya," *International Journal of Middle East Studies*, 16, no. 3 (August 1984), pp. 325–348; James A. Field, Jr., "A Scheme in Regard to Cyrenaica," *Mississippi Valley Historical Review*, 44, no. 3 (December 1957), pp. 445–468; Michel Le Gall, "The Ottoman Government and the Sanusiyya: A Reappraisal," *International Journal of Middle East Studies*, 21, no. 1 (February 1989), pp. 91–106; and John Wright, "Murzuk and the Saharan Slave Trade in the 19th Century," *Libyan Studies*, 29 (1998), pp. 89–96.

Ali Abdullatif Ahmida, *The Making of Modern Libya: State Formation, Colonization, and Resistance, 1830–1932* (Albany: State University of New York, 1994) explores the nature of the state and political economy of Libya after 1830, emphasizing the impact of Ottoman state centralization, the decline of the Saharan trade, and the penetration of European financial capital. His work contributes to an understanding of Cyrenaican tribal structures and the Libyan response to Italian colonialism. Ahmida later expanded his analysis in *Forgotten Voices: Power and Agency in Colonial and Postcolonial Libya* (London and New York: Routledge, 2005).

The most comprehensive study of the Sanusi Order is Knut S. Vikor, *Sufi and Scholar on the Desert Edge: Muhammad b. Ali al-Sanusi and his Brotherhood* (Evanston, IL: Northwestern University Press, 1995). Also recommended is Emrys L. Peters, *The Bedouin of Cyrenaica: Studies in Personal and Corporate Power* (Cambridge: Cambridge University Press, 1990), a collection of essays edited by Jack Goody and Emanuel Marx.

Traditional studies of the Sanusi Order include E. E. Evans-Pritchard, *The Sanusi of Cyrenaica* (Oxford: Oxford University Press, 1949) and Nicola A. Ziadeh, *Sanusiyah: A Study of a Revivalist Movement in Islam* (Leiden: E. J. Brill, 1983).

For the troubled history of Libyan Jews, the reader should begin with Renzo de Felice, *Jews in an Arab Land: Libya, 1835–1970* (Austin: University of Texas Press, 1985). Two more recent studies, Harvey E. Goldberg, *Jewish Life in Muslim Libya: Rivals and Relatives* (Chicago, IL: University of Chicago Press, 1990) and Rachel Simon, *Change within Tradition among Jewish Women in Libya* (Seattle: University of Washington Press, 1992) are also recommended. Simon's book, which examines the changing status of Jewish women from the second half of the nineteenth century until 1967, is a pioneering study of Jewish women in an Arab state. The record of Jewish life kept by the Talmudic scholar and itinerant peddler, Mordechai Hakohen (1856–1929), and translated by Harvey E. Goldberg, *The Book of Mordechai: A Study of the Jews of Libya* (Philadelphia, PA: Institute for the Study of Human Issues, 1980) offers insight into the life of the Jewish community in Libya.

The standard English language history of the Italian occupation remains Claudio G. Segré, *Fourth Shore: The Italian Colonization of Libya* (Chicago, IL: University of Chicago Press, 1974). Sources on the early years of war and occupation include William C. Askew, *Europe and Italy's Acquisition of Libya, 1911–1912* (Durham, NC: Duke University Press, 1942); Thomas Barclay, *Turco-Italian War and Its Problems* (London: Constable & Company, 1912); and Timothy W. Childs, *Italo-Turkish Diplomacy and the War over Libya, 1911–1912* (Leiden: E. J. Brill, 1990). On the transition period from Turkish to Italian rule, see Lisa Anderson, "The Development of Nationalist Sentiment in Libya, 1908–1922," in *The Origins of Arab Nationalism*, ed. Rashid Khalidi et al. (New York: Columbia University Press, 1991), pp. 225–242; Lisa Anderson, "The Tripoli Republic, 1918–1922," in *Social and Economic Development of Libya*, ed. E. G. H. Joffé and K. S. McLachlan (Wisbech, Cambridgeshire: Middle East & North African Studies Press, 1982), pp. 43–65; Habib Hesnawi, "Italian Imperial Policy towards Libya, 1870–1911," in *Modern and Contemporary Libya: Sources and Historiographies*, ed. Anna Baldinetti (Rome: Istituto Italiano per L'Africa e L'Oriente, 2003), pp. 49–62; and Rachel Simon, *Libya between Ottomanism and Nationalism: The Ottoman Involvement in Libya during the War with Italy (1911–1919)* (Berlin: Klaus Schwarz Verlag, 1987).

On the Italian colonial experience, see Leonard Appleton, "The Question of Nationalism and Education in Libya under Italian Rule," *Libyan Studies*, 10 (1979), pp. 29–33; David Atkinson, "The Politics of Geography and the Italian Occupation of Libya," *Libyan Studies*, 27 (1996), pp. 71–84; Duncan Cumming, "Libya in the First World War," in *Libya in History*, ed. Fawzi F. Gadallah (Benghazi: University of Libya, 1968), pp. 383–392; Mohammed Taher Jerary, "The Libyan Cultural Resistance to Italian Colonization: The Consequences of Denying the Values of Others," in *Modern and Contemporary Libya: Sources and Historiographies*, ed. Anna Baldinetti (Rome: Istituto Italiano per L'Africa e L'Oriente, 2003), pp. 17–36; Brian L. McLaren, *Architecture and Tourism in Italian Colonial Libya: An Ambivalent Modernism* (Seattle and London: University of Washington Press, 2006); Enzo Santarelli et. al., *Omar al-Mukhtar: The Italian Reconquest of Libya*, trans. John Gilbert (London: Darf Publishers, 1986); Claudio G. Segré, *Italo Balbo: A Fascist Life* (Berkeley: University of California Press, 1974); and John Wright, "Mussolini, Libya and the 'Sword of Islam,'" *Maghreb Review*, 12, no. 1–2 (January–April 1987), pp. 29–33. For a discussion of the Italian occupation from a Libyan viewpoint, see Ahmed M. Ashiurakis, *A Concise History of the Libyan Struggle for Freedom* (Tripoli: General Publishing, Distributing & Advertising Company, 1976). For a broader view of Italian colonial policy, see Denis Mack Smith, *Mussolini's Roman Empire* (London: Longman, 1976) and R. J. B. Bosworth, *Mussolini's Italy: Life under the Dictatorship, 1915–1945* (London: Penguin, 2005).

On the transition from colony to independent state, Scott L. Bills, *Libyan Arena: The United States, Britain, and the Council of Foreign Ministers, 1945–1948* (Kent, OH: Kent State University Press, 1995), Adrian Pelt, *Libyan Independence and the United Nations: A Case of Planned Decolonization* (New Haven, CT: Yale University Press, 1970), and Benjamin Rivlin, *The United Nations and the Italian Colonies* (New York: The Carnegie Endowment for International Peace, 1950) are invaluable. Annie Lacroix-Riz, *Les protectorates d'Afrique du Nord entre la France et Washington* (Paris: Editions L'Harmattan, 1988) and Martin Thomas, "Defending a Lost Cause? France and the United States Vision of Imperial Rule in French North Africa, 1945–1956," *Diplomatic History*, 26, no. 2 (Spring 2002), pp. 215–247 detail Franco-American relations in the run-up to Libyan independence and the immediate post-independence period. Other useful sources include Lisa Anderson, "'A Last Resort, an Expedient and an Experiment': Statehood and Sovereignty in Libya," *Journal of*

Libyan Studies, 2, no. 2 (Winter 2001), pp. 14–25; Ann Dearden, "Independence for Libya: The Political Problems," *The Middle East Journal*, 4, no. 4 (October 1950), pp. 395–409; C. Grove Haines, "The Problem of the Italian Colonies," *The Middle East Journal*, 1, no. 4 (October 1947), pp. 417–431; Benjamin Rivlin, "Unity and Nationalism in Libya," *The Middle East Journal*, 3, no. 1 (January 1949): 31–44; and Ronald Bruce St John, "The United States, the Cold War & Libyan Independence," *Journal of Libyan Studies*, 2, no. 2 (Winter 2001), pp. 26–45.

John Wright, *Libya: A Modern History* (Baltimore, MD: Johns Hopkins University Press, 1982) has long been the only general history of modern Libya available in English. Expanding the story begun in his 1969 book, entitled *Libya*, Wright focuses on the post-1900 era. A more recent addition to the literature, Dirk Vandewalle, *A History of Modern Libya* (Cambridge: Cambridge University Press, 2006) begins the story in the 1900s but concentrates on the post-1969 political economy of Libya. In the French language, André Martel, *La Libya, 1835–1990: Essai de géopolitique historique* (Paris: Presses Universitaires de France, 1991) is strongly recommended.

For the history of the United Kingdom of Libya (1951–69), the reader is well advised to begin with Majid Khadduri, *Modern Libya: A Study in Political Development* (Baltimore, MD: Johns Hopkins University Press, 1963) which focuses on Libya's formation as an independent state. John Norman, *Labor and Politics in Libya and Arab Africa* (New York: Bookman Associates, 1965); Henry Serrano Villard, *Libya: The New Arab Kingdom of North Africa* (Ithaca, NY: Cornell University Press, 1956); and Nicola A. Ziadeh, *The Modern History of Libya* (London: Weidenfeld & Nicolson, 1967) are standard works. *The Life and Times of King Idris of Libya* by E. A. V. De Candole, published privately by Mohamed Ben Ghalbon in 1990, is a favorable treatment of the monarchy. For those familiar with the Italian language, Massimiliano Cricco, *Il Petrolio dei Senussi: Stati Uniti e Gran Bretagna in Libia dall'indipendenza a Gheddafi (1949–1973)* (Florence: Edizioni Polistampa, 2002) is useful regarding foreign affairs.

On the monarchical era, the following are also recommended: Mustafa Ahmed Bin Halim, *Libya: The Years of Hope* (London: AAS Media, 1998); Stephen Blackwell, "Saving the King: Anglo-American Strategy and British Counter-subversion Operations in Libya, 1953–59," *Middle Eastern Studies*, 39, no. 1 (January 2003), pp. 1–18; Ann Dearden,

"Independence for Libya: The Political Problems," *The Middle East Journal*, 4, no. 4 (October 1950), pp. 395–409; Alison Pargeter, "Anglo-Libyan Relations and the Suez Crisis," *Journal of North African Studies*, 5, no. 2 (Summer 2000), pp. 41–58; Salaheddin Hasan Sury, "A New System for a New State: The Libyan Experiment in Statehood, 1951–1969," in *Modern and Contemporary Libya: Sources and Historiographies*, ed. Anna Baldinetti (Rome: Istituto Italiano per L'Africa e L'Oriente, 2003), pp. 179–194; and John Wright, "Libya's Short Cut to Independence," *Journal of Libyan Studies*, 2 no. 2 (Winter 2001), pp. 77–88. On the final days of the monarchy, see William H. Lewis, "Libya: The End of Monarchy," *Current History* 58 (January 1970), pp. 34–38, 50.

For an introduction to contemporary Libya, see Dirk Vandewalle, *Libya since Independence: Oil and State-Building* (Ithaca, NY: Cornell University Press, 1998) and Mansour O. El-Kikhia, *Libya's Qaddafi: The Politics of Contradiction* (Gainesville: University Press of Florida, 1997). Vandewalle concentrates on the domestic policies of the Qaddafi regime while El-Kikhia also covers foreign policy. Dirk Vandewalle, ed., *Qadhafi's Libya, 1969 to 1994* (New York: St. Martin's Press, 1995) provides background and detail to the broader issues raised in more recent works.

The English language biographies of the Libyan leader, Mu'ammar al-Qaddafi, including Mirella Bianco, *Gadafi: Voice from the Desert* (London: Longman Group, 1975); David Blundy and Andrew Lycett, *Qaddafi and the Libyan Revolution* (London: Weidenfeld & Nicolson, 1987); and George Tremlett, *Gadaffi: The Desert Mystic* (New York: Carroll & Graf Publishers, 1993), are all dated. Edmond Jouve provides a contemporary portrait in *Mouammar Kadhafi: Dans le concert des nations* (Montréal: L'Archipel, 2004). Guy Georgy, *Kadhafi: Le Berger des Syrtes* (Paris: Flammarion, 1996) is also recommended.

The ideology of the Libyan revolution, sometimes referred to as the Third Universal Theory, is best introduced through a reading of the three slender volumes of Qaddafi's *Green Book*. Published independently after 1975, these books are collected in Henry M. Christman, ed. *Qaddafi's Green Book: An Unauthorized Edition* (Buffalo, NY: Prometheus Books, 1988). Mohamed El-Khawas, *Qaddafi: His Ideology in Theory and Practice* (Brattleboro, VT: Amana Books, 1986) provides a detailed analysis of the Third Universal Theory, and Mahmoud Mustafa Ayoub, *Islam and the Third Universal Theory: The Religious Thought of Mu'ammar al-Qadhafi* (London: KPI Limited, 1987) places the Third Universal

Theory in a religious context. Helpful on the formative years of the revolution is Ronald Bruce St John, "The Ideology of Mu'ammar al-Qadhdhafi: Theory and Practice," *International Journal of Middle East Studies*, 15, no. 4 (November 1983), pp. 471–490. Muammar Gaddafi with Edmond Jouve, *My Vision* (London: John Blake, 2005) is a controversial statement of the Libyan leader's ideological journey since 1969.

For the history of the One September Revolution, Ruth First, *Libya: The Elusive Revolution* (London: Penguin, 1974) is the place to start. Other helpful studies of the early years of the revolution include Jonathan Bearman, *Qadhafi's Libya* (London: Zed Books, 1986); John K. Cooley, *Libyan Sandstorm: The Complete Account of Qaddafi's Revolution* (New York: Holt, Rinehart, and Winston, 1982); and Salah El Saadany, *Egypt and Libya from Inside, 1969–1976* (Jefferson, NC: McFarland & Company, 1994). Omar I. El Fathaly, Monte Palmer, and Richard Chackerian, *Political Development and Bureaucracy in Libya* (Lexington, MA: Lexington Books, 1977) and Omar I. El Fathaly and Monte Palmer, *Political Development and Social Change in Libya* (Lexington, MA: Lexington Books, 1980) explore revolutionary political structures. Marius K. Deeb and Mary Jane Deeb, *Libya since the Revolution: Aspects of Social and Political Development* (New York: Praeger Publishers, 1982) provide valuable information on the role of women, education, and Islam. Lillian Craig Harris, *Libya: Qadhafi's Revolution and the Modern State* (Boulder, CO: Westview Press, 1986) and Martin Sicker, *The Making of a Pariah State: The Adventurist Politics of Muammar Qaddafi* (New York: Praeger Publishers, 1987) survey history, politics, and society. Helpful French language studies include G. Albergoni et al., *La Libye nouvelle: Rupture et continuité* (Paris: Editions du Centre National de la Recherche Scientifique, 1975); Juliette Bessis, *La Libye contemporaine* (Paris: Editions L'Harmattan, 1986); and Moncef Djaziri, *État et Société en Libye* (Paris: Editions L'Harmattan, 1996).

For an examination of post-1969 sociopolitical events, the single most rewarding volume is John Davis, *Libyan Politics: Tribe and Revolution* (London: I. B. Tauris, 1987). Focusing on the Zuwaya tribe, the author analyzes life under a revolutionary government in a society in which any kind of government is a fairly recent phenomenon. Amal Obeidi, *Political Culture in Libya* (Richmond: Curzon Press, 2001) surveys university students in one of the few empirical studies of popular attitudes published since Qaddafi came to power. Dirk Vandewalle, ed., *Libya since 1969: Qadhafi's Revolution Revisited* (New York: Palgrave, 2008) examines contemporary domestic and foreign policy issues. Ronald Bruce St John, "Libya: Reforming the Economy, Not the Polity," in *North Africa: Politics, Region and the Limits of Transformation*, ed. Yahia Zoubir and Haizam Amirah Fernández (London and New York: Routledge, 2008), pp. 53–70, explores recent socioeconomic and political reforms in Libya.

The economic history of contemporary Libya is explored in J. A. Allen, *Libya: The Experience of Oil* (London: Croom Helm, 1981); Judith Gurney, *Libya: The Political Economy of Oil* (Oxford: Oxford University Press, 1996); and Frank C. Waddams, *The Libyan Oil Industry* (London: Croom Helm, 1980). Selected aspects of the economy are discussed in J. A. Allan, ed., *Libya since Independence* (London: Croom Helm, 1982); Bichara Khader and Bashir El-Wifati, ed., *The Economic Development of Libya* (London: Croom Helm, 1987); E. G. H. Joffé and K. S. McLachlan, *Social and Economic Development of Libya* (Wisbech, Cambridgeshire: Middle East & North African Studies Press, 1982); M. M. Buru, S. M. Ghanem, and K. S. McLachlan, ed., *Planning and Development in Modern Libya* (Wisbech, Cambridgeshire: Middle East & North African Studies Press, 1982); Ronald Bruce St John, "Libya's Oil & Gas Industry: Blending Old and New," *The Journal of North African Studies*, 12, no. 2 (June 2007), pp. 239–254; and Ronald Bruce St John, "The Libyan Economy in Transition," in *Libya since 1969: Qadhafi's Revolution Revisited*, ed. Dirk Vandewalle (New York: Palgrave, 2008).

Ronald Bruce St John provides the most comprehensive examination to date of the prolonged, often tortured relationship between Libya and the United States in *Libya and the United States: Two Centuries of Strife* (Philadelphia: University of Pennsylvania Press, 2002). A broader analysis of Libyan foreign policy, still valuable but increasingly dated, can be found in Ronald Bruce St John, *Qaddafi's World Design: Libyan Foreign Policy, 1969–1987* (London: Saqi Books, 1987). P. Edward Haley, *Qaddafi and the United States since 1969* (New York: Praeger Publishers, 1984) focuses on post-1969 Libyan foreign policy toward the United States. Mahmoud G. ElWarfally, *Imagery and Ideology in U.S. Policy toward Libya, 1969–1982* (Pittsburgh, PA: University of Pittsburgh Press, 1988) covers related ground from a totally different perspective. Also of interest are Brian L. Davis, *Qaddafi, Terrorism, and the Origins of the U.S. Attack on Libya* (New York: Praeger Publishers, 1990); Ronald Bruce St John, "'Libya Is Not Iraq': Preemptive Strikes, WMD and Diplomacy," *The Middle East Journal*, 58, no. 3 (Summer 2004), pp. 386–402; Ronald Bruce St John, "Libyan Foreign Policy," *Orbis*, 47, no. 3 (Summer 2003), pp. 463–477; and Joseph T. Stanik, *El Dorado Canyon: Reagan's Undeclared War with Qaddafi* (Annapolis, MD: Naval Institute Press, 2003.

On the long history of Libyan involvement in Africa, see J. Millard Burr and Robert O. Collins, *Africa's Thirty Years' War: Chad, Libya, and the Sudan, 1963–1993* (Boulder, CO: Westview, 1999); Mary-Jane Deeb, *Libya's Foreign Policy in North Africa* (Boulder, CO: Westview, 1999); Bernard Lanne, *Tchad-Libye: La querelle des frontières* (Paris: Karthala, 1982); René Lemarchand, ed., *The Green and the Black: Qadhafi's Policies in Africa* (Bloomington: University of Indiana Press, 1988); René Otayek, *La Politique Africaine de la Libye (1969–1985)* (Paris: Éditions Karthala, 1986); Ronald Bruce St John, "Libya in Africa: Looking Back, Moving Forward," *Journal of Libyan Studies,* 1, no. 1 (Summer 2000): 18–32; and John Wright, *Libya, Chad and the Central Sahara* (London: Hurst & Company, 1989).

On the history of architecture, see Ashil M. Barbar, *Islamic Architecture in Libya* (Monticello, IL: Vance, 1979); Federico Cresti, "City and Territory in Libya during the Colonial Period: Sources and Research Documents," in *Modern and Contemporary Libya: Sources and Historiographies,* ed. Anna Baldinetti (Rome: Istituto Italiano per L'Africa e L'Oriente, 2003), pp.141–168; J. Martin Evans, "The Traditional House in the Oasis of Ghadames," *Libyan Studies,* 7 (1976), pp. 31–40; Nora Lafi and Denis Bocquet, "Local Élites and Italian Town-Planning Procedures in Early Colonial Tripoli, 1911–1912," *Journal of Libyan Studies,* 3, no. 1 (Summer 2002), pp. 59–68; Brian L. McLaren, *Architecture and Tourism in Italian Colonial Libya: An Ambivalent Modernism* (Seattle: University of Washington, 2006); and J. B. Ward-Perkins, "Pre-Roman Elements in the Architecture of Roman Tripolitania," in *Libya in History,* ed. Fawzi F. Gadallah (Benghazi: University of Libya, 1968), pp. 101–116.

On the arts and artisanship of Libya, see Tertia Barnett, "Rock-art, Landscape and Cultural Transition in the Wadi al-Ajal, Fazzan," *Libyan Studies,* 33 (2002), pp. 71–84; Monique Brandily, "Music and Social Change," in *Social and Economic Development of Libya,* ed. E. G. H. Joffé and K. S. McLachlan (Wisbech, Cambridgeshire: Middle East & North African Studies Press, 1982), pp. 207–214; Philip Ciantar, "Continuity and Change in the Libyan Ma'luf Musical Tradition," *Libyan Studies,* 34 (2003), pp. 137–146; A. Pesco et. al. *Pre-historic Rock Art of the Libyan Sahara* (Stoughton, WI: Oleander Press, 1974); Taher El Amin El Mughrabi, Ali Mustafa Ramadan, and Ali Ammar El-Abani, *Shadows and*

Lights from Libyan Arab Republic (Tripoli: Arabic House for Book, 1977); and H. M. Walda and S. Walker, "Ancient Art and Architecture in Tripolitania and Cyrenaica," *Libyan Studies*, 15 (1984), pp. 81–92.

The body of Libyan literature available in the English language is small but growing: Ahmed Fagih, *Charles, Diana and Me and Other Stories* (London and New York: Kegan Paul International, 2000); Ahmed Fagih, *Gazelles and Other Plays* (London and New York: Kegan Paul International, 2000); Ahmed Fagih, ed, *Libyan Stories: Twelve Short Stories from Libya* (London and New York: Kegan Paul International, 2000); Ahmed Fagih, *Valley of Ashes* (London and New York: Kegan Paul International, 2000); Ahmed Fagih, *Who's Afraid of Agatha Christie? and Other Stories* (London and New York: Kegan Paul International, 2000); Ibrahim al-Koni, *The Bleeding of the Stone* (New York: Interlink Books, 2002); Hisham Matar, *In the Country of Men* (New York: Dial Press, 2007); and Muammar Qaddafi, *Escape to Hell and Other Stories* (New York and Montreal: Stanké, 1998).

NOTES

CHAPTER 1

1. Quoted in Michael Brett and Elizabeth Fentress, *The Berbers* (Oxford: Blackwell, 1997), p. 82.
2. Abdallah Laroui, *The History of the Maghrib: An Interpretative Essay*, translated from the French by Ralph Manheim (Princeton, NJ: Princeton University Press, 1977), p. 87.
3. Ali Abdullatif Ahmida, *The Making of Modern Libya: State Formation, Colonization, and Resistance, 1830–1932* (Albany: State University of New York Press, 1994), pp. 11–18, esp. pp. 16–17.

CHAPTER 2

1. Richard B. Parker, *Uncle Sam in Barbary: A Diplomatic History* (Gainesville, FL: University Press of Florida, 2004), p. 6.
2. C. R. Pennell, *Piracy and Diplomacy in Seventeenth-Century North Africa: The Journal of Thomas Baker, English Consul in Tripoli, 1677-1685* (Rutherford, NJ: Associated University Press, 1989).
3. Kola Folayan, *Tripoli during the Reign of Yusuf Pasha Qaramanli* (Ile-Ife, Nigeria: University of Ife Press, 1979), pp. 47–77.
4. Lisa Anderson, *The State and Social Transformation in Tunisia and Libya, 1830–1980* (Princeton, NJ: Princeton University Press), pp. 70–76, 87–95, 104–113; Lisa Anderson, "Nineteenth-Century Reform in Ottoman Libya," *International Journal of Middle East Studies*, 16, 3, August 1984, pp. 325–348.
5. Michel Le Gall, "The Ottoman Government and the Sanusiyya: A

Reappraisal," *International Journal of Middle East Studies*, 21, 1, February 1989, pp. 91–106, esp. pp. 96–101.

6. Nahum Slouschz, *Travels in North Africa* (Philadelphia, PA: Jewish Publication Society of America, 1927), quoted in John Wright, ed., *Travellers in Libya* (London: Silphium Books, 2005), p. 228.

7. Dirk Vandewalle, *A History of Modern Libya* (New York: Cambridge University Press, 2006), p. 20.

CHAPTER 3

1. Alessandra Mussolini is the daughter of Romano Mussolini, son of fascist leader Benito Mussolini, and a prominent politician in contemporary Italy.

2. Domenico Tumiati, *Nell'Africa Romana: Tripolitania* (Milan: Fratelli Treves, 1911), quoted in *Travellers in Libya*, ed. John Wright (London: Silphium Press, 2005), p. 236.

3. R. J. B. Bosworth, *Mussolini's Italy: Life under the Dictatorship, 1915–1945* (New York: Penguin, 2006), p. 43.

4. Enrico Corradini, *L'Ora di Tripoli* (Milan: Fratelli Treves, 1911), quoted in *Travellers in Libya*, pp. 233–234.

5. Ali Abdullatif Ahmida, *Forgotten Voices: Power and Agency in Colonial and Postcolonial Libya* (London and New York: Routledge, 2005), pp. 27–30.

6. Bashir al-Hashmi, "Screams in our Village," in *Libyan Stories: Twelve Short Stories from Libya*, ed. Ahmed Fagih (London and New York: Kegan Paul International, 2000), pp. 31–34.

7. For additional detail, see Lisa S. Anderson, "The Tripoli Republic, 1918–1922," in *Social & Economic Development of Libya*, ed. E. G. H. Joffé and K. S. McLachlan (Wisbech: Middle East & North African Studies, 1982), pp. 43–65.

8. Bosworth, *Mussolini's Italy*, p. 381.

9. Ali M. Almisrati, "An Extract from Mussolini's Nail," *Libyan Stories*, p. 30.

10. John Wright, "British and Italians in Libya in 1943," *Maghreb Review*, 15, 1–2, 1990, p. 32.

11. On the 1945 riots, see Harvey E. Goldberg, *Jewish Life in Muslim Libya: Rivals & Relatives* (Chicago, IL: University of Chicago Press, 1990), pp. 97–122.

12. Lisa Anderson, "The Development of Nationalist Sentiment in Libya, 1908–1922," in *The Origins of Arab Nationalism*, ed. Rashid Khalid et al. (New York: Columbia University Press, 1991), pp. 225–242.

13. Fagih, "Background Notes on Modern Libyan Literature," *Libyan Stories*, p. 2.

14. Brian L. McLaren, *Architecture and Tourism in Italian Colonial Libya: An Ambivalent Modernism* (Seattle and London: University of Washington Press, 2006), p. 41.

CHAPTER 4

1. Majid Khadduri, *Modern Libya: A Study in Political Development* (Baltimore, MD: The Johns Hopkins Press, 1963), pp. 28–52.
2. Scott L. Bills, *The Libyan Arena: The United States, Britain, and the Council of Foreign Ministers, 1945–1948* (Kent, OH: The Kent State University Press, 1995), pp. 1–33.
3. James Reston, "U.S. Chiefs Divided on Italy's Colonies," *The New York Times*, 2 September 1945.
4. Wm. Roger Louis, *The British Empire in the Middle East, 1945–1951: Arab Nationalism, the United States, and Postwar Imperialism* (Oxford: Clarendon Press, 1984), pp. 105, 300–302.
5. Khadduri, *Modern Libya*, pp. 120–124.
6. Ronald Bruce St John, *Libya and the United States: Two Centuries of Strife* (Philadelphia: University of Pennsylvania Press, 2002), pp. 57–59.
7. On the UN negotiations, see Adrian Pelt, *Libyan Independence and the United Nations: A Case of Planned Decolonization* (New Haven, CT: Yale University Press, 1970).
8. Henry Serrano Villard, *Libya: The New Arab Kingdom of North Africa* (Ithaca, NY: Cornell University Press, 1956), pp. 33–34.
9. Ann Dearden, "Independence for Libya: The Political Problems," *The Middle East Journal*, 4, 4, October 1950, p. 408.

CHAPTER 5

1. Benjamin Howard Higgins, *The Economic and Social Development of Libya* (New York: United Nations Technical Assistance Programme, 1953), p. 6.
2. Shukri Ghanem, "The Libyan Economy before Independence," in *Social and Economic Development of Libya*, ed. E. G. H. Joffé and K. S. McLachlan (Wisbech, Cambridgeshire: Middle East & North African Studies, 1982), pp. 141–159.
3. Khadduri, *Modern Libya*, pp. 217–220.
4. John Wright, *Libya: A Modern History* (Baltimore, MD: Johns Hopkins University Press, 1982), p. 89.

5. Hisham B. Sharabi, *Nationalism and Revolution in the Arab World* (Princeton, NJ: D. Van Nostrand Company, 1965), pp. 48–50.
6. Henry Serrano Villard, *Libya: The New Arab Kingdom of North Africa* (Ithaca, NY: Cornell University Press, 1956), p. 9.
7. Mustafa Ahmed Ben Halim, *Libya: The Years of Hope* (London: AAS Media Publishers, 1998), pp. 147–176 and 201–223, quote p. 149.
8. Fagih, "Background Notes on Modern Libyan Literature," *Libyan Stories*, pp. 6–7
9. Ronald Bruce St John, *Qaddafi's World Design: Libyan Foreign Policy, 1969–1987* (London: Saqi Books, 1987), pp. 16–17.
10. Renzo De Felice, *Jews in an Arab Land: Libya, 1835–1970* (Austin: University of Texas Press, 1985), pp. 185–233.
11. John Norman, *Labor and Politics in Libya and Arab Africa* (New York: Bookman Associates, 1965), p. 66.

CHAPTER 6

1. Ambassador David L. Mack, interview with author, Washington DC, 16 November 2005.
2. Ruth First, *Libya: The Elusive Revolution* (Harmondsworth, Middlesex: Penguin Books, 1974), pp. 119–124.
3. Mu'ammar al-Qaddafi, "The Village," in *Escape to Hell and Other Stories* (New York: Stanké, 1998), p. 50.
4. Patrick Seale and Maureen McConville, *The Hilton Assignment* (London: Fontana/Collins, 1974), pp. 144–145, 152, 170–173.
5. Mu'ammar al-Qaddafi, "Address Delivered by Col. Mu'ammar al-Qaddafi in Tripoli on 4 Sha'ban 1389 = 16 October 1969," in *The Libyan Revolution: A Sourcebook of Legal and Historical Documents, Vol. I: 1 September 1969 – 30 August 1970*, eds. Meredith O. Ansell and Ibrahim Massaud al-Arif (Stoughton, WI: Oleander Press, 1972), p. 90.
6. St John, *Libya and the United States*, pp. 107–108.
7. Mu'ammar al-Qaddafi, "Address Delivered by Col. Mu'ammar al-Qaddafi in Tripoli on 4 Sha'ban 1389 = 16 October 1969," p. 95.
8. John Anthony Allan, *Libya: The Experience of Oil* (London: Croom Helm, 1981), pp. 186–187.
9. Taoufik Monastiri, "Teaching the Revolution: Libyan Education since 1969," in *Qadhafi's Libya, 1969–1994*, ed. Dirk Vandewalle (New York: St. Martin's Press, 1995), pp. 68–72.
10. Dirk Vandewalle, *Libya since Independence: Oil and State-Building* (Ithaca, NY: Cornell University Press, 1998), pp. 72–73.
11. St John, *Qaddafi's World Design*, pp. 49–58.

12. Mu'ammar al-Qaddafi, "Escape to Hell," in *Escape to Hell and Other Stories*, pp. 63–64.
13. Omar I. El Fathaly and Monte Palmer, *Political Development and Social Change in Libya* (Lexington, MA: Lexington Books, 1980), pp. 71–116.
14. Mo'ammar el-Gadhafi, *I. Broad lines of the Third Theory; II. The Aspects of the Third Theory; III. The Concept of Jihad; IV. The Divine Concept of Islam* (Tripoli: Ministry of Information and Culture, 1973).
15. Marius K. Deeb and Mary Jane Deeb, *Libya since the Revolution: Aspects of Social and Political Development* (New York: Praeger Publishers, 1982), pp. 93–108.

CHAPTER 7

1. Quotations from part one of *The Green Book* come from Mu'ammar al-Qaddafi, *The Green Book, Part 1: The Solution of the Problem of Democracy – "The Authority of the People"* (London: Martin Brian & O'Keefe, 1976).
2. Quotations from part two of *The Green Book* come from Mu'ammar al-Qaddafi, *Part 2: The Solution of the Economic Problem – "Socialism"* (London: Martin Brian & O'Keefe, 1978).
3. Quotations from part three of *The Green Book* come from Mu'ammar al-Qaddafi, *Part 3: The Social Basis of the Third Universal Theory* (Tripoli: Public Establishment for Publishing, Advertising, and Distribution, 1979).
4. Vandewalle, *Libya since Independence*, pp. 83, 87–88, 100.
5. Hisham Matar, *In the Country of Men* (New York: Dial Press, 2007), p. 198.
6. Hanspeter Mattes, "The Rise and Fall of the Revolutionary Committees," in *Qadhafi's Libya, 1969–1994*, ed. Dirk Vandewalle (New York: St. Martin's Press, 1995), pp. 89–112.
7. Matar, *In the Country of Men*, p. 235.
8. Vandewalle, *Libya since Independence*, pp. 104–105.
9. Ambassador William L. Eagleton, interview with author, Taos, New Mexico, 31 May 2006.
10. St John, *Libya and the United States*, pp. 106–119.
11. Mary-Jane Deeb, *Libya's Foreign Policy in North Africa* (Boulder, CO: Westview Press, 1991), pp. 100–105.
12. Ronald Bruce St John, "The Libyan Debacle in Sub-Saharan Africa," in *The Green and the Black: Qadhafi's Policies in Africa*, ed. René Lemarchand (Bloomington: Indiana University Press, 1988), pp. 125–138.
13. J. Millard Burr and Robert O. Collins, *Africa's Thirty Years War: Libya, Chad and the Sudan, 1963–1993* (Boulder, CO: Westview Press, 1999), pp. 82–98.
14. George P. Schultz, *Turmoil and Triumph: My Years as Secretary of State* (New York: Charles Scribner's Sons, 1993), p. 677.

CHAPTER 8

1. On economic and political liberalization in the 1980s, see Dirk Vandewalle, "The Failure of Liberalization in the Jamahiriyya," in *Qadhafi's Libya, 1969–1994*, ed. Dirk Vandewalle (New York: St. Martin's Press, 1995), pp. 203–222.
2. St John, *Libya and the United States*, 138–146.
3. Ann Elizabeth Mayer, "In Search of Sacred Law: The Meandering Course of Qadhafi's Legal Policy," in *Qadhafi's Libya, 1969–1994*, ed. Dirk Vandewalle (New York: St. Martin's Press, 1995), pp. 123–131.
4. On the early years of the chemical weapons dispute, see Thomas C. Wiegele, *The Clandestine Building of Libya's Chemical Weapons Factory* (Carbondale and Edwardsville: Southern Illinois University Press, 1992), esp. pp. 12–55, 113–136.
5. For an overview of the Lockerbie dispute, see Khalil I. Matar and Robert W. Thabit, *Lockerbie and Libya* (Jefferson, NC: McFarland & Company, 2004).
6. Sam C. Nolutshungu, *Limits of Anarchy: Intervention and State Formation in Chad* (Charlottesville: University Press of Virginia, 1996), pp. 143–144.
7. Mu'ammar al-Qaddafi, *Part 3: The Social Basis of the Third Universal Theory* (Tripoli: Public Establishment for Publishing, Advertising, and Distribution, 1979), p. 14.
8. For background on the Gulf of Sirte dispute, see Joseph T. Stanik, *El Dorado Canyon: Reagan's Undeclared War with Qaddafi* (Annapolis, MD: Naval Institute Press, 2003), esp. pp. 26–65, 120–142.

CHAPTER 9

1. St John, *Libya and the United States*, pp. 175–184.
2. Amal Obeidi, *Political Culture in Libya* (Richmond, Surrey: Curzon, 2001), pp. 103–106, 129–133.
3. George Joffé, "Libya's Saharan Destiny," *The Journal of North African Studies*, vol. 10, no. 3–4 (September–December 2005), pp. 613–614.
4. Jeremy Keenan, "Waging War on Terror: The Implications of America's 'New Imperialism' for Saharan Peoples," *The Journal of North African Studies*, vol. 10, no. 3–4, September–December 2005, pp. 641–642.
5. Muammar al-Qaddafi, "Statement by Brother Leader of the Revolution on the Occasion of the Opening of the Fifth Ordinary Session of the Assembly of the African Union," Sirte, Libya, 4 July 2005, p. 10, http://www.africa-union.org, accessed 1 September 2005.
6. Pamela Chasek, "Revolution across the Sea: Libyan Foreign Policy in Central

America," in *Central America & the Middle East: The Internationalization of the Crises*, ed. Damián J. Fernández (Miami: Florida International University Press, 1990), pp. 150–176.

7. Haizam Amirah Fernández, "Libya's Return: Between Change and Continuity," *Real Instituto Elcano de Estudios Internacionales y Estratégicos*, 1 June 2006, http://www.realinstitutoelcano.org, accessed 23 October 2006.

8. Sara Hamood, "African Transit Migration through Libya to Europe: The Human Cost," *The American University in Cairo, Forced Migration and Refugee Studies*, January 2006, http://www.aucegypt.edu, accessed 25 June 2007.

9. Ronald Bruce St John, "'Libya Is Not Iraq': Preemptive Strikes, WMD and Diplomacy," *The Middle East Journal*, vol. 58, no. 3, Summer 2004, pp. 396–402.

10. World Bank, "Socialist People's Libyan Arab Jamahiriya: Country Economic Report," *Country Economic Report No. 30295/LY*, July 2006, Internet edition, http://www.worldbank.org, accessed 8 September 2006, p. i.

11. Ronald Bruce St John, "Libya's Oil and Gas Industry: Blending Old and New," *The Journal of North African Studies*, vol. 12, no. 2 (June 2007), pp. 203–218.

12. Ray Takeyh, "Qadhafi's Libya and the Prospect of Islamic Succession," *Middle East Policy*, vol. 7, no. 2, February 2000, pp. 154–164.

13. Human Rights Watch, "Libya, Words to Deeds: The Urgent Need for Human Rights Reform," vol. 18, no. 1, January 2006, p. 2, http://hrw.org, accessed 25 June 2007.

14. Alison Pargeter, "Libya: Reforming the Impossible?" *Review of African Political Economy*, vol. 33, no. 108, June 2006, p. 224.

INDEX

5/11

DATE DUE

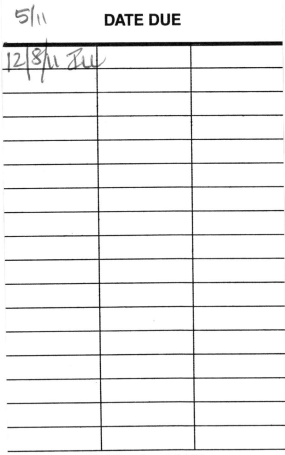

12/8/11 Jill